Viola Desmond's Canada

Viola Desmond
By permission of Joe and Wanda Robson

Viola Desmond's Canada

A History of Blacks and Racial Segregation in the Promised Land

Graham Reynolds
with Wanda Robson

Fernwood Publishing
Halifax & Winnipeg

Editing: Curran Faris
Text design: Brenda Conroy
Cover photo: U.N.I.A. Marching Band Whitney Pier,
Nova Scotia, 1921, courtesey of Beaton Institute
Cover design: John van der Woude
Printed and bound in Canada

Published by Fernwood Publishing
32 Oceanvista Lane, Black Point, Nova Scotia, B0J 1B0
and 748 Broadway Avenue, Winnipeg, Manitoba, R3G 0X3

www.fernwoodpublishing.ca

Fernwood Publishing Company Limited gratefully acknowledges the financial support of the Government of Canada through the Canada Book Fund and the Canada Council for the Arts, the Nova Scotia Department of Communities, Culture and Heritage, the Manitoba Department of Culture, Heritage and Tourism under the Manitoba Publishers Marketing Assistance Program and the Province of Manitoba, through the Book Publishing Tax Credit, for our publishing program.

Library and Archives Canada Cataloguing in Publication

Reynolds, Graham, 1944-, author
Viola Desmond's Canada : a history of blacks and racial segregation in the promised land / Graham Reynolds with Wanda Robson.

Includes bibliographical references and index.

Issued in print and electronic formats.
ISBN 978-1-55266-837-5 (paperback).--ISBN 978-1-55266-857-3 (kindle).--
ISBN 978-1-55266-856-6 (epub)

1. Desmond, Viola, 1914-1965. 2. Blacks--Canada--History. 3. Blacks--Segregation--Canada--History. 4. Segregation--Canada--History. 5. Slavery-Canada--History. 6. Canada--Ethnic relations--History. I. Robson, Wanda, 1926-, author. II. Title. III. Title: Canada.

FC106.B6R49 2016   971.00496   C2015-908280-3
C2015-908281-1

To John and Eunice Harker, for their sustained commitment to human rights, and to Catherine Arseneau, Jane Arnold and the staff of the Beaton Institute at Cape Breton University, for their dedication to preserving and sharing the archival treasures of Atlantic Canada's and Canada's multicultural heritage.

Contents

Acknowledgements ix

Foreword: Towards That Elusive Just Society *by George Elliott Clarke* xiii

Introduction 1

PART I: A NARRATIVE HISTORY 13

1   A Narrative of Race in Canadian History
    from Slavery to the Underground Railroad 14
    The Institution of Slavery in New France.................................... 14
    Slavery and Freedom Under British Rule 17
    The Decline of Slavery in Canada... 23
    The Underground Railroad... 26

2   The Many Faces of Jim Crow:
    Racial Segregation in Canada 1880–1960 35
    The Origin of Jim Crow in the Southern United States................. 36
    Canada's "Indigenous" Black Communities
    During the Late Victorian Era... 39
    Modernization, Immigration and Canada's "Negro Problem"........ 43
    Canada's New Culture of Segregation... 49
    The Struggle to End Racial Segregation in Canada....................... 56

3   My Early Memories of Race, My Sister Viola
    and My Journey of Self-Discovery *by Wanda Robson*................. 69
    My First Experiences of Racial Prejudice.................................... 71
    My Sister Viola and the Incident at the Roseland Theatre............ 75
    My Personal Journey of Self-Discovery
    through Education and Raising Public Awareness........................ 81

PART II: A DOCUMENTARY HISTORY 87

4   Marie Marguerite Rose: What Her Inventory of Material
    Possessions Tells Us About Slavery and Freedom
    in Eighteenth Century New France 88

5   West Indian Immigration to Canada, 1900–1920:
    What the Census Figures Don't Tell Us 114

6   The Culture of Racism in Canada: Burning Crosses,
    Blackened-Faced Actors and Minstrel Shows..146

7   Pearleen Oliver: Pioneer in the Fight to End Racial Discrimination....163

Epilogue...175

Appendix: The Promised Land Project Symposium
    Roundtable Discussion...177

References 188

Index..196

Acknowledgements

I am indebted to a great number people, and without their support *Viola Desmond's Canada* would not have been possible. In June of 2010, John Harker, former president of Cape Breton University, provided the initial encouragement for this book by appointing me as the first Viola Desmond Chair in Social Justice. The creation of the Chair followed the Nova Scotia Government's action of granting an apology and free pardon to the late Viola Desmond in April 2010. President Harker's initiative was inspired, in part, by the role that Cape Breton University graduate and Viola Desmond's youngest sister, Wanda Robson, played in this historic event.

I first met Wanda in 2000 when she became a student in my race relations course. We quickly formed a close student-mentor bond that, over the years, has evolved into a lasting friendship and collaborative relationship. I am grateful to Wanda for the substantive contribution she has made to this book and to her husband Joe who provided important family documents and much helpful advice.

The research for *Viola Desmond's Canada* draws heavily on the archival holdings at the Cape Breton University Beaton Institute, which includes the Fortress of Louisbourg as well as the Black Nova Scotian Holdings. Catherine Arseneau, the Director of the Beaton Institute, and archivist Jane Arnold offered invaluable advice and assistance throughout all phases of the project. I also received very helpful assistance from Parks Canada historian, Anne Marie Lane Jonah and Elizabeth Tait, the Curator of Textiles at the Fortress of Louisbourg National Historic Site. Both these Parks Canada specialists provided me with valuable information and insights into the role of women in eighteenth-century Ile Royale as well as details regarding the life of Marie Marguerite Rose. Anne Marie translated the inventory of Rose's material possessions, and she generously provided me with the French and English translation of the eighteenth century merchant Pierre Lapouble's letter that she discovered while conducting her own research.

The story of Marie Marguerite Rose came to my attention through the research of retired Fortress of Louisbourg historian Kenneth Donovan. My own study of the early history of Blacks in Canada, which is presented in chapters 1 and 4, has benefitted greatly from his pioneering work on the history of slavery and from the many discussions we have had over the years.

The office of the President of Cape Breton University, the former Dean of Research, Dale Keefe and the former Dean of the School of Arts and Social Science, Rod Nicholls, provided financial assistance to this project. This support enabled me to hire three research assistants and to conduct interviews and research in several provinces. In the initial stage of this project, Anna MacNeil helped locate and retrieve important documents relating to West Indian immigration to Canada. Meghan Donovan later transcribed oral interviews I conducted, helped with translations of French documents and compiled newspaper articles. In the final phase of completing the book, Courtney MacIsaac assisted in obtaining documents at the New Brunswick Provincial Archives and in ferreting out important newspaper articles. She also creatively formatted the Rose inventory in order to make it into a much more reader-friendly document.

Several public libraries and archives assisted my research for *Viola Desmond's Canada*, including the Toronto Public Library, the City of Vancouver Archives, the New Brunswick Provincial Archives, The Public Archives of Nova Scotia and Library and Archives Canada. I am also very grateful to the dedicated staff at the Cape Breton University Library, especially for the support and specialized expertise I received from Mary Dobson, Barry Gabriel and Mary Campbell.

Viola Desmond's Canada incorporates several interviews as well as a roundtable discussion that took place at the fourth annual Promised Land Project Symposium, held at the Black Cultural Centre in Dartmouth, Nova Scotia. I would like to thank Virginia Travis, Philip Alexander, Marie Carter, Sylvia Hamilton and Les Oliver for their generosity and willingness to share their deeply personal early childhood recollections involving racial prejudice. I am especially thankful to Boulou Ebanda de B'beri, Professor of Media, Communication and Cultural Studies at the University of Ottawa, for preparing the audio file of the roundtable discussion that he recorded at the Promised Land Project Symposium.

I am very grateful to George Elliott Clarke, Professor of English at the University of Toronto, for kindly agreeing to write the Foreword to *Viola Desmond's Canada*. I am also indebted to all those who gave of their time to read and offer constructive criticisms on all or parts of the book manuscript, including Jessica Antony, managing editor at Fernwood Publishing, the anonymous reviewers, as well as Afua Cooper, associate professor and James Robinson Johnston Chair in Black Canadian Studies at Dalhousie University, Harvey Amani Whitfield, associate professor of history at the University of Vermont, Anne Marie Lane Jonah, Mike Hunter, editor of Cape Breton University Press, Patrick Howard, associate professor of Education at Cape Breton University, Tom Henderson, African Canadian Studies Coordinator for the Nova Scotia Department of Education, Tony Colaiacovo, owner and editor of Effective Publishing in Halifax and Don Nerbas, Assistant Professor of History at Cape Breton University. Don also provided valuable insights into the history of the Ku Klux Klan and its relationship to New Brunswick party politics during the 1920s and 1930s.

I am especially grateful to my colleague, Andy Parnaby, associate professor of history at Cape Breton University, who showed a keen interest in this project from the beginning. He read all the key portions of the manuscript and provided many valuable insights and encouragement as well as his expertise as an accomplished writer and editor.

Finally, I am deeply indebted to my wife, Terri Macgregor, for her support and for keeping me well grounded and focused throughout the duration of this project.

Foreword

Towards That Elusive Just Society

George Elliott Clarke

The story that Dr. Graham Reynolds reveals in *Viola Desmond's Canada: A History of Blacks and Racial Segregation in the Promised Land* is a peculiar saga, one that seems bizarre because it narrates and depicts aspects of Canada that we must consider aberrant, inhuman and obscene. It is eye opening to read, for instance, of the advertised sale of a "Negro wench ... creole born," who can cook and clean and do "every other thing that can be expected from such a slave." Canadians have long understood that African-heritage female slaves could be fondled, raped, even impregnated by masters and overseers "down South," or on Caribbean isles of sugar and sun. But the cited advertisement is from a 1752-vintage Halifax, NS newspaper. Canadians take pride in the nation's colonial-era status as the terminus of the Underground Railroad that ferried tens of thousands of African-American fugitive slaves "to freedom" in the Province of Canada. Yet, we are less aware of the discriminatory practices that discouraged those impromptu "settlers" from staying. (How different Canadian history would have been had a "Black Belt" of towns and villages taken serious root in what is now Southern Ontario.) Nor do we understand that the surveillance and pursuit of escaping ex-slaves by "professional slave hunters called patrollers" in the mid-nineteenth century led to the rise of the bounty hunter (including TV's *Dog the Bounty Hunter* and like bloodhounds). However, it also led to the inherent, white view of all Blacks as being perpetual "suspects," and thus to the endless shooting of unarmed Black people by law enforcement, and even to the Toronto, ON, police policy of "carding" — keeping tabs on — mainly young blacks. Weirder still, we Canucks like to imagine ourselves as automatic slave liberators, if not by cannon and rifle and bayonet (as was the case in the U.S.), then by Their Royal Britannic Majesties' law courts. The reality is that colonial Canada had a schizoid attitude to slavery. In the U.S., emancipation was a matter of Christian Abolitionists — saints marching in, really — pushing and pushing the State to make good on the equality lingo in its Constitution. In British North America, emancipation was a result of elites — judges and politicians — following the precedents of Lord Mansfield's Somerset decision (1772) that had the effect of saying essentially that no man could breathe England's air and be a slave. However, one must note that Lord Mansfield's words didn't free a single slave in the West Indies or in British North America. Instead, as in Nova Scotia and New Brunswick, a laissez-faire system of slavery developed: if you could keep your slaves, good for you; if your slaves escaped, too bad for you. It wasn't humanitarianism that freed colonial Canadian slaves, but their own willingness to run off. Thus, by 1805, slavery had declined so much in Nova Scotia that the legislature refused to hear a petition from slaveholders for stronger laws to return runaways. Nevertheless, slavery did not legally end in British North America until the British Empire moved its abolition in 1834.

Dr. Reynolds unfolds, with research and relish, and without equivocation or euphemism, the fact of anti-Black bias in our Canadian history, even after slavery ended. His study indicates that African-Canadian freedom and equality remain more a privilege than a right, and that racism continues, even if it is inconsistent in its force and often invisible in its identification (though not in its effects).

Again, Canadians know well the images of Ku Klux Klan "knights" and night-riders — terrorists — torching homes and lynching alleged Black violators of "white womanhood." But we are woefully ignorant of the truth that, says Dr. Reynolds, "the Klan ... had branches in nearly every province" of Canada in the 1920s, that the "Edmonton-based Klan newspaper, *The Liberator*, claimed to have a circulation of 250,000, and by 1925 there were as many as 8,000 Klan members in the City of Toronto alone." One is tempted to think, "Well, that's the 1920s." Sure, but how many great-grandchildren of those 8,000 Canuck Klansmen ended up joining the Toronto police?

Moreover, Canadian popular culture was infected by Klan-style, anti-coloured propaganda. Dr. Reynolds reminds us that D.W. Griffiths' historic, pro-KKK film, *The Birth of a Nation*, played to "packed movie houses across Canada," 1915 to 1927. It could only have reinforced the bifurcated, slavery-borne images of Blacks as a) lazy, imbecilic, shiftless and b) violent, crafty, criminal. (No wonder, then, that, in 2010 in Ontario, a Royal Canadian Legion thought it was okay to award a prize, for Best Halloween Costume, to a tandem of Klansman and would-be, blackface lynchees.) In turn, the popular (white) reception of these images could only have encouraged socio-economic marginalization (including sometimes legislated segregation) as well as police brutality and legalized lynchings (death-by-hanging sentences disproportionately dished out to Black defendants).

Dr. Reynolds informs us, for instance, of the long campaign by a Dresden, ON, restauranteur to reserve the right to refuse service to Black would-be patrons. The restauranteur was so adamant about maintaining segregation that he became Br'er Rabbit assaulting, vainly and farcically, the Tar Baby of justice.

But Dr. Reynolds is most engaged by, and rightfully so, the story of Nova Scotia's Viola Desmond. The prosperous, hard-working beautician became, by accident, a champion of integration, by refusing — as America's Rosa Parks would famously do nine years later — to move from a "white" seating area to a "coloured" one. The incident occurred in a cinema in New Glasgow, NS, in 1946, where Desmond inadvertently took a seat in the whites-only downstairs section of the Roseland Theatre. Advised to move to the "Negro" balcony, Desmond refused, and was eventually manhandled out by a town cop and the cinema manager and jailed. The next day, she was fined a total of $26.00, not for having failed to accept a Jim Crow seating arrangement, but for having violated the provincial amusement tax law by failing to pay the penny difference in tax between the "white" seats downstairs and the "coloured" seats upstairs. Dr. Reynolds quotes a provincial judge who summed up the case as constituting "a surreptitious endeavour to enforce Jim Crow rule by misuse of a public statute." Clearly, Dr. Reynolds sees Viola Desmond as a bona fide heroine, and he is right. For unlike the case of Ms. Parks in 1955, in Montgomery, Alabama, there was no cadre of civil-rights activists and social-gospel clergy to come to her defence. She was a lone businesswoman confronting the enmity of a racially prejudiced province. Her allies were few and far. In contrast, Rosa Parks' refusal to move from her seat on a segregated bus touched off the Montgomery Bus Boycott and the ascension of a rookie preacher, Rev. Dr. Martin Luther King, Jr., to the prominence of, a decade later, a Nobel Peace Prize Laureateship. Ms. Parks became the figurehead of a historic socio-political movement that guaranteed, eventually, the right to vote for millions of black people, a fact that, eventually, helped elect an African-American president. Yet, Desmond could trigger no mass protest. She struggled — and suffered — alone. She was no symbol; she was a martyr.

But Nova Scotia — and Canada — evolved. Later, as Dr. Reynolds documents, Ms. Desmond an official provincial government apology and a royal pardon (both posthumously); in February 2012, her image appeared on a Canada Post stamp. Her story — and Dr. Reynolds's history — underline again that anti-racism in Canada succeeds when renegades' protests meet with, sooner or later, elite accommodation.

Importantly, Dr. Reynolds canvasses the story of a slave woman at Fort Louisbourg, on what is now Cape Breton Island, in the 1740s; explores Black immigration issues (including the insistent efforts of some politicians and bureaucrats to bar all potential Black immigrants); recounts the Canadian activities of the pan-Africanist Universal Negro Improvement Association; and discusses "The Culture of Racism in Canada." Valuably, too, Dr. Reynolds presents us with the biography of Dr. Pearleen Oliver, an African-Nova Scotian (or Africadian) clergywoman whose Christianity inspired her dismantling of barriers to black women becoming nurses in Canada.

One applauds Dr. Reynolds for fielding his insights into the history of Negrophobia or anti-Black oppression in Canada. His facts are black ink that crosses the eyes like lightning, not blindingly, but to enlighten. Once enlightened, it is up to us to act. If not to bring about Martin Luther King's Promised Land, then to secure Pierre Elliott Trudeau's Just Society.

— *Dr. George Elliott Clarke, O.C., ONS, PhD.*
E.J. Pratt Professor of Canadian Literature
University of Toronto

Introduction

On April 15, 2010, the province of Nova Scotia granted an apology and free pardon to the late Viola Desmond, a Black businesswoman who has come to symbolize the struggle for civil rights and racial equality in Canada. In 1946, Viola Desmond was wrongfully arrested after she refused to give up her seat in a racially segregated theatre in New Glasgow, Nova Scotia. The action of the Nova Scotia legislature marked a significant moment in Canadian history and brought the long forgotten practice of racial segregation that existed in Nova Scotia and elsewhere in Canada into public consciousness. The free pardon granted to Viola Desmond is also unlike any other pardon in that, instead of forgiving an unlawful act, it is intended to correct a judicial error and "right a wrong." Above all, it is an acknowledgement of Viola's innocence as well as the injustice done to her by the government of Nova Scotia.[1]

Most Canadians are familiar with Rosa Parks, the American civil rights icon who refused to give up her seat on a racially segregated bus in Montgomery, Alabama. Viola Desmond's singular act of courage in resisting a similar practice of racial segregation in the town of New Glasgow occurred nine years before Rosa Parks' famous protest, but, until the recent granting of her free pardon, her story was not well known, even in Nova Scotia. The Viola Desmond incident is not an isolated example of our national ignorance regarding racial segregation and the struggle for racial equality in Canada.

Three years after Viola's resistance and wrongful arrest in Nova Scotia, the Black activist and war veteran Hugh Burnett and his supporters formed the National Unity Association in Ontario in order to fight for civil rights and to end the practice of racial segregation in the town of Dresden, Ontario. Hugh Burnett's fight for civil rights in Ontario occurred almost a generation before Martin Luther King Jr.'s "I Have a Dream" speech, yet very few Canadians are aware of this important chapter in Canadian history. There are many others of Viola Desmond and High Burnett's generation who struggled for racial equality and social justice and who are little or not known to most Canadians. On the subjects of race and racial segregation, Canadians seem to exhibit a form of collective amnesia.[2]

Historically, Blacks in North America have regarded Canada as the "Promised Land," a place of freedom and opportunity. The phrase has biblical origins, and it refers to the land of Canaan, where Moses led the ancient Israelites from Egypt and out of slavery. This vision of Canada became a powerful and inspiring metaphor for freedom among enslaved Africans in the United States, and it gained universal meaning during the period of the Underground Railroad.[3] The Promised Land also refers to the search for freedom among other Black immigrants, including the Black Loyalists who came to Nova Scotia in the closing months of the American Revolutionary War. Unfortunately, for most of these Black Loyalists, as well as many of the fugitive slaves, the reality of life in Canada fell far short of their hopes and expectations. Indeed, over the long course of Canadian history, there has been a strong undercurrent of racial discrimination toward Blacks, and this provides a troubling testimony to how difficult and, at times, illusive the quest for the Promised Land of freedom and opportunity has been.

Although unfamiliar to many students of Canadian history, the subject of race and the history of segregation in Canada have received the attention of scholars over the past number of years. Almost half a century ago, Robin Winks published his highly acclaimed and now classic study *Blacks in Canada: A History* (1971), which is the first and most comprehensive history of Blacks in Canada.[4] Since then, several other important works have been published that, together, have helped extend our understanding of the significant role Blacks have played in the history of Canada. James W. St. G. Walker's *The Black Loyalists: The Search for a Promised Land in Nova Scotia and Sierra Leone, 1783–1870* (1976) provides a detailed history of the dramatic and epic journey of over 3,000 former slaves who made their way in the aftermath of the American Revolutionary War to Nova Scotia and Sierra Leone in the quest of a Promised Land.[5] Afua Cooper's pioneering work, *The Hanging of Angelique: The Untold Story of Canadian Slavery and the Burning of Old Montreal* (2006), offers new and important insights into the history of slavery in Canada.[6] Harvey Amani Whitfield's well researched and engaging study *Blacks on the Border: The Black Refugees in British North America, 1815–1860* (2006) tells the story of the Black refugees who came to Canada following the War of 1812 and settled in the Atlantic region.[7] Most recently, Sarah-Jane Mathieu has written a history of the Black experience in Canada during the era in which racial segregation was persistent throughout most regions of the country.[8] Her book, *North of the Color Line; Migration and Black Resistance in Canada, 1870–1955* (2010) focuses on the railway industry in Canada and documents the nearly century-long history of discrimination against Blacks as porters, redcaps and railway laborers together with their struggle to seek racial equality and social justice through the organized labour movement. In addition to these general works, there have been numerous regionally focused and specialized studies in the form of scholarly articles and books.[9] One of the most notable is Constance Backhouse's *Colour-Coded: A Legal History of Racism in Canada, 1900–1950* (1999).[10] Her book is the first major study focusing on the racial prejudice and presumption of white supremacy that had a firm hold on Canada's legal system throughout the first half of the twentieth century.

Backhouse examines in detail six court cases involving African-Canadian, Aboriginal, Inuit and Chinese-Canadian individuals whose legal ordeals represent "central moments in the history of racism in Canada."[11] Her research has brought to light several obscure but important legal cases that, until her publication, were little known, even among members of Canada's legal profession. Backhouse is the first scholar to thoroughly examine the details and historical significance of the case of Viola Desmond, and largely as a result of her pioneering study, this important chapter in the legal history of racial segregation in Canada has been brought to the attention of the larger academic community interested in the history of race relations in Canada.[12]

Despite the cumulative efforts of these and other scholars over the past fifty years, the study of Blacks in Canada has not been a part of the mainstream of Canadian history, and it remains a marginalized subject, largely overshadowed by the study of other racial- ethnic groups.[13] For this reason, the history of racial segregation and the experience of Blacks in Canada are not well understood, and what Canadians do know is often the American example or merely a fragment of the larger narrative. The story of the Underground Railroad, for example, figures prominently in most courses and textbooks in Canadian history, but very little, if any, attention is given to the larger context of this history, particularly to the struggle among former slaves and other Black immigrants against severe economic hardships and the persistent and dehumanizing effects of racial discrimination and segregation that they experiences after arriving in Canada.[14]

More recently, the story of the Black Loyalists has been the subject of a popular historical narrative written primarily for an American audience as well as in Lawrence Hill's *The Book of Negroes*, a prize-winning book of historical fiction.[15] Hill recounts the life of Aminata Diallo, a fictional character who is kidnapped at the age of eleven from her village near the Grain Coast in West Africa and sold into slavery. Aminata is an accurate historical representation of the Black Loyalist experience, and Hill vividly describes her difficult and often traumatic journey from her homeland to her enslaved life in the southern United States to her search for the Promised Land in Nova Scotia and later Sierra Leone. Hill's novel is also a story of the protagonist's personal quest of self- discovery involving her African identity and roots. *The Book of Negroes* is an inspiring account that brings to life for its readers, through the genre of fiction, the dramatic and real-life experiences of Black Loyalists and other enslaved Africans.

Hill's novel and other recent books have succeeded in raising general interest in the history of the Black Loyalists; however, most of these accounts focus exclusively on the exodus of the Black Loyalists who departed Nova Scotia after only a few years.[16] It is important to acknowledge that the majority of Black Loyalists did not in fact leave with the flotilla of ships bound for Sierra Leone. Over 2,000 Black Loyalists stayed behind and became a part of the sizable and permanent Black community in Atlantic Canada. These Black Loyalists joined other free and enslaved immigrants of African descent on their own quest for the Promised Land. History shows that in Canada this journey was to become a difficult and enduring struggle for acceptance, equality and social justice.

The intention of this book is to provide general readers and students of Canadian history with a narrative of race that illustrates important aspects of the history of the Black experience in Canada. This is a deliberately selective narrative that focuses exclusively on the African-Canadian experience in relation to the history of racial segregation in Canada. The issue of racial prejudice in Canada encompasses, of course, a number of racial and ethnic groups, and Canadian history includes not one but several distinct narratives of race. Since the 1970s, the nation's attention on the subject of race and race relations has rightly focused mainly on Canada's First Nations. Due to the concerted and collective efforts of aboriginal elders, historians and educators, together with provincial and federal governments in Canada, there has been a steady increase in public awareness regarding the prejudice and injustices that Canada's Indigenous peoples have experienced since the arrival of Europeans over 400 years ago. Today, the history and culture of the First Nations of Canada have come to be understood to a much greater extent than in the past, and the difficult process of healing and reconciliation has now finally begun.[17] Unfortunately, the same cannot be said in regard to other racial-ethnic groups. In sharp contrast to Canada's First Nations, for example, Blacks have had largely an invisible presence in Canada. Until the Nova Scotia legislature granted a free pardon to Viola Desmond in 2010, few Canadians were even aware of the fact that Canada had its own form of Jim Crow segregation that was similar to that of the southern United States. Coincidentally, 2010 also marks another important date in the Black experience and history of racial segregation in Canada: in February of that year, the city of Halifax issued an official apology for the expropriation and destruction of Africville, a Black community that had existed along the northeastern shore of the Bedford basin on the outskirts of Halifax. The community can be traced back to the 1840s, and its long history, in many respects, is representative of the pattern of racial discrimination, segregation and neglect that African-Canadians endured for so many years.[18]

It is important for all Canadians to have a fuller understanding of the continuity and history of the Black experience in Canada. This narrative of race is part of a critical subtext of our larger national history, and it chronicles the centuries long struggle for freedom and racial equality in pursuit of the Promised Land. The narrative begins with the institution of slavery under the French and British rule during the seventeenth century and extends through the era of segregation in the twentieth century until the present day.

The roots of racial prejudice run deep in the history of North America, and although the struggle for racial equality and human rights has made significant advances, the spectre of racism is never very far below the surface. This is evidenced in the racial violence that erupts periodically in some of our schools, as well as fire bombings and cross burnings that have occurred as recently as a few years ago in Nova Scotia.[19] Most Canadians are unaware of the fact that, until very recently in our history, being born an African-Canadian was almost universally associated with negative childhood experiences. With few exceptions, children of mixed race or Black parents, born only a generation ago, experienced early in their lives the psychological effects of the stigma of being different and less acceptable in the eyes of whites, simply because of the colour of their skin. The impact of this arbitrary but socially important distinction of colour was often the first and singularly most defining racial event in the lives of Black children.

For Wanda Robson, the youngest sister of Viola Desmond, this moment of racial awareness occurred in a racially mixed neighbourhood in Halifax when she was seven or eight years old and was told she could not play with her white friend across the street because her friend's father would not allow her in their house. For Virginia Travis, a retired nurse who grew up in Dresden, Ontario, during the late 1930s and early 1940s, the first memory of racial consciousness came in the feelings of insecurity and exclusion she felt after being told by her grade one teacher that she could not play in the sand box with her white classmates. And for Philip Alexander, a Black resident of Buxton, Ontario, the defining moment of his racial identity occurred when he was a young teenager. He and a white friend went to a Tarzan movie that was popular during the 1950s, and his friend made reference to the wildly exaggerated African scenes depicted in the movie as a place he could relate to because, after all, he was Black and he came from Africa.[20]

As these painful episodes indicate, racial prejudice has had a profound and lasting influence on the lives of Black children and on Canadian society as a whole. These and other recent expressions of racial prejudice are deeply rooted in our country's past and they are a stark reminder of a time not too long ago when the colour of one's skin was a mark of enslavement.

In Canada, during the period in which slavery was permitted, children of slaves were born into a life of human bondage and servitude. The life of African children abducted and sold into slavery was even more tragic because they would carry with them the earliest memories of their violent capture and the loss or permanent separation from their closest loved ones. The scene depicting the kidnapping of Aminata Diallo, told so poignantly by Lawrence Hill, happened to a countless number of African children during the nearly 300 year history of the slave trade and the resulting African diaspora that brought an estimated 10.5 million enslaved Africans to America.[21] A similar story is told by Olaudah Equiano in his famous slave narrative that was later used to raise public awareness in the fight to abolish the slave trade within the British Empire.[22] In chapter one of this book, readers are told about the remarkable life of Marie Marguerite Rose, a female slave who lived in Ile Royale (Cape Breton) during the eighteenth century. Marie had been abducted from her native Guinea and sold into slavery when she was a teenager. She eventually became the property of Jean Loppinot, a French officer serving with his family at the Fortress of Louisbourg. Marie gained her freedom at the age of 38, and shortly thereafter she married a Mi'kmaq named Jean Baptiste Laurent. Together they opened a tavern in the Fortress of Louisbourg.

All these accounts are representative of the brutality of the slave trade that systematically and violently uprooted African men, women and children from their native villages and transported them, in the most cruel and inhumane manner, across the Atlantic Ocean in order to be sold as slaves. In addition to documenting the extreme hardships of slavery, these accounts show the strength and resilience of the human spirit and provide testimony to the fact that many enslaved Africans were able to gain some measure of freedom, autonomy and self-dignity in their lives. Some of these stories, and others, will be told in the following pages.

The institution of racial slavery in North America has cast a long and indelible shadow over the history of Canada, and it has, and will continue to have, a lasting influence on successive generations of African-Canadians. Blacks in Canada or in the United States who are in search of their family history or African roots are invariably drawn back to the lives of their enslaved ancestors. Understanding this family history for Blacks creates a deeply personal human bond between slavery, the lives of their ancestors and the freedom, dignity and rights they have in their own lives today. This connection is described by Carmelita Carvey Robertson, a former assistant in the Nova Scotia Museum Black Database Research Project, which sought to develop the genealogical history of the descendants of Black Loyalists. After joining the project in 1995, Carmelita discovered details regarding her own family connection to the Black Loyalists, and she was able to trace this family genealogy to a former plantation in South Carolina. Inspired by her discovery, Carmelita visited this place where her ancestors had been slaves. Asked later in an interview how she felt when she stepped onto the plantation and shared the same ground with her ancestors, Carmelita replied: "It was a moment of returning to that place where my ancestors had been enslaved and saying, you made it to your freedom. Your blood runs through me. Your freedom comes through me. I'm here [and] we have survived. Thanks for your strength."[23]

Carmelita's experience is a reminder for all Canadians about the essential connections we have to those who have come before us, and as one of the most important lessons of history, it teaches us that our rights and freedoms have come to us as a result of the struggles, suffering and sacrifices of those of the past. Carmelita's quest to discover her family history illustrates, so profoundly, the extent to which historical consciousness is shaped by our own personal interests and experiences. Historical understanding is determined primarily by the questions we pose that set us on the path of historical inquiry, and often this is the direct result of the close connections we have to the people and the periods of time we study.

This personal aspect of historical consciousness is very much behind the writing of this book. Growing up in the 1960s, I was deeply influenced by Martin Luther King Jr. and the civil rights movement, and I have maintained a personal and scholarly interest in this area of study ever since. I have taught courses on the history of race relations in North America for the past several decades, and although I cannot say with certainty that I have inspired the majority of my students, I have succeeded in introducing them to new historical perspectives as well as to my own enthusiasm for the teaching and learning about this area of study. One of my students was Viola Desmond's youngest sister, Wanda Robson, who audited my course on the history of race relations in the spring term of 2000. Wanda was 73 years old at the time and had not attended university since her freshmen year, over a half century before. I soon discovered Wanda's family connection to Viola and brought this to the attention of the class. Wanda was only 19 years old when her sister was arrested for refusing to give up her seat in the white's only section of the Roseland theatre, and although she has been well informed about the facts of the case, it was only after she returned to university that she became fully aware of the significance of the incident in the larger historical context of the struggle for racial equality in Canada. As the next four years would prove, university education for Wanda became a part of her own personal journey of historical awareness and self-discovery.

Since graduating from Cape Breton University in 2004, Wanda has been instrumental in raising public awareness about the events surrounding her sister and the struggle for racial equality in Nova Scotia. Wanda published her own book, *Sister to Courage: Stories from the World of Viola Desmond, Canada's Rosa Parks,* in 2010.[24]

As this book will document, the eventual granting of the free pardon to Viola Desmond by the Nova Scotia Government in 2010 was largely the result of Wanda's efforts to correct the injustices of the past. In many important respects, Wanda's own personal life and the story of her sister Viola Desmond show how the metaphor of the Promised Land continues to capture the reality of the Black experience in Canada.

The book is divided into two complementary parts: a narrative history and a documentary history. Chapters 1 and 2 of Part I trace the narrative of race from the institution of slavery under French rule in the late seventeenth century to the widespread practice of racial segregation and the struggle for racial equality in Canada during the twentieth century. Chapter 3 presents the personal reminiscences of Viola Desmond's youngest sister, Wanda Robson. She relates her childhood experiences of race, her memories of her sister Viola and her personal journey of self-discovery through education and community involvement.

The documentary history provides a detailed discussion of important but littleknown or previously unpublished primary sources. It begins with a commentary on the inventory of the material possessions of Marie Marguerite Rose, a freed female African slave in eighteenth century Ile Royale. This document accompanies the commentary, and it is the only known inventory of a freed African female slave in Canada. The inventory is evidence of the life of a remarkable woman, and it provides a number of insights into slavery and society in eighteenth century Ile Royale. Chapter 5 focuses on West Indian immigration to Canada during the early twentieth century. It documents, through a series of letters and reports, the efforts of William D. Scott, Canada's Superintendent of Immigration from 1903–1924, to restrict the immigration of Blacks to Canada on the grounds that they were unsuited to the climate and culture of Canada. The correspondence and other evidence presented in this chapter supports the fact that, in spite of Canada's racially restrictive immigration policy, there was a steady flow of Black immigration to Canada during the first two decades of the twentieth century. The chapter illustrates the fact that although Blacks experienced widespread racial discrimination during this period there was an emerging cultural self-identity and pride among Canada's Black population as well as the growth of distinct Black communities in most major urban areas of the country. Chapter 6 focuses on the culture of racism in Canada and the "Americanization" of Canadian racial attitudes during the twentieth century. The commentary discusses how the American sphere of influence fostered a number of racial stereotypes that have had a significant and enduring presence in Canada. The final chapter is based, in part, on an unpublished interview with Pearleen Oliver, one of Canada's most important but little-known civil rights activists in the twentieth century.

Pearleen Oliver was a pioneer in the fight for racial equality, and she is largely responsible for breaking the colour barrier that prevented Blacks from training and practicing the profession of nursing in Canada.

NOTES

1. "The Late Viola Desmond Granted Apology, Free Pardon," Nova Scotia Canada, April 15, 2010. Retrieved from <novascotia.ca/news/smr/2010-04-14-pardon.asp>. See also the document section of the book.

2. Ignorance regarding the history of race relations in Canada has helped foster the myth that, in matters of race, Canada is superior to the United States. See Joseph Mensah, *Black Canadians: History, Experience, Social Conditions,* second edition (Black Point, NS: Fernwood Publishing, 2010), p. 2. Jeffrey Reitz and Raymond Breton have compared American and Canadian attitudes toward race and have concluded that Canadians and Americans are similar in their attitudes and behaviors toward racial minorities. See Jeffrey Reitz and Raymond Breton, "Prejudice and Discrimination in Canada and United States: A Comparison," in Vic Satzewich (ed.), *Racism and Social Inequality in Canada: Concepts, Controversies and Strategic Resistance* (Toronto: Thompson Educational Press, 1998), p. 65.

3. This aspect of Canada's image as the Promised Land was a result of the *Anti-Slavery Act* of 1793, which partially abolished slavery in Upper Canada. Knowledge of this act spread through word of mouth to all slave-holding regions of the United States, and it helped in the creation of the Underground Railroad. The Act of 1793 is discussed more fully in Chapter 1.

4. Robin Winks, *The Blacks in Canada: A History,* 2nd edition (Montreal: McGill-Queen's Press, 1997).

5. James W. St. G. Walker, *The Black Loyalists: The Search for a Promised Land in Nova Scotia and Sierra Leone, 1783–1870* (Toronto: University of Toronto Press, 1993).

6. Afua Cooper, *The Hanging of Angelique: The Untold Story of Canadian Slavery and the Burning of Old Montreal* (Toronto: Harper Perennial, 2006).

7. Harvey Amani Whitfield, *Blacks on the Border: The Black Refugees in British North America, 1815–1860* (Burlington, VT: University of Vermont Press, 2006).

8. Sarah-Jane Mathieu, *North of the Color Line: Migration and Black Resistance in Canada, 1870–1955* (Chapel Hill: The University of North Carolina Press, 2010).

9. For a thorough discussion of the historiography of Blacks in Atlantic Canada, see Harvey Amani Whitfield, "Reviewing Blackness in Atlantic Canada and the African Atlantic Canadian Diaspora," *Acadiensis* 37 (Summer/Autumn, 2008): pp. 1–9. Other noteworthy publications in African Canadian History include Peggy Bristow, *We're Rooted Here and They Can't Pull Us Up: Essays in African Canadian Women's History* (Toronto: University of Toronto Press, 1994); Nina Reid-Maroney, *The Reverend Janice Johnson and African Canadian History, 1868–1967* (Rochester: University of Rochester Press, 2013); Adrienne Shadd, *The Journey from Tollgate to Parkway: African Canadians in Hamilton* (Toronto: Dundurn, 2010); Barrington Walker, ed., *The African Canadian Legal Odyssey: Historical Essays* (Toronto: University of Toronto Press, 2012); Dorothy Williams, *The Road to Now: A History of Blacks in Montreal* (Montreal: Vehicule Press, 1997).

10. Constance Backhouse, *Colour-Coded: A Legal History of Racism in Canada, 1900–1950* (Toronto: Published for the Osgoode Society for Canadian Legal History by University of Toronto Press, 1999).

11. Constance Backhouse, *Colour-Coded* (Toronto: University of Toronto Press, 1999), p. i.
12. Constance Backhouse's research on the Viola Desmond case first appeared in an article published in *Dalhousie Law Review* in 1994. See Constance Backhouse, "Racial Segregation in Canadian Legal History: Viola Desmond's Challenge, Nova Scotia, 1946," *Dalhousie Law Review* 17 (1994): pp. 299–362.
13. Owen Thomas, "Cultural Tourism, Commemorative Plaques, and African–Canadian Historiography: Challenging Historical Marginality," *Social History/Histoire Sociale* 29 (1996): pp. 431–32.
14. This historical void has partially been addressed by research conducted under The Promised Land Project, a community-university alliance (CURA) focusing on the contributions of nineteenth century Black pioneers in Chatham, Chatham Townships and Dawn Settlement. See The Promised Land Project at <huronuc.on.ca/research/promised_landproject/>.
15. Simon Schama, *Rough Crossing: Britain, the Slaves and the American Revolution* (New York: Harper Collins, 2006); Lawrence Hill, *The Book of Negroes* (Toronto: Harper Collins, 2007).
16. One important exception to this historiographical trend is Ruth Holmes Whitehead's *Black Loyalists: Southern Settlers of Nova Scotia's First Free Black Communities* (Halifax: Nimbus Publishing, 2013). Whitehead's study is the partial culmination of the work she began in 1991 under the Nova Scotia Museum's Black Heritage Resource database project. This project has helped establish a genealogical history of people of African descent living in Nova Scotia. Whitehead's study traces the Black Loyalist population from their lives under slavery in South Carolina, Georgia and Florida to their descendants in all the Maritime Provinces.
17. This is particularly the case in relation to the past Government of Canada's policies regarding cultural assimilation and Residential Schools. See The Truth and Reconciliation Commission of Canada website at <trc.ca/website/trcinstitution/index.php?=3>.
18. The history of Africville is discussed in Chapter 2.
19. In 2006, the Black Cultural Centre in Dartmouth and the Black Loyalist Heritage Society's office in Birchtown, Nova Scotia, were firebombed. For a fuller discussion of these incidents, see Jennifer J. Nelson, *Razing Africville: A Geography of Racism* (Toronto: University of Toronto Press, 2008) pp. 148–150. In February 2010, a cross burning occurred in Hants County, Nova Scotia. See "Burning Cross Ignited Racial Tension in Nova Scotia," *Globe and Mail* (February 24, 2010). For the most recent racial incident, see "Employees at Leon's Furniture Outlet Fired for Lynching Black Statue," *National Post* (September 5, 2013). According to Statistics Canada, in 2010, Blacks were the most commonly targeted racial group in Canada. There were 271 racial incidents reported that year, and Blacks accounted for approximately 40 percent of the total. See Cara Dowden and Shannon Brennan, "Police-Reported Hate Crime in Canada, 2010," Statistic Canada, retrieved from <Statcan.gc.ca/pub/85-001-x/2012001/article/11635- eng.htm#5>. In Toronto Black males are three times more likely to be carded by police. See "By the Numbers: Facts about Racial Discrimination in Canada," United Federation of Canadian Workers (March 17, 2013), retrieved from <Ufcw.ca/

index- php?option=com_content&viewarticle&id=3324Aby-the-numbers—facts-about-racial- discrimination-in-can>.

20. Wanda Robson discusses in detail her first experience of racial prejudice in Chapter 3. References to Virginia Travis and Philip Alexander are from oral interviews conducted in Buxton and Chatham, Ontario, June 15–19, 2012. Virginia Travis also discusses her childhood experiences of racial prejudice in her comments in the Promised Land Project Symposium roundtable discussion. See the Appendix section of the book.

21. Estimates of the total number of Africans forcibly removed and transported to the Americas between the sixteenth and nineteenth centuries has been the subject of intense debate over the years. The current estimate of over 10.5 million is based on the latest data and analysis of the Trans-Atlantic Slave Trade Database Project led by David Eltis and Martin Halbert at Emery University. See <slavevoyages.org>. For a fuller discussion of the debate over these estimates, see Davis Eltis and David Richardson (editors), *Extending the Frontiers: Essays on the New Transatlantic Slave Trade Database* (New Haven: Yale University Press, 2008), pp. 5–8; 37–44.

22. Olaudah Equiano, *The Interesting Narrative of the Life of Olaudah Equiano: Or, Gustavus Vassa, The African* (1789) (New York: Random House, 2004).

23. Graham Reynolds and Richard MacKinnon, *The Peopling of Atlantic Canada* [CD ROM] (Sydney, NS: Folkus Atlantic, 2000), Family Roots, p. 8. Carmelita Carvey Robinson's search for her family roots is a story involving a remarkable coincidence of family origins and history. After joining the Black Heritage Resource Files Project, she discovered that the Director of the project, Ruth Holms Whitehead, shared similar roots from the same location in North Carolina. They both travelled together to visit their ancestral home and their extraordinary account of family connection and history later became the subject of a National Film Board of Canada video documentary. See Lesley Ann Patten, Director, *Loyalties* (Toronto: National Film Board of Canada, 1999). For Ruth Holms Whitehead's account of her collaboration with Carmelita Carvey Robinson, see *Black Loyalists: Southern Settlers of Nova Scotia's First Free Black Communities*, pp. 181–83.

24. Wanda Robson, *Sister to Courage: Stories from the World of Viola Desmond, Canada's Rosa Parks* (Wreck Cove, NS: Breton Books, 2010).

PART I

A NARRATIVE HISTORY

Chapter 1

A Narrative of Race in Canadian History from Slavery to the Underground Railroad

Canadians usually associate extreme forms of racism such as slavery and segregation with the history of the United States. These are seen as part of an historical narrative that extends from slavery, the Civil War and Jim Crow laws to the civil rights movement of the 1960s. Although it is still not widely acknowledged, much of this historical narrative also applies to Canada. The following discussion traces the narrative of race in Canadian history from the establishment of slavery under French rule in the eighteenth century through the decline of slavery and the growth of the Underground Railroad in the nineteenth century. Chapter 2 continues the discussion of the narrative of race in the twentieth century and it focuses, in particular, on the emerging pattern of racial discrimination and segregation in Nova Scotia and Ontario.

The Institution of Slavery in New France

The European "discovery" of America in 1492 initiated a new era of commercial expansion that was facilitated and sustained through slavery. This expansion was based upon a distinctive pattern of transatlantic trade that linked together Europe, Africa and the Americas wherein the resources and agricultural commodities such as sugar, tobacco and cotton flowed from the western hemisphere to Europe's expanding consumer markets. The labourers who produced these goods were overwhelmingly enslaved Africans who were the victims of the transatlantic slave trade. Over the course of three centuries, ending with the abolition of the slave trade in 1807, more than 10.5 million Africans were forcefully uprooted from their tribal homelands in order to be transported to the New World and sold into slavery. The French, along with the British, Dutch, Spanish and Portuguese were major players in the slave trade. Over 1 million Africans were transported and sold by the French as slaves, and although most French slaves worked on plantations in

Louisiana and the West Indies, over one thousand Africans were brought to Canada as slaves during the seventeenth and eighteenth centuries.[1]

The importation of African slaves to Canada began officially in 1687 following a formal request to Louis XIV by Marquis de Denonville, the Governor of New France. Governor Denonville argued that African slaves were required to fill the increasing demand for labour and that they would supplement the relatively large number of existing slaves that had been drawn from Canada's aboriginal peoples (known as *panis*). Louis XIV felt that African slaves were too far removed from their native homeland and were unsuitable for work in the harsh winter climate of Canada; however, he reluctantly agreed to the Governor's request. Over the next century, a small but steady stream of African slaves were brought to all regions of New France.[2]

In Ile Royale (known today as Cape Breton Island), the institution of slavery was, in many respects, typical of most French settlements in Canada. Unlike the French West Indies, where slaves worked tirelessly on plantations, slaves at Ile Royale were mainly domestic servants and labourers. In the fortified town of Louisbourg, on Ile Royale, there were 266 slaves and approximately 90 percent of them were Black. Some of these slaves had been born in Africa, but the vast majority had been born in the French West Indies. Historian Kenneth Donovan has spent a number of years researching the history of slavery in eighteenth century Louisbourg, and he has concluded that slavery formed an integral part of the social fiber of Louisbourg; yet, unlike other slave holding regions of the New World, Louisbourg had the distinction of being "a society with slaves, not a slave society."[3]

Owning slaves in Louisbourg was a symbol of social status, and most of the governing elite as well as many officers and members of the middle class owned slaves. Although most slaves were bought by individuals to work as domestic servants, some were purchased by the government. In 1740, for example, François Bigot, Louisbourg *Commissaires-ordonnateur,* arranged for a slave by the name of François to be sent from the West Indies to serve as the town executioner. This was a socially repugnant occupation, and it was usually reserved for social outcasts like slaves and convicted criminals. François had been convicted of manslaughter as a young boy and he was given the choice of being executed or taking on the job of hangman at Louisbourg. Francois "voluntarily" accepted the job, and after arriving at Louisbourg he was given food rations, an annual salary of 300 *livres* and a small log house with a fenced yard and garden. Later, government authorities arranged for him to marry the widow of a British officer.[4]

One of the most notable slaves at Louisbourg was Marie Marguerite Rose, who has recently been recognized by the Government of Canada as a person of national historic significance. Marie was a remarkable woman. She was born in 1717 in Guinea, a small country on the west coast of Africa, and as a young girl she was captured and transported to North America in order to be sold into slavery. In 1736, at the age of nineteen, she was purchased by Jean Loppinot, a French officer who was living with his family in Louisbourg. Marie, like many of the domestic slaves at Louisbourg, was baptized Catholic, and she lived in the Loppinot residence in order to cook and help with domestic chores. Two years after Marie arrived in Louisbourg, she gave birth to a son, Jean-Francois, who, because of his mother's status, immediately became a slave in the Loppinot household. Although the boy's father is listed as "unknown," it is likely that Jean Loppinot was the birth father.

Jean-Francois grew up in the Loppinot family, and he helped his mother with the domestic chores. Shortly after the first siege of Louisbourg in 1745, Jean-Francois died at the age of thirteen. After his death, Marie continued as a domestic slave in the Loppinot household, and during her nearly twenty years of service, she helped raise the Loppinot's twelve children. In 1755, at the age of thirty-eight, Marie was given her freedom. Later during that year, she married Jean Baptiste Laurent, a Mi'kmaq, and together they opened a tavern in a house they rented next to the Loppinot's home. As a tavern operator, Marie demonstrated a wide range of business and management skills. Although she could not read or write, Marie was able to maintain records and purchase all the supplies for her tavern. Marie's success as a businesswoman and tavern owner demonstrates that freed slaves had some degree of opportunity and could gain acceptance in the wider community. Owning and operating a tavern was one occupation available to free Black women in New France. The precedence for this had already been established in the West Indies before Marie and her husband started their tavern in Louisbourg.[5]

Unfortunately, Marie's life as a free Black woman was very short lived. In 1757, just two years after gaining her freedom, Marie died suddenly at the age of forty. Upon her death, the local French authorities entered her residence and, in accordance with the law, conducted a detailed inventory of Marie's material possessions. This document, as Kenneth Donovan notes, is a unique historical record in Canada and "is the only inventory of a women who had been recently freed from slavery."[6]

From the clothing and other material possessions that Marie left behind, it is possible to gain a glimpse of her life and her extraordinary repertoire of talents. The receipts, tavern supplies and vast assortment of cloth, dye, articles of clothing and other material possessions reveal that, in addition to being a successful tavern operator, Marie was a cook and a gardener and, like many other women in eighteenth century Louisbourg, she was skilled at making and mending clothes. It is also interesting to note that the inventory of her dye, wool and cotton cloth indicate that she was accustomed to making bright coloured and patterned clothing that was popular in her native homeland of Guinea.

Marie's personal wardrobe, handkerchiefs and necklaces provide evidence that, in the manner of her appearance, she maintained her African identity. This aspect of Marie's life raises a number of fascinating questions about the self-identity and sense of community among slaves in Ile Royale. We know from the work of Ken Donovan that there was at least one other female slave at Louisbourg from Guinea. Given the tight knit social structure of eighteenth century Louisbourg and the relatively large number of slaves, it is reasonable to assume that, to some extent, a slave community existed and Marie would have had an opportunity to form a social bond with other enslaved Africans, particularly those from her native homeland. Apart from these speculations, we know that, in many respects, Marie is representative of the ingenuity, perseverance and autonomy, together with the wide range of skills, possessed by Blacks in the new world; her life also demonstrates that there were limited opportunities available to free Blacks at Louisbourg and elsewhere in New France.[7] Marie's inventory of material possessions offers new insights into the nature of slavery and freedom in eighteenth century New France, which is discussed in more detail in Chapter 4.

Slavery and Freedom Under British Rule

The institution of slavery in Canada continued under British rule during the eighteenth century. We don't know a great deal about the history of slavery during this period, and the very existence of slaves in the British settlements of Canada has been largely overshadowed by the dramatic events of the Revolutionary War and the epic story of the exodus of Black Loyalists to Nova Scotia.[8] By 1784, approximately 3,500 Black Loyalist had come to Nova Scotia, and by the winter of 1792, nearly one-third of the these Black Loyalists had gone to Sierra Leone. The Loyalist migration also brought over 1,500 slaves to Nova Scotia, New Brunswick and Prince Edward Island. This was, on a much larger scale, a continuation of the earlier settlement pattern that brought Loyalists and their slaves to various regions of Nova Scotia, Quebec and Lower Canada. The institution of slavery under British rule was an extension of the slave trade and, accordingly, African slaves could be bought or sold in all regions of Canada or purchased in the West Indies or elsewhere and transported directly to Canada.[9]

The sale and purchase of slaves is well documented through the record of transactions and the advertisements that appeared in newspapers in Lower Canada, Quebec and Nova Scotia. As early as 1752, an advertisement appeared in the *Halifax Gazette* that announced the sale of six slaves who had been recently imported from the West Indies by the merchant Joshua Mauger. The group consisted of a woman (age 35), two boys (ages 12 and 13), two teenage males (age 18) and one man (age 30). The young boys are described as "healthy and well shaped and understand [sic] some English," and the two other older boys are described as having "agreeable tempers and fit for any kind of business." The women is described as a

"Negro wench ... creole born [who] has been brought up in a Gentleman's family, and capable of doing all sorts of work ... [such as] needle-work, and in the best manner; also washing, ironing, cookery, and *every other thing that can be expected from such a slave*" [emphasis added].[10] This advertisement is subtly suggestive of the kind degradation and sexual exploitation female slaves were subjected to under all forms of slavery. Slaves of mixed race (commonly referred to as creoles) were of special value because of their lighter complexion, and slave traders would market them for a higher price as housekeepers or mistresses. It should be noted, however, that the very nature of the institution of slavery meant that *all* female slaves were vulnerable to some degree of sexual exploitation. As it was likely the case with Marie Marguerite Rose in Ile Royale, domestic female slaves frequently gave birth to the children of their masters. Among the seventy female slaves in Ile Royale, for example, thirty-six gave birth to a total of forty-eight "illegitimate" children.[11]

Historian Amani Whitfield has researched the history of Black communities in Nova Scotia, and he notes that slavery existed throughout all regions of Loyalist Nova Scotia. In the agriculturally rich regions of the Annapolis Valley, for example, slaves provided the labour to several of the farms. Although most Loyalist slaveholders brought only a few slaves with them to Nova Scotia, there are a few documented examples of Loyalists who brought dozens of slaves as well as numerous indentured servants. It is clear from the recent research by Whitfield, Cahill and others that Nova Scotia evolved both as a free society and a society with slaves.[12]

The Loyalist migration brought nearly 30,000 new immigrants to the eastern shores of Nova Scotia. In addition to causing economic, political and administrative problems for the colonial government, the Loyalist migration had a profound and lasting effect on race relations in Nova Scotia. The arrival of Loyalist slaveholders expanded the institution of slavery and reinforced negative racial stereotypes that portrayed Blacks as inherently inferior and incapable of handling the responsibilities of freedom. Such views echoed the commonly held defence of slavery in America that argued, in the words of Thomas Jefferson, that the institution of slavery was a "necessary evil." Blacks, according to Jefferson, were "inferior to the whites in the endowments of both body and mind" and needed the paternal guidance of their white masters.[13] This defence of slavery developed into the so-called "positive good" argument that became popular among slave holders during the nineteenth century. It also contributed to the creation of the "Sambo" racial stereotype that portrayed Blacks as being childlike, docile, lazy in nature and unfit for freedom. This image of Blacks became so widespread in North America — Canada included — that nearly a century later it influenced aspects of the character Tom in New England abolitionist Harriet Beecher Stowe's popular *Uncle Tom's Cabin*. Tom was inspired by the real life figure Josiah Henson, a fugitive slave who figured prominently in the development of the Underground Railroad and the establishment of an independent and self-reliant Black community in Ontario during the nineteenth century. Stowe reflected the racial views of her generation, and in her novel, the majority of fugitive slaves who sought exile in Canada were of mixed blood. She believed that it was the seed of freedom contained in the white blood that flowed through the veins of mixed race fugitives that led them to seek the Promised Land.[14]

In late eighteenth century Nova Scotia, the views of Loyalist slaveholders came into sharp conflict with the spirit, values and aspirations of freedom that were held by the Black Loyalists and other free Blacks in the colony. This tension between freedom and slavery played out in the personal and collective struggles of Blacks throughout the maritime region. The story of the Black Loyalist journey from slavery is well documented in the personal accounts of Black Loyalists like Boston King, David George and John Marrant and in the work of historians James Walker and, more recently, Simon Schama. All these accounts record the hardships and extraordinary courage of an entire population of former slaves who settled in a dozen or more communities in Nova Scotia, New Brunswick, Prince Edward Island and Cape Breton.[15]

The first major wave of Loyalists brought approximately 2,000 whites, 1,000 Blacks and 800 disbanded soldiers to Roseway Harbour on the south shore of Nova Scotia on May 14, 1783. Soon after their arrival, the Loyalists, under the employment of the colonial administration, commenced an ambitious effort to construct houses and other community structures in the new town of Shelburne. In an area close to Shelburne, the Black Loyalists began the settlement of Birchtown, which was home to nearly 1,500 free Blacks and was the largest African urban community in North America.[16] Loyalist and Chief Surveyor of Shelburne, Benjamin Marston, recorded the rapid progress of settlement and noted that from the spring of 1783 to the early summer of 1784 the Loyalists had built nearly 1,500 houses in Shelburne as well as public buildings such as barracks and jailhouses. A sizable portion of the workforce consisted of the Black Loyalists referred to as "Birchtowners" who were organized into twenty-one companies each under the command of a Black captain. In addition to being well disciplined, many of the Black Loyalists were skilled tradesmen. Marston wrote in his diary that he preferred Black Loyalist workers over white Loyalists because "they work very hard and labour cheaply."[17]

Marston's comment reveals a critical source of racial tension that would soon lead to racial violence. The white Loyalists together with the disbanded soldiers were angered by the fact that the Blacks were willing to work for lower wages. They were also frustrated by the inaction of the colonial administration in fulfilling the promise of providing land to all those who supported the British in the American Revolutionary War. On July 26, 1784, violence erupted when a mob of disbanded soldiers attacked free Blacks and destroyed approximately twenty of their newly constructed homes. Marston witnessed the event and wrote in his diary that the race riot was "an attempt by the unruly disbanded soldiers to drive the Negroes out of town because they labour cheaper than they will."[18]

This event was the first recorded race riot in North America and, in some important respects, marks the beginning of a pattern of racial conflict that extended well into the twentieth century. At the end of the First World War, for example, racial violence erupted in east St. Louis, Chicago and dozens of other cities and towns in northeastern United States. Whites in these northern states feared that Blacks migrating from the south would work for lower wages and be hired as "scabs" in order to undermine the efforts of labour unions to improve wages and working conditions. The situation was similar in Canada after the WWI and racial violence occurred in several industrial towns that had relatively large Black populations, although on a much smaller scale.[19]

The race riot in July of 1784 is similar to modern urban racial tensions in yet another important respect: the rioting white mob sought to drive Blacks out from the town itself. This may very well be the first example of an action of violence and discrimination by a group of white residents to forcefully remove Blacks from their community. As a consequence, this reinforced a pattern of racial segregation. It also represented an important turning point for Black Loyalists, especially the residents of Birchtown. The events of July 1784 not only forced free Blacks from their homes in Shelburne but also ended employment opportunities for a large number of the residents of Birchtown. In partial response to the discontent among the white Loyalists and former soldiers, the colonial administration increased its efforts to distribute parcels of land according to the agreement for expatriation and settlement in Nova Scotia. The Black Loyalists were not so fortunate in receiving their promise of land. They were the last to receive land grants, and what they did receive was substantially smaller and far less suitable for farming than the land that other Loyalists received.[20]

With little or no suitable land to farm and limited opportunities for employment, the residents of Birchtown, and elsewhere, were not well equipped to survive the winter months. It should be noted that the winters of 1783–1784 were unusually harsh, even for those who were accustomed to the climate in Nova Scotia.[21] The severe winters were followed by several years with poor growing conditions that led to widespread crop failures. In January 1787, the living conditions were so bad that people died from starvation or exposure to the elements. The famous Black Loyalist, Boston King described the situation in biblical terms as a "dreadful famine" that "prevailed" at Birchtown and in other Black settlements in Nova Scotia. "Many of the poor," King wrote in his memoirs, "were compelled to sell their best gowns for five pounds of flour, in order to support life. When they had parted with all their clothes, even to their blankets, several of them fell down dead in the streets, thro' hunger."[22]

The poverty and distress in Birchtown was so severe that Boston King was forced to leave in search of any kind of employment. He eventually encountered Captain Selex, who hired him to build a chest. King provided the following description of the incident in his memoirs, which were published in 1798:

I rejoiced at the offer, and returning home, set about it immediately. I worked all night, and by eight o'clock next morning finished the chest, which I carried to the Captain's house, thro' the snow which was three feet deep. But to my disappointment he rejected it. However he gave me directions to make another. On my way home, being pinched by hunger and cold, I fell down several times, thro' weakness, and expected to die upon the spot. But even in this situation, I found my mind resigned to the divine will, and rejoiced in the midst of tribulation; for the Lord delivered me from all murmurings and discontent, altho' I had but one pint of Indian meal left for the support of myself and wife. Having finished another chest, I took it to my employer the next day; but being afraid he would serve me as he had done before, I took a saw along with me in order to sell it. On the way, I prayed that the Lord would give me a prosperous journey, and was answered to the joy of my heart, for Captain Selex paid me for the chest in Indian-corn; and the other chest I sold for 2s.6d. and the saw for 3s.9d. altho' it cost me a guinea; yet I was exceeding thankful to procure a reprieve from the dreadful anguish of perishing by famine. O what a wonderful deliverance did GOD work for me that day! And he taught me to live by faith, and to put my trust in him, more than I ever had done before.[23]

King's description is testimony to his remarkable perseverance and ability to adapt to difficult circumstances, and it provides a vivid glimpse into the life experiences of the Black Loyalists. It also reveals the role of faith as a source of strength in partially mitigating the extraordinary hardships that Blacks had to endure during this period.

King, like many other residents at Birchtown, had come under the influence of Moses Wilkinson, the Methodist evangelist. Following his wife's conversion, King joined the faith in 1785. He eventually moved to Preston and became a Methodist preacher in 1791. King and Baptist preacher David George, along with other Black religious leaders, were instrumental in persuading a large number of their followers to join in the movement led by British abolitionists to relocate Black Loyalists in Sierra Leone. In their continued quest for a promised land of freedom, Blacks from communities in Nova Scotia and a small number from New Brunswick made their way to the port of Halifax in December 1791. John Clarkson, the brother of renowned abolitionist Thomas Clarkson, arranged for a convoy of fifteen ships carrying 1,196 people, including 383 children, to set sail for Sierra Leone on January 9, 1792. The departing flotilla was an impressive scene for the residents of Halifax, and it was the beginning of an entirely new phase in the lives of the voyagers. The exodus, in the words of Simon Schama, was "not just about an escape from bondage ... it would be an experimental voyage of social transformation."[24] A population who had lived a life of slavery and servitude was now in a situation that did not allow for distinctions based on race. Free from the tethers of bondage, the pioneers to Africa were now the true masters of their own fate, and each individual was considered an equal and valued member of society.

The exodus of Black Loyalists had an immediate impact on the remaining population of Nova Scotia. Birchtown was almost completely depopulated, and there were not enough residents or employment opportunities to sustain the growth of the town over the long term. The town of Preston, the former home of Boston King and his Methodist following, was reduced to a handful of residents, but its proximity to Halifax provided a variety of employment opportunities that insured its survival. The departure of Black Loyalists also reinforced negative white attitudes towards Blacks. For many whites, the experience of Black Loyalists and the dramatic departure of such large numbers of them demonstrated that they could not handle the responsibilities of freedom. This confirmed the commonly held view, especially among slave-holding Loyalists, that free Blacks could not work as effectively as slaves and they would eventually become a permanent tax burden on the community. The situation was made even worse by the fact that the exodus of Black Loyalists left behind the most disadvantaged among the Black population. According to James Walker, this segment of the population included "slaves, indentured servants, and sharecroppers ... and the weak, the aged, the indebted, and the unskilled." These people were in an economically vulnerable situation and "were neither free to choose their employment nor capable of bargaining an equitable share in Nova Scotia's economy."[25]

It is clear that this first encounter with a large population of Blacks in Nova Scotia resulted in "distrust, anger, and resentment among peoples of African descent and the white population."[26] These sentiments were reinforced with the arrival of more than 500 Jamaican Maroons in 1796 that were exiled to Nova Scotia because of their resistance to British rule in Jamaica. The Maroons found life in Nova Scotia difficult. The climate and soil were not suitable for farming the kind of food they were accustomed to in Jamaica. As a result, most of the Maroons were forced to work for low wages as labourers. In 1800, they took advantage of the opportunity to leave Nova Scotia in order to resettle in Sierra Leone.

The Decline of Slavery in Canada

The exodus of Black Loyalists and Maroons fragmented the Black settlements in Nova Scotia. Churches, schools and other community organizations were shattered to the point that for the next several decades, as Walker notes, "there were no longer in existence large and isolated concentrations of Black people served by institutions under their own effective control."[27] In positive contrast to this situation, the departure of Blacks had the temporary effect of diminishing racial tensions. At least until the next major wave of Black migration that occurred with the flood of Black refugees during the War of 1812, which pitted the United Sates against Britain, Blacks had a less visible presence in Canada. Slavery continued but on a much smaller scale, and for the majority of free Blacks, there were clear signs that their lives were improving. By the beginning of the nineteenth century, most indentured terms of service had been completed and many Blacks began to develop trades for the expanding economies of Nova Scotia and Upper Canada. The War of 1812 benefited Blacks by increasing wages and the demand for labour. Support for the war was nearly universal among Black communities, and the willingness of Black men to serve in defence of Canada against American aggression won the approval of most of the white population.

In Nova Scotia, a Black company was created under the first battalion of Halifax militia, and it attracted 120 eager volunteers.[28] In Upper Canada, there was widespread fear among the Black community that an American victory over the British would result in the reintroduction of slavery in Canada. Black volunteers rushed to enlist in the military and many of these recruits, "Black men in red coats," became the first line of defence in guarding the Detroit and Niagara frontiers.[29]

Although slavery and racial prejudice persisted in Canada, there were clear signs that anti-slavery sentiments were increasing throughout all regions of the country.[30] Toward the close of the eighteenth century, slavery was still firmly rooted in Nova Scotia, New Brunswick and Lower Canada; however, there was persistent opposition to slavery among some judges and government officials. In Nova Scotia, Chief Justices Thomas Andrew Strange, who served from 1791 to 1796, and Sampson Salter Blowers, who served from 1797 to 1833, were staunch anti-slavery advocates. Both Justices engaged in a "judicial war of attrition upon slave-owners."[31] The Justices together with impassioned efforts of Rev. James MacGregor, a Scottish Presbyterian minister, waged a campaign against slavery through the power of the pulpit, the pen and judicial opinion.

The fight to end slavery took place on both sides of the Atlantic, and even before the Revolutionary War, it was clear that England's — and thus Canada's — position on slavery was beginning to diverge from that of the United States. This was evident from a case brought before the Court of King's Bench (Britain's highest criminal court) in 1772. The case involved James Somerset, a Virginia slave who had been brought to England by his master and had escaped only to be recaptured and placed on board a ship bound for Jamaica. A lower court had ordered Somerset free until a higher court could hear his case. Within a few months, the case went before Lord Chief Justice Mansfield, one of England's most able and respected judges who is acknowledged today as the father of modern commercial law. Mansfield knew the importance of the case because it pitted the protection of property against the right of liberty on English soil. He ultimately ruled in favor of Somerset, and although he was careful to limit his ruling to the unique circumstances of this case, it was immediately seen by many in England as a legal precedent that freed all slaves in England. Historian Adam Hochschild regards Mansfield's decision as a watershed in the fight to abolish slavery, not because of the Judge's deliberate intentions but because of the widespread public perception that followed: "This was a case in which what people *thought* was decided proved more important than the actual wording. Almost everyone believed that Mansfield had indeed outlawed slavery in England, including many lower-court judges who subsequently ruled against more than a dozen masters trying to assert ownership over slaves on English soil."[32] The Somerset case may well have given many Americans cause for concern, and for slave owners, in particular, it could certainly be regarded as one more argument in support of American independence.

One of the most significant milestones in the struggle to end slavery in Canada involved the efforts of John Graves Simcoe, Upper Canada's first lieutenant governor. Simcoe was a staunch Tory loyalist and former commander of The Queen's Rangers, a New York Loyalist regiment that fought in the American Revolutionary war. Prior to becoming lieutenant governor of Upper Canada, Simcoe had served nine years in the British Parliament. As a member of parliament, Simcoe became a close friend and ally of William Wilberforce, the outspoken and renowned abolitionist, and supported the movement to end Britain's role in the transatlantic slave trade. Simcoe firmly believed that slavery was a fundamental violation of Christianity as well as the British constitution.[33]

In March of 1793, after returning to Canada from England and assuming the office of lieutenant governor of Upper Canada, Simcoe heard of an incident involving the violent apprehension of a fugitive slave girl by the name of Chloe Cooly who, after being bound, was forcefully taken by her former master from Canada back across the Niagara River to the United States. Simcoe was deeply moved by this incident, and he vowed to introduce legislation to end slavery in Upper Canada. Although he lacked widespread public support as well as the support of his cabinet, several members of which were slave owners, Simcoe and his small circle of supporters managed to work out a compromise that was passed into law later in the year. The legislation did not abolish slavery outright, but, as the actual wording of the *Anti-Slavery Act of 1793* stated, it was intended "to Prevent the Further Introduction of Slavery, and to Limit the Term of Contracts for Servitude" in Upper Canada. The Act went into effect on July 9, 1793, and it provided the legal grounds for the gradual abolition of slavery by limiting the institution to existing slaves. Children of this population of slaves were given their freedom after they turned twenty-five, and their children were free at birth.[34]

The Act of 1793, like the Somerset ruling, represented a watershed in the effort to abolish slavery in Canada, and it quickly became a powerful symbol in creating the image of Canada as the Promised Land. As word of mouth spread to nearly all regions of the slave states, there was a growing awareness among slave communities that the dream of freedom could be realized in Canada.[35]

There were two other events in 1793 that had a lasting influence on the institution of slavery in the United States and on shaping the destiny of Canada as the Promised Land. First, as Canada moved toward the gradual abolition of slavery, the Congress of the United Sates, under pressure from slave owners and the southern slave states, passed the *Fugitive Slave Act,* which gave additional powers under the Constitution to apprehend fugitive slaves, many of whom were headed north. The Act also strengthened the penalties for aiding and harbouring runaway slaves. This legislation aimed at strengthening the laws to protect the "property" of slave owners, and it came at a time when many Americans began to question the morality of the institution of slavery.[36]

The idea of the gradual abolition of slavery was gaining popularity in northern states and even among whites in slave holding states. However, any hope that this trend would lead to concrete action to abolish the institution of slavery was quickly dispelled by another event that occurred that same year. In 1793, Eli Whitney introduced the cotton gin, a mechanized drum that removed seeds from the raw cotton fiber. This invention revolutionized the cotton industry by shifting the burden of labour from removing seeds to picking cotton. With Eli Whitney's simple but remarkable invention only one slave was required to operate the rotating drum. The immediate effect of the cotton gin dramatically expanded the production of cotton as well as the demand for slaves to work in the cotton fields. This technological innovation ushered in the era of "King Cotton" and insured that the southern economy and way of life would depend, more than ever, on the institution of slavery.[37] In Mississippi, for example, there was a direct correlation between cotton production and the expansion of slavery. From 1821 to 1859, cotton production increased from 20,000 bales to 960,000 bales, nearly one fourth of national output.[38]

During the same period, the slave population more than doubled each decade. A similar process occurred throughout the cotton-growing states of the south, and by the outbreak of the Civil War, the total number of slaves in the southern United States increased from 900,000 in 1800 to over 4 million in 1860.[39]

The Underground Railroad

It is impossible to give an exact date to the beginning of the Underground Railroad. It had its origins well before the introduction of the railroad and the metaphor that so aptly describes its organization and operations. From the very beginning of the establishment of the institution of slavery in North America, there were instances of slave rebellion and escape on the part of individuals and groups who either spontaneously or through careful planning broke from their chains of bondage in the pursuit of freedom.

Some of the more fortunate fugitives would receive food, shelter and guidance from sympathetic whites, free Blacks or fellow slaves. Eventually, many of these runaway slaves made their way to relatively safe locations in states where anti-slavery sentiments were taking firm root, such as Pennsylvania, Illinois, Ohio and New England. The loosely structured network that eventually became known as the Underground Railroad began with these isolated and singular accounts of courage on the part of slaves, together with the sympathetic acts of kindness and humanity among a vast array of individuals.

We might reasonably mark the beginning of the Underground Railroad with the scene witnessed by a young Quaker boy by the name of Levi Coffin in 1805, who watched a procession of slaves pass by the front of his farm in North Carolina. The procession was a frequent event in the process of relocating slaves to new plantation settlements in the western frontier regions. Levi learned from his father that slave husbands and their wives and children were forced apart in order to be sold separately and sent to different plantations. The scenes of personal suffering he witnessed outside his house in the Quaker community in North Carolina stayed with him all his life. Later as a young man, Levi became a prominent leader in the anti-slavery movement and one of earliest pioneers in organizing the Underground Railroad. Levi eventually was given the unofficial title of "President" of the Underground Railroad, an office he held until 1870 when, at age 73, he witnessed the adoption of the 15th Amendment to the American Constitution, extendeding suffrage to African Americans and thus making the Underground Railroad no longer necessary. Over his life-long service in the Underground Railroad, Levi Coffin helped an estimated 3,000 fugitives in their passage to freedom.[40]

Another possible starting point for the Underground Railroad occurred almost a decade earlier than the incident involving the young Levi Coffin. This event centred on another young boy by the name of Josiah Henson and his father. Born into slavery in Kentucky, Henson recalled much later in his autobiography that one of his first memories as a child was seeing his father returning home after being brutally beaten by his master. He wrote that his father appeared one day "with his head bloody and his back lacerated" and "was beside himself with mingled rage and suffering."[41] Some days before this incident, Josiah's father had attacked his master when he encountered him in the act of physically assaulting his wife. In slave states, it was almost an unthinkable crime for a Black man to threaten or strike a white man, and, in Josiah's words, such an incident was "enough to set a whole county afire; no question is asked about provocation." According to Josiah, following this incident "the authorities were soon in pursuit of my father. The penalty was one hundred lashes on the bare back, and to have the right ear nailed to the whipping-post, and then severed from the body."[42] After assaulting his master in order to protect his wife, Josiah's father escaped into the woods. A few days later he was captured and shortly thereafter he received the appointed penalty. After being whipped by a local blacksmith who was brought in because of his expertise and strength in delivering this kind of brutal punishment, Henson's father's ear was nailed to the whipping post, his master drew his knife, and with the cheers of a crowd of white on lookers, severed his ear, shouting: "That's what he's got for striking a white man."[43]

Josiah Henson went on to become one of most celebrated figures in the history of slavery, the abolitionist movement and the Underground Railroad. After escaping from the bondage of slavery in Kentucky he made his way to Canada and eventually settled near Dresden, Ontario. In 1849, he published his autobiography that quickly became a best seller among abolitionists. Harriet Beecher Stowe was so moved after reading this account that she shaped her main character, Tom, in her famous *Uncle Tom's Cabin*, on the life of Josiah Henson.

The expansion of the institution of slavery in the United Sates and the concerted efforts on the part of Washington to enforce the *Fugitive Slave Act* gave sustained stimulus to the growth of the anti-slavery movement and the development of the Underground Railroad. The government of Upper Canada was persistent in resisting the efforts of slave owners and the U.S. Government to arrest fugitive slaves in Canada in order to return them to the United States. In 1819, John Beverley Robinson, the Chief Justice of Upper Canada, drafted the *Fugitive Offenders Act*, which protected the rights of fugitives in accordance with the principles of due process guaranteed under the British Constitution. The Act protected runaway slaves from arbitrary arrest and removal from Canada.

According to Karolyn Smartz Frost, author of a prize-winning history of the Underground Railroad, Chief Justice Robinson "Was the most important lawmaker in Upper Canada." He was a staunch Tory and defender of the principles of British jurisprudence. "It is not overstating the case to say," writes Frost, "that the Underground Railroad could not have found its main terminus in Canada had it not been for the legal decisions made by John Beverley Robinson."[44]

In the decades that followed the *Fugitive Slave Act* until the American Civil War, a vast system of passageways to Canada developed, and the image of Canada as the "Promised Land" became firmly established. The infrastructure of the Underground Railroad consisted of a fluid network based on a hierarchy of command (passengers, conductors and station masters) who harboured, clothed, fed and guided fugitive slaves in their dangerous and arduous journey to freedom. Under the organizational skills of Quakers like Levi Coffin and other religious leaders, the Underground Railroad developed into an efficient and collaborative grassroots organization involving local free Blacks and slaves together with a vast network of white sympathizers. The system operated through a connecting web of family-based units that passed fugitives "up the line" from one locality to the next. The success of the Underground Railroad depended on its secrecy and the anonymity of the conductors and stationmasters, each of whom operated as independent cells connected through family and religious affiliations.

In the beginning, the organization of the Underground Railroad was spotty at best, and there were only a few established corridors for the passage of fugitives to safe communities in the northern states and Canada. Fugitive slaves from the deep south and from frontier regions like Kentucky had a much more difficult time making their way over the long journey to the north. It is almost impossible to imagine the hardships and obstacles these courageous individuals experienced in their struggle to seek the Promised Land. They made their way, often at night through difficult and unfamiliar terrain, guided most of the way only by the North Star. At every point in their journey they faced the long reach of the *Fugitive Slave Act* and the threat of arrest from local authorities. They were constantly pursued by professional slave hunters called patrollers who followed them to northern states and, in some cases, even into Canada.

There are many vivid personal accounts of fugitive slaves, and like those of Frederick Douglas and Josiah Henson, many of these became popular autobiographies. Perhaps the most famous account that serves as a lasting testimonial to the courage and sacrifice of all those who were part of the Underground Railroad is that of Harriet Tubman. This remarkable woman rose from historical obscurity to becoming a prominent symbolic figure in the civil rights and women's movements during the 1950s and 1960s, and today, as her recent biographer notes, she has achieved the status of "a heroine without equal" and "has become part of the core American memory."[45] What is remarkable is the fact that her life is a Canadian as well as an American story, and although she is barely mentioned in most Canadian history texts, she deserves a place of prominence in the mainstream of Canadian history.

Unlike the published autobiographies of other fugitives, Harriet Tubman remained illiterate all her life, and what we know about her extraordinary life is based on personal interviews and the research of her biographers and historians. Fergus Bordewich states that "her story survived only in the memories and impressions of others." Despite our incomplete understanding of Tubman's life, "her story shaped both the legend as well as the myth of the Underground Railroad." Bordewich observes that Tubman "eventually became a kind of metaphor for the entire underground, endowed — a remarkable individual by any measure — with virtually superhuman personal qualities, while her uniquely brilliant work evolved into a template for the entire system."[46]

Born into slavery in 1822 on Maryland's eastern shore, Harriet grew up under the constant reign of terror by a particularly cruel master. She received a half dozen, or more, beatings a day, and after seeing her sisters taken away, she lived in the constant fear that she too would be carried away by a white man. As a young girl, Harriet was unintentionally struck in the head by a heavy stone that was thrown in an act of rage by her master at another slave. The injury left her with lifelong symptoms similar to epilepsy that included blackouts and episodes of delirium. The disability gave Harriet a larger than life mystique, and during particularly difficult moments in her life, she drew spiritual strength from her condition.[47]

In 1849, after an attempt to escape with her two brothers had failed, Harriet fled alone. With the help of a local Quaker woman she made her way to Delaware. From Delaware, Harriet was passed from a succession of conductors until she arrived in a safe community in Pennsylvania. Instead of settling into her new life of freedom, Harriet soon returned to Maryland, and over the course of several trips, she successfully rescued her brothers and eleven other slaves. Within a year of own escape, Harriet and her company of fellow fugitives arrived in Canada. Over the following years, Harriet successfully established a network of activists that included Quakers and other white sympathizers together with a cadre of slaves and free Blacks. With the support of this network, Harriet made thirteen separate trips and brought over seventy slaves to the Promised Land.[48]

The northern movement of Blacks during the era of Underground Railroad represented the largest wave of Black migration in Canadian history. It is estimated that 20,000 to 23,000 Blacks came to Canada during the four decades prior to the outbreak of the Civil War. Some of these immigrants were educated and well-to-do free Blacks who came to Canada following the passage of the *Fugitive Slave Law* of 1850. Many of these Blacks were from northern cities like Boston, and they moved to Canada out of fear of being kidnapped by rogue bounty hunters and sold into slavery. Karolyn Frost makes the important observation that the passage of the *Fugitive Slave Law* "was the single greatest impulse to African American migration to Canada during the antebellum period, effectively doubling the Black population of what is now Ontario within a decade."[49]

One of the most notable Blacks who came to Canada during this period was

Henry Bibb, a former slave from Kentucky. Bibb and his wife moved to Canada from Boston in 1850 as a direct consequence of the *Fugitive Slave Law,* which was passed that same year. Bibb immediately became involved in the anti-slavery movement in Canada and founded *The Voice of the Fugitive,* the first Black newspaper in Upper Canada. In 1852, Bibb was elected president of the Windsor Anti-Slavery Society, an office he held until his premature death in 1854.[50]

For the vast majority of fugitive slaves, the terminus for the Underground Railroad extended across the Detroit River into settlements in the region that is presently southeastern Ontario. Harriet Tubman established a residence in St. Catherine's, while many others like Josiah Henson settled near Chatham. Henson devoted his later life to the improvement of Blacks, and with the help of Levi Coffin and others, he founded the British-American Manual Training Institute at Dawn Mills near Dresden, Ontario. The Institute, later known simply as the Dawn Settlement, was one of the first planned Black self-help communities in Canada. It had approximately 500 Black settlers who occupied fifteen hundred acres of land. The Dawn Settlement was built on Henson's vision of Black improvement through education and self-reliance. The community had its own school, and its graduates were expected to become future teachers in order educate the new members of the community.[51]

From the period of French settlement to the end of the nineteenth century, the narrative of race in Canadian history has involved the ongoing tension between slavery and freedom. In many important respects, this narrative was shaped by the dramatic events that were taking place in the United States that centred on slavery, the abolitionist movement together with the efforts of the U.S. Federal Government to maintain national unity through the creation and enforcement of Fugitive Slave laws. The narrative of race in Canada and the United States intersected at many critical points, and in the case of the Underground Railroad, the central characters of the story have a place in the history of both nations. A strong claim can also be made that slavery, abolitionism and the Underground Railroad served as the catalyst for the creation of the first civil rights movement in both Canada and the United States. In the United States, one important impetus behind this movement for civil rights stemmed from the deeply held religious belief among Quakers, Methodists, Baptists and other Christian faiths that all human beings are equal in the eyes of God. However, in contrast to the United States, the struggle from slavery to freedom in Canada was guided largely by lawmakers, judges and religious leaders who sought to extend human rights and the principles of justice and due process under the British constitution to all those who set foot on Canadian soil.

The similarity between the narratives of race does not end with the Underground Railroad. As we will see in the following chapters, this historical similarity extends from the period following the U.S. Civil War until well into the twentieth century.

Both countries have experienced a persistent pattern of racial prejudice and discrimination. Unlike the United States, racism in Canada rarely erupted into large-scale incidents of violence; nevertheless, expressions of racism were (and still remain) close to the surface, and its occurrence is in direct relation to the proximity and relative size of the Black population. In Nova Scotia, as we have seen, the arrival of Black Loyalist and Maroons increased racial tensions that eventually led to the large scale out-migration of Blacks to Sierra Leone. The remaining population experienced a persistent pattern of discrimination in all areas of life, and in respect to schools, churches and housing, there were informal as well as legislated forms segregation.

In the aftermath of the War of 1812, large numbers of Black refugees arrived in Nova Scotia. The majority of these newcomers to Canada joined existing Black communities in the region around Halifax. There is some evidence to suggest that refugees from the War of 1812 were among the first to settle in an area that later became known as Africville. Although Africville became an autonomous and self-determining Black community, it represents an early example of urban segregation, and those who lived there were deliberately and almost entirely out of sight and mind of the white residents of Halifax.[52]

In Canada West, the largest concentrations of the Black population settled in rural farming communities such Dawn, Buxton and on family run farms near Chatham and Dresden. There was a growing urban Black community as well, especially in the rapidly expanding city of Toronto. Some slave fugitives, like Thornton Blackburn, were successful in business and were respected members among the entire community. However, the veneer of acceptance was often very thin. One Black observer stated that racism in Canada is worse than the United States because it is so "polite."[53] This particularly Canadian brand of discrimination was more subtle than racism in the U.S., but it was equally pervasive in the social interactions between the two races. In 1852, Josiah Henson wrote in a letter published in the *British Banner* that in Canada the racial prejudice was present in "the everyday intercourse of the Black man and white man." In formal and informal situations "it is the invariable rule to refuse [the Black man's] association with the white at the dinner table [or] in the salon of the steam vessel."[54]

Josiah Henson's observations aptly capture the reality of race relations in Canada, and they underscore the difficult journey that lay ahead for Blacks in their search of the Promised Land.

NOTES

1.   In 1759, there were 3,604 slaves in New France, and 1,132 of these slaves were of African origin. This information was provided by the historian Ken Donovan. For additional sources on slavery in New France, see Frank Mackey, *Done With Slavery: The Black Fact in Montreal 1760–1840* (Montreal and Kingston: McGill-Queen's University Press, 2006); Dobie Madeleine, *Trading Places: Colonization and Slavery in Eighteenth Century in Eighteenth Century French Culture* (Ithica: Cornell University Press, 2010); Marcel Trudel, *L'Esclavage Au Canada Francais: Histoire et Conditions de L'Esclavage* (Quebec: Les Presses Universitaires Laval, 1960); Ken Donovan, "Slaves in Ile Royale, 1713–1758," *French Colonial History* 5 (2004), pp. 25–42; Ken Donovan, "Slaves and Their Owners in Ile Royale, 1713–1760," *Acadiensis* xxv, n1 (1995), pp. 3–32.

2.   Robin Winks, *The Blacks in Canada: A History* 2nd ed. (Montreal, Kingston: McGill-Queen's University Press, 1997). pp. 4–5.

3.   Ken Donovan, "Marie Marguerite Rose and Slavery in Louisbourg, 1713–1768" (unpublished manuscript, Parks Canada, Fortress of Louisbourg, 2010), p. 3.

4.   Ken Donovan, "Slaves and Their Owners in Ile Royale, 1713–1760," 1995, p. 19.

5.   Ken Donovan, "Slaves and Their owners in Ile Royale, 1713–1760," 1995, p. 29.

6.   Ken Donovan, "Marie Marguerite Rose and Slavery in Louisbourg, 1713–1768," 2010, p. 16.

7.   Ken Donovan, "Marie Marguerite Rose and Slavery in Louisbourg, 1713–1768," 2010, p. 17.

8.   The history of slavery in eighteenth century Canada is the subject of a recent article by Harvey Amani Whitefield. He states that although the scholarship on slavery has burgeoned over the last twenty years, "the most basic aspects of Maritime slavery remain unknown" (p. 19). Whitfield argues that "slavery has not become a part of the national narrative ... because the historiography of slavery in Canada still lacks the basic overviews that allowed scholars of American slavery to pursue complicated topics" (p. 18). Whitfield's article adds a great deal to our understanding of slavery during this period, and it goes a long way toward correcting this weakness in the historiography of slavery in Canada. See Harvey Amani Whitfield, "The Struggle Over Slavery in the Maritime Colonies," *Acadiensis* 41 (Summer/Autumn, 2012) pp. 17–44.

9.   Harvey Amani Whitfield, *Blacks on the Border: The Black Refuges in British North America, 1815–1860* (Burlington: University of Vermont Press, 2007), p. 130, n. 42; Robin Winks, *The Blacks in Canada*, pp. 24–60; "Black Loyalists, 1783–1792," Nova Scotia Archives <novascotia.ca/archives/virtual/africans'results.asp/>.

10.   *Halifax Gazette* (May 17, 1752), p. 2, "African Nova Scotians," Nova Scotia Virtual Archives <gov.ns.ca/nsarm/virtual/africans/arcives.asp?ID=4>.

11.   Ken Donovan, "Female Slaves as Sexual Victims in Cape Breton, 1713–1810," paper presented to the Old Sydney Society, 28 February 2013.

12.   Barry Cahill, "Habeas Corpus and Slavery in Nova Scotia: *R v. Hecht Ex Parte Rachel, 1798*," *University of New Brunswick Law Journal* 44 (1995), p. 193; Harvey Whitfield, *Blacks on the Border*. p. 21.

13.   Thomas Jefferson, *Notes on the State of Virginia and Related Documents*, edited with an

introduction by David Wallstreiker (New York: Bedford/St. Martins Press, 2002), quarry XIV and XVIII, pp. 189–90.

14. Elizabeth Amnons, *Harriet Beecher Stowe's Uncle Tom's Cabin: a Casebook* (New York: Oxford University Press, 2007), pp. 240ff.

15. James W. St. G Walker, *The Black Loyalists: The Search for a Promised Land in Nova Scotia and Sierra Leone, 1783–1870.* (London: Longman and Dalhousie University Press, 1976); James W. St. G Walker, "The Establishment of a Free Black Community in Nova Scotia, 1783–1840," *The African Diaspora: Interpretive Essays,* edited by Martin L. Kilson and Robert I. Rotberg (Cambridge, MA: Harvard University Press, 1976); Simon Schama, *Rough Crossings: Britain, the Slaves and the American Revolution* (New York: Harper Collins, 2006); for journals and memoirs of Black Loyalists, see "Black Loyalists," Canada's Digital Collections, at <blackloyalist.com/Canadiandigitalcollection/index.htm>.

16. B. Pachai, *Peoples of the Maritimes: Blacks* (Tantallon, NS: Four East Publications, 1993), p. 12.

17. Benjamin Marston, Diary, September 14, 1783. The Black Loyalists, Canada's Digital Collection.

18. Benjamin Marston, Diary, July 26, 1784.

19. Racial violence erupted in the industrial towns of Glace Bay and New Glasgow, Nova Scotia, in 1919. A fuller discussion of these events is provided in chapter 2.

20. James Walker, "The Establishment of a Free Black Community in Nova Scotia, 1783–1840," pp. 210–12.

21. The winters of 1783–1784 have been described as among the worst of the entire eighteenth century, and this may have been a result of the Laki eruption in Iceland. See Thorvaldur Thordarson and Stephen Self, "Atmospheric and Environmental Effects of the 1783–1784 Laki Eruption: A Review and Reassessment," *Journal of Geophysical Research* (2003), 108(D1), pp. 1–29; W.R. Baron, "Historical Climate Records from the North Eastern United States, 1640–1900" in *Climate Since A.D.1500,* edited by R.S. Bradley and P.D. Jones (New York: Rutledge, 1992) pp. 74–91.

22. Boston King, Memoirs, The Black Loyalists, Canada's Digital Collection.

23. Boston King, Memoirs.

24. Somon Schama, *Rough Crossing,* p. 308.

25. James Walker, "The Establishment of a Free Black Community in Nova Scotia, 1783–1840," 1976, p. 224.

26. Harvey Whitfield, *Blacks on the Border,* 2006, p. 22.

27. James Walker, "The Establishment of a Free Black Community in Nova Scotia, 1783–1840," 1976, p. 226.

28. James Walker, "The Establishment of a Free Black Community in Nova Scotia, 1783–1840," 1976, p. 227.

29. Karolyn Smardz Frost, *I've Got a Home in Glory Land: A Lost Tale of the Underground Railroad* (New York: Farrar, Strauss and Giroux, 2007), p. 196.

30. Harvey Amani Whitfield argues that with the decline of slavery racial prejudice actually increased throughout the Maritime colonies. He states that "the struggle over slavery resulted in the creation and further development of an insidious racism, which attempted to marginalize and isolate people of African descent on poor lands and deny

an opportunity for social mobility. Although most whites eventually opposed slavery in the Maritimes, they also rejected anything resembling equality with their Black neighbors." Harvey Amani Whitfield, "The Struggle over Slavery in the Maritimes," p. 43.

31. Robin Winks, *The Blacks in Canada*, 1997, p. 102.

32. Adam Hochschild, *Bury the Chains: Prophets and Rebels in the Fight to Free an Empire's Slaves* (New York: Houghton Mifflin Company, 2006) p. 50.

33. Robin Winks, *The Blacks in Canada*, 1997, p. 96.

34. Robin Winks, *The Blacks in Canada*, 1997, p. 98; Karolyn Frost, *I've Got a Home in Glory Land*, 2007, pp. 195–96.

35. Karolyn Frost, *I've Got a Home in Glory Land*, 2007, p. 24.

36. Karolyn Frost, *I've Got a Home in Glory Land*, 2007, p. 23.

37. Karolyn Frost, *I've Got a Home in Glory Land*, 2007, p. 24; Fercus M. Bordewich, *Bound for Canaan: The Epic Story of the Underground Railroad, America's First Civil Rights Movement* (New York: Harper Collins, 2005), pp. 41–45.

38. Fercus Bordewich, *Bound for Canaan*, 2005, p. 42.

39. Fercus Bordewich, *Bound for Canaan*, 2005, p. 43.

40. Fercus Bordewich, *Bound for Canaan*, 2005, p. 402.

41. Josiah Henson, "Uncle Tom's Story of His Life:" An Autobiography of the Rev. Josiah Henson (London: "Christian Age" office, 1876) p. 14.

42. Josiah Henson, "Uncle Tom's Story of His Life:" An Autobiography of the Rev. Josiah Henson," 1876, p. 15.

43. Josiah Henson, "Uncle Tom's Story of His Life:" An Autobiography of the Rev. Josiah Henson," 1876, 15.

44. Karolyn Frost, *I've Got a Home in Glory Land*, 2007, p. 204.

45. Kate Cifford Larson, *Bound for the Promised Land: Harriet Tubman, Portrait of an American Hero* (New York: Random House, 2004), p. iv.

46. Fercus Bordewich, p. 347.

47. Kate Larson, *Bound for the Promised Land*, pp. 42–45.

48. Fercus Bordewich, *Bound for Canaan*, 2005, p. 351.

49. Karolyn Frost, *I've Got a Home in Glory Land*, 2007, p. 281.

50. Karolyn Frost, *I've Got a Home in Glory Land*, 2007, pp. 291–97.

51. Fercus Bordewich, *Bound for Canaan*, 2005, p. 264.

52. For a further discussion of Africville, see Chapter 2.

53. Samuel Ringgold Ward, "Canadian Negro Hate," *Voice of the Fugitive*, October 21, 1852. Retrieved from <http://ink.ourontario.ca/brouse/vf/reel1/00118>.

54. Josiah Henson to John Campbell, "Condition of the Blacks in Canada," *British Banner*, August 25, 1852, quoted in Frost, p. 236.

Chapter 2

The Many Faces of Jim Crow
Racial Segregation in Canada 1880–1960

In 1903, Black scholar and activist, W.E.B. Du Bois wrote *The Souls of Black Folk*, which today is regarded as one of the great literary classics and commentaries on race in American history.

The opening sentence of the second chapter of the book begins with these prophetic words: "The problem of the twentieth century is the problem of the colour line-the relation of the darker to the lighter races of men in Asia and Africa."[1] The history of America in the twentieth century has borne out the truth of Du Bois' observation. Although slavery ended with President Lincoln's famous Emancipation Proclamation on January 1, 1863, racial discrimination continued, and in the American South, a new pattern of racial segregation emerged that eventually evolved into a widespread system of so-called Jim Crow laws.

The term "Jim Crow" refers to a minstrel show act created by Thomas D. Rice during the 1830s. Rice assumed a racist caricature of a Black person by blackening his face and performed a song and dance act with accompanying music called "Jump Jim Crow." Rice's act toured the United States throughout the 1830s and 1840s, and it was so popular that the term "Jim Crow" became a widely used racial epithet for Blacks. Rice's Jim Crow act and the general popularity of minstrel shows with blackened faced performers are indicative of the popular cultural trends of the period as well as the underlying current of racism that ran throughout all regions of the United States after the formal abolition of slavery.[2] Developments during the twentieth century brought this current to the surface in both the northern as well as in the southern states and in the first decades of the century race riots broke out in dozens of northern cities. The Ku Klux Klan, which was originally founded in 1865, underwent a revival in 1915 and by the 1920s it had gained wide spread support in the most regions of the United States; its membership is estimated to have peaked at four million.[3]

In Canada, a similar pattern of race relations was occurring and, although less dramatic than in the United States, it is nonetheless clear that W.E.B. Du Bois' words can also be used to describe the history of Canada during the twentieth century. There were no "official" Jim Crow laws in Canada; however, a similar *ad hoc* pattern of racial segregation developed that spread unevenly to those regions of the country that had relatively large Black populations, especially in Ontario and Nova Scotia. As we will see, in Canada, the pattern of racial segregation mimicked the practice of "Jim Crow" segregation in the southern United States that evolved in a piecemeal and customary manner during the decades immediately following the Civil War.

The Origin of Jim Crow in the Southern United States

The aftermath of the American Civil War brought an era of uncertainty, change and turmoil to the southern states. With the end of slavery, so ended the long-standing system of social controls that had defined and entrenched the master and slave relationship between whites and Blacks throughout the slave states. The Reconstruction Era that followed the Civil War gave rise to a new generation of Blacks who sought to assume the full rights of citizenship afforded to them under the constitution and the civil rights legislation that followed the Civil War. For whites in the south, the assertiveness and independence of what they regarded as "uppity" Blacks was met with various degrees of distain and resistance. Blacks of the older generation, so accustomed to mores and controls of racial slavery, were more likely to maintain some degree of deference and even subservience to the whites. Their own life experiences and the violence of the past had taught them the prudence of avoiding actions and public gestures that would call attention to themselves. For this reason, in part, the emerging pattern of race relations followed a general tendency for both races to avoid unnecessary contact and to live their lives separately.

In the immediate aftermath of the Civil War, white legislators in southern states attempted to enact restrictive Black codes and segregation laws, but these were successfully challenged in the courts. In spite of these legal setbacks, there was widespread grassroots support among both races for maintaining the line of colour in many areas of life. Even in state legislatures that supported civil rights and the principle of racial equality, there was no interest in legally enforcing racial integration upon the unwilling citizens of the south. Although the term "segregation" was not used to describe the practice of racial segregation until the beginning of the twentieth century, it was clear that through a process of trial and error, or "forays and retreats," that a new system of racial segregation was gradually evolving in virtually all regions of the south.[4] In some communities, the solution to the problem of racial contact in public places was the outright banning of Blacks to these areas. In some parks, for example, Blacks were denied access completely or they were given access only at designated times.[5] Slavery may have ended, but the practice of maintaining the power relationship of superiority and inferiority among whites and Blacks continued unabated. Leon Litwack describes the history of segregation in the south and states that "law and custom interacted to keep Blacks in their place."[6] The practice of racial segregation varied from place to place and this required all Black citizens to be aware of local customs. As one Black educator wrote: "Every town had its own mores, its own unwritten restrictions. The trick was to find out from local people what the rules were."[7]

The gradual transformation of this uneven pattern of segregation based largely on custom to a widespread system of Jim Crow laws that were enforced throughout the south began in the area of public transportation. In most other areas of racial contact, etiquette and custom clearly defined the manner of social behavior and racial interaction. When Blacks were permitted, on certain occasions, to enter whites-only places, they did so not as social equals but as servants, chauffeurs or nannies. Trains and trolley cars, however, were "contested" spaces, and they temporarily brought both races together as social equals out of the necessity of travel.[8]

The expansion of the railroads and urban trolley cars was part of the new industrial age, and these were the most efficient and desirable means of travel. Railroad cars were conveniently divided into first class and second class. First-class cars afforded passengers the greatest comfort: seats were cushioned and upholstered; ceilings were raised; doors at each end of the car were padded and windows were adorned with drapes. Passengers had clean air to breath and fresh water to drink. Second-class cars, in contrast, had none of these comforts; the cars were fitted with hard wooden benches and were reserved for economy class passengers and men who smoked or chewed tobacco. Second-class cars were usually behind the engine and they were frequently part of the baggage car separated by only a temporary partition. Initially, Blacks were permitted to buy first-class tickets, and those who did so sat in the same cars with white first-class passengers. This practice gave an uneasy appearance of social equality among the races, and it was often met with some form of resistance on the part white passengers and railroad personnel. White porters frequently tried to intimidate Black first-class passengers, forcing them to move to second-class cars or, in some instances, violently remove them from the train altogether.

Many Black passengers knew they had the legal right to travel in first class, and they had the courage to assert that right by refusing to leave. Whites generally were uncomfortable travelling in such close proximity with Blacks, and it was particularly upsetting if a white female had to sit near a Black male. As a New Orleans newspaper stated in 1890: "A man that would be horrified at the idea of his wife or daughter seated by the side of a burly negro in the parlor of a hotel or restaurant cannot see her occupying a crowded seat in a car next to a negro without the same feeling of disgust."[9]

Eventually, beginning in the 1880s, municipal and state legislatures passed legislation sanctioning the creation of racially segregated areas on trains and on urban trollies. On the railroads, Blacks were relegated to the second-class "smoking" cars, and on most trolley cars there were partitions separating the races or signs posted directing Blacks to sit at the back of the car. The practice of racial segregation spread very quickly to waiting rooms and public lavatories. Signs were clearly posted indicating "White" and "Black" entrances, but later the terms "Negro" or "coloured" were used because they were seen to be more inclusive of all shades of colour.[10]

Racial segregation spread to almost every conceivable area where both races came into contact: parks and all public recreational places, schools, hospitals, asylums, churches, workplaces, saloons and all forms of public transportation. "The legislation of Jim Crow," writes Litwack, "affected all classes and ages, and it tended to be thorough, far-reaching, even imaginative: from separate public school textbooks for Black and white children and Jim Crow Bibles on which to swear in Black witnesses in court, to separate telephone booths … and Jim Crow elevators in office buildings."[11]

Blacks mounted a concerted effort to challenge the practice of racial segregation on the railroads in both the state legislatures and in the courts. Individuals who had been denied their right to travel in first-class cars took the railroads and their employees to court but, in most instances, they lost their cases. In 1892, two Black equal rights activists in Louisiana decided to challenge the state's railroad racial segregation law. They enlisted the support of a light-skinned Black man named Homer Plassy who purchased a ticket in order to board the first-class car. Railroad authorities were informed in advance, and Plassy was arrested and later that same year he was tried and found guilty in a Louisiana court. Plassy's case eventually made its way under appeal to the Supreme Court of the United States. In 1896, it was the subject of the now-infamous *Plassy v. Ferguson* ruling that established the legal basis for racial segregation under the principle of "separate but equal." By the time of this Supreme Court ruling, state legislatures had already passed racial segregation laws in every southern state except Virginia and the Carolinas. *Plassy v. Ferguson* gave sanction under the authority of the highest court of the land to all forms of Jim Crow laws, and it was immediately clear that the principle of "separate but equal" was in practice "separate and grossly unequal." On the railroads, as one southern newspaper admitted, Jim Crow cars were "universally filthy and uncomfortable" and a sign of "indignity, disgrace, and shame."[12]

The history of Jim Crow illustrates the deep-seated and widespread nature of racial prejudice in the southern United States, and it demonstrates that, in many respects, Jim Crow laws merely gave sanction to the existing customs and habits of racial segregation. A similar pattern of racial segregation developed in Canada but at a much later date and in a more subtle and uneven manner. As we will see in the following sections of this chapter, the appearance of more overt forms of enforced racial segregation became firmly established in the era of rapid industrialization during the first decades of the twentieth century.

Canada's "Indigenous" Black Communities During the Late Victorian Era

Traditionally, Blacks have not been considered to be a significant aspect of Canadian history. In terms of size and extent, however, it is important to acknowledge that by the time of Confederation, Blacks represented the sixth-largest population group in Canada, and they had a presence in virtually all regions of the country.[13] Although most Canadians are aware of the Black presence in the eastern portion of the country, few are aware of the role Blacks played in the development of Canada's west. In 1858, for example, the Governor of the Colony of Vancouver Island, Sir James Douglas, who was himself of mixed-race ancestry, invited thirty-five Black men and women to the colony from San Francisco. This was the beginning of Black immigration to the west coast of Canada, and by 1860 over 600 Black immigrants had come to the colony in order to pursue a new life free from the discrimination and lack of opportunities they had experienced in the United States. Blacks figured prominently in communities from Victoria, New Westminster and Kamloops to Salt Spring Island, and by the early 1860s there were significant numbers of Blacks in Victoria to form the (Black) Pioneer Rifle Corp.[14]

Blacks have always been part of Canadian history, and their presence in Canada can be traced back to the period of European exploration and first settlement.[15] Black scholar and poet, George Elliott Clarke, argues that as a self-described "Africadian," he regards himself as "an indigenous Black Nova Scotian."[16] Although Clarke's use of the term "indigenous" was intended to stress the interconnected history and experiences of Black Nova Scotians with the Mi'Kmaw First Nations, his identification also captures the salient aspects of the character and continuity of the Black experience in Canada.

Black immigration to Canada began with the arrival of Europeans during the seventeenth century, and ever since this time there has been a continuous Black presence in Canada. The term "indigenous" is an accurate counterweight to the view that, unlike European cultures, Blacks are seen as refugees whose presence is regarded, in many respects, as temporary. There is a tendency among some writers of Black history to see the history of Blacks in Canada as a series of largely disconnected waves of refugees beginning with the Black Loyalists and the Maroons, followed by the refugees of the War of 1812 and the steady stream of fugitive slaves who came to Canada through the Underground Railroad during the nineteenth century.[17] During the twentieth century, the Black immigration from the United States continued, but a new wave of immigration came from the West Indies.

This view of Black history does not fully account for the fact that the African diaspora to Canada began much earlier with the arrival of slaves under French and British rule and that some of these early Black immigrants, like Marie Marguerite Rose, obtained their freedom and became accepted and free contributing members of the community. As mentioned in the previous chapter, under French and early British rule, slaves and free Blacks lived in close proximity and provided an important and lasting dynamic in Canadian society. It is also important to remember that although many of the Black Loyalists left Canada for Sierra Leone, nearly two-thirds of them remained in Canada. In the nineteenth century, Black immigration to Canada flowed almost exclusively from the United States, and many of these immigrants had no thoughts of ever returning to their previous country of residence. Some, like Black abolitionists Henry and Mary Bibb, were relatively well-off, while others like Thornton and Lucie Blackburn came to Canada poor but became well-established and successful entrepreneurs. Thornton and his wife Lucie settled in Toronto in the 1830s and started the first taxi company that served the entire city.[18]

In light of these facts, Black immigration to Canada should be seen as part of an extended process of acculturation and adaptation, with occasional out-migrations as well as large-scale infusions of new immigrants. Like other immigrant experiences, the process is one of adaptation to new circumstances and a partial integration and assimilation into the larger Canadian culture as well as into regional ethnic and racial cultures. This process is illustrated in the formation of language dialects, and it gives credence to what Clarke refers to as the "existence of African-Nova Scotian vernacular English, a version of African-American vernacular English that is as distinct as the variants spoken in Liberia and Sierra Leone."[19] Black Nova Scotians represent the oldest documented and most continuous population of African descent in Canada, and like the Black population in Ontario, with loyalist roots, Black Nova Scotians retained a strong sense of Britishness throughout late eighteenth and the nineteenth century.

Unlike in the United States before the Civil War, Blacks during the nineteenth century came to Canada of their own free will, and many developed a sense of national identity and pride toward their newly adopted country. There was strong support within Black communities for British institutions, especially for the British constitution that affirmed the principles of justice and equality under the law. In Ontario, for example, Blacks enthusiastically supported the defence of their new homeland in the War of 1812, and they formed their own military regiment in order to defend the southern border of Canada against American aggression. In the Rebellions of 1837–1838, the sense of Britishness led a group of loyal Blacks to form their own "Coloured Regiment" in defence of Upper Canada.[20] In contrast to the United States, Blacks in Canada achieved a much fuller degree of participation in various aspects of Canadian life. In communities with relatively large Black populations, local residents formed a variety of civic and fraternal associations that helped gain for them acceptance and respectability. In the rural towns of Chatham and Amherstburg in Southwestern Ontario, Blacks joined the Freemasons; however, because they were denied the privileges of full membership, they eventually formed their own racially segregated Masonic lodges. These fraternal associations encouraged a strict moral code of conduct and stressed the values of manhood and being a good father, husband and member of the community. In rural Black communities, there was strong spirit of equality among all members of the community, and for this reason, membership in Masonic lodges was open to all males, regardless of their occupation. There was also the opportunity for wives and other female relatives to form auxiliary organizations or to join women's social clubs that were popular toward the end of the nineteenth century.[21]

In urban areas with large Black populations, there was a similar quest for respectability through community involvement and by joining self-improvement or fraternal associations such as the Freemasons, Oddfellows and Templers lodges; however, unlike in rural areas, there was a well-defined social stratification based on occupation, education and residence. In her study of the Black community in late Victorian Halifax, Judith Fingard observed that Blacks were "united by colour [but] clearly divided by attitude and behaviour."[22]

Toward the end of the nineteenth century, Canada entered a prolonged period of sustained urban and industrial development that over the next several decades had the effect of radically transforming nearly every aspect of life. For Blacks, this provided many new opportunities for employment and social mobility. In the Maritimes, the employment focus shifted away from traditional jobs in seafaring to employment in the steel and coal mining industries as well as in the railroad industry. The urban areas provided employment in labour and skilled trades together with business opportunities. According to the census records of 1881, there were 1,039 Blacks living in Halifax. However, there were nearly one-and-a-half times as many Blacks living in the surrounding areas outside the city, and many of these Blacks commuted to Halifax for work.[23] The city also provided opportunities for social contact and racial interaction. Although racial integration was limited, by the late nineteenth century there were many mixed race marriages.

These marriages provided a means for greater social acceptance and mobility for the lighter-skinned offspring, and perhaps for this reason, as Fingard speculated, some of the prominent members of the Black elite were not identified as "coloured" in the gathering of the census records.[24]

In addition to their membership in fraternal organizations, Blacks in Halifax, like their counterparts in rural Southwestern Ontario, also sought respectability by becoming active in the temperance movement, the church and in local politics. In Halifax, participation in all these activities and organizations helped to delineate the differences between an emerging class of respectable civic-minded Black citizens from the poorer and more transient members of the Black community. "What set them apart from their lesser brethren," according to Fingard, "was not great wealth or more prestigious occupations but their devotion to respectability. The worthy Black citizens of Halifax considered respectability to be the key, not only to their superiority over their rough brethren, but to equality with whites, dignity in status, and justice in the public sphere."[25]

The quest for respectability in Victorian Halifax is perhaps most evident in the controversy over school segregation during the 1870s and 1880s. For the Black middle class, respectability was an expression, in part, of the duties and responsibilities of citizenship, and one of the primary concerns of tax-paying Black citizens of Victorian-era Halifax was the education of their children. Traditionally, the education of Black children was limited to elementary school, and in accordance with the *School Act of 1865*, racially segregated schools were created throughout the city of Halifax. In some instances, when parents wanted to extend their children's education beyond the elementary level, they were able to send their children to secondary schools in predominantly white neighbourhoods of the city. During the 1870s, there was growing resistance to allowing these kinds of exceptions to the practice of racial segregation in schools. However, following the closure of a Black school in the north end of Halifax, the members of the Black elite successfully petitioned the Halifax school authorities in 1883 to allow their children to attend white schools.[26] Although this was only a short-lived victory, it demonstrates the relative degree of acceptance and influence of a small group of Black residents of Halifax. This stands in sharp contrast to other members of the Black community, especially those on the outskirts of the city in areas such Preston, Hammond Plains and Campbell Road, later known as Africville.

The history of Africville, in particular, illustrates the nature and extent of racism in Nova Scotia over a 150-year period, and it provides insight into the overall pattern of race relations in Canada. The first settlers of Africville were related to a group of eight founding families, most of whom moved to the area from the racially segregated Black communities of Preston and Hammonds Plains. The exact date of settlement is not clear, but there is evidence that some members of the original eight families were living on the land prior to its purchase in 1848.[27] Many of the early residents of Africville were decedents of the refugees of the War of 1812 who came to Nova Scotia from the Chesapeake Bay-area of Maryland. William Brown and William Arnold, two prominent members of the initial group of settlers, each bought approximately six acres that together formed the permanent boundary of

Africville. The land was situated within the Halifax city limits but in the remote area along the shore of Bedford Basin. The settlers moved to this site in order to escape the economic hardships they had experienced in Preston and Hammonds Plains. Africville had better soil conditions than in other Black communities, and its close proximity to the city provided opportunities for work. The Bedford Basin also was a rich fishery resource and it provided the residents of Africville a plentiful supply of many species of fish common to the Atlantic region.[28]

Africville was a close knit and self-sustaining community that gradually grew from eight original families in 1850 to over fifty families in 1964, the same year the Government of Nova Scotia relocated the residents and ordered the destruction of the buildings. Historically, Africville residents had strong ties to Seaview African United Baptist Church, which was the centre of the community. By the 1860s, in addition to the church, Africville had its own school, a post office and a community store. However, as a segregated Black settlement, it became increasingly marginalized as a community of outsiders.[29] Through isolation, neglect and prejudice, Africville underwent a process of ghettoization, and the residents were left to fend for themselves without many of the basic essentials such as running water and police service. In periods of economic decline, the community drew a number of unemployed and dislocated people in search of cheap housing.

In the white public's eyes, Africville was seen as a slum community consisting of "transients and squatters," and in the words of one city official, it was "A national blot on the city of Halifax."[30] During the latter decades of the nineteenth century, the city of Halifax witnessed a process of sustained economic expansion that led to several major encroachments on Africville. Over the next century, a fertilizer plant, slaughterhouse and a dumpsite with an incinerator were built very near to the community. Also, the expansion of the railroad along the Bedford Basin opened the entire area for industrial development. Eventually a rolling mill, nail factory, coal piers and foundries were built within short distance from Africville. The final and fatal blow to the community occurred when it was targeted for demolition in order to make way for the construction of a new bridge connecting Halifax and Dartmouth.

Modernization, Immigration and Canada's "Negro Problem"

At the end of the nineteenth century and during the first decades of the twentieth century, North America witnessed an unprecedented process of urban industrialization that transformed virtually every aspect of life. Major cities in the north grew at a staggering pace; Chicago, for example, grew from a small cross roads town of several thousand in the 1840s to a modern bustling city with skyscrapers and over one million people by 1910. New industrial towns like Pittsburgh and Bethlehem in Pennsylvania and Hamilton, Ontario, and Sydney, Nova Scotia, developed rapidly around state-of-the-art steel mills, and like the larger industrial cities of the North, they attracted workers from other regions of North America and from Britain and Europe.

From a Black historical perspective, perhaps the most appropriate defining symbol of this era is the railroad. Not only was the railroad a great agent for industrialization and national unity, it also created a lasting pattern of race relations. As we have seen, with the origin of Jim Crow laws in the United States, the railroad introduced new contested spaces of racial contact that led to the creation and strict enforcement of racial segregation laws. The railroad was also the major conduit that brought millions of Blacks from the cities and rural regions of the south to the industrial cities of the north. This exodus, known as the Great Migration, brought six million Blacks northward in search of employment and a better way of life over a period of sixty years beginning in 1910.[31]

In Canada, the railroad also shaped the Black experience. Although the pattern of segregation developed differently and there was no large-scale movement of Blacks from the United States to Canada in this era, the railroad nevertheless played a significant role in creating the culture of Jim Crow racial segregation in Canada that lasted for more than a century.

The completion of the Canadian Pacific Railway (CPR) was a momentous technological achievement, and it was seen at the time as an instrument for national unity and progress.[32] It was regarded as a great triumph of British, Anglo-Saxon civilization and domination over a rugged terrain and unyielding forces of nature. Anglophone Canadians took pride in being part of the British Empire, and national governments of the day set out to make Canada a racially homogeneous nation built on British institutions as well as Anglo-Saxon financial and technological ingenuity. There was perhaps no greater symbol of this feeling of national identity than the completion of the transcontinental railroad. This view, of course, gave little or no recognition to the fact that thousands of immigrant Chinese workers were responsible for building the roadbed and laying the continent-wide rail line. The completion, operation and expansion of the Canadian railway system required the blood and sweat of a vast army of workers, including many Blacks who provided their labour and skills in the construction and maintenance of the railroads and who worked in the extended hierarchy of service jobs as red caps and sleeping car porters. The CPR, Grand Trunk and other regional railroads were the main employers of Blacks from the late 1880s through the first half of the twentieth century.[33] Through regular employment or limited term work contracts, the railroad industry generated a new public presence of Blacks, and it was chiefly responsible for a dramatic rise in the urban Black population in all major Canadian cities that were serviced by the railroads. Cities that served as connecting railroad hubs drew large numbers of Blacks from the United States, the West Indies and from other parts of Canada. In the years leading up to World War II, Montreal's Black population grew by 49 percent, Toronto's by 21 percent and Winnipeg's grew by a staggering 96 percent. These rates of growth are remarkable, especially given the concerted efforts on the part of both Liberal and Conservative governments to severely restrict the immigration to Canada on racial grounds.[34]

Historically, the indigenous Black population of Canada resided mainly in segregated rural and urban areas of Ontario and Nova Scotia, and like Africville, these communities were largely out of sight and out of mind to the vast majority of Canadians. With the process of modernization, the pattern of Black settlement shifted to new areas, and due to the railroads and government policies, in particular, Blacks had a more sizable and visible presence in communities where few or none had resided in the past. In the prairie provinces, the presence of large groups of Black immigrants was a relatively new phenomenon, and it was the direct result of the Canadian homestead policy that was implemented by the Liberal Government of Wilfrid Laurier in 1896.

Laurier and his cabinet designed a plan to attract large numbers of immigrants and thus expand rural agriculture settlements in the west, especially in the newly created provinces of Saskatchewan and Alberta. The homestead policy aggressively targeted the United States, Great Britain and Europe and offered the most desirable immigrants 160 acres of land for a nominal fee of $10.00 if they agreed to engage in farming. From 1896 to 1911, the program, together with Canada's open immigration policies, helped to attract nearly 2 million white immigrants to predominantly rural regions of Canada.[35] Although Canada's immigration policies favoured whites, the homestead policy attracted a significant number of Black immigrants who sought to escape the Jim Crow laws and racial violence of the south.[36] The Underground Railroad was fresh in the memory of many American Blacks, and in spite of a racially restrictive immigration policy, Canada was still perceived as a Promised Land founded on British ideals of justice and due process of law.

In 1911, a large company of Blacks arrived in Canada from Oklahoma, Arkansas and Texas. The group was led by Henry Sneed, a Baptist minister, who had a well-conceived plan to create a Black farming community in northern Alberta. The Sneed party travelled to Canada on a train carrying 194 Black passengers and seven freight cars of farm equipment and animals, including cattle, horses and mules.[37] These immigrants were only one of several well-organized groups of Blacks who made their way to Canada during this period. The appearance of this group of Black settlers did not, of course, go unnoticed at the time and, indeed, it raised alarm among many, especially among a vocal and influential minority of nativists. Canadian newspapers warned that the Sneed party was a "Black Peril" and a menacing vanguard for an even greater "Invasion of Negroes."[38] In Alberta, a well-known businessman, F.D. Fisher, joined with the Edmonton Board of Trade in presenting a resolution to Prime Minister Laurier, requesting that the government "take such steps as will effectively prevent the advent of negroes to western Canada; and that such negroes as are now on homestead lands in the country be segregated in a certain defined area … from which white settlers be removed."[39] The resolution reflected the widely held nativist sentiment that the presence of Blacks was a threat to the peace and security of the country, and it was soon followed by a petition organized by members of the Edmonton Board of Trade that demanded the total exclusion of Blacks to Canada.[40] The Edmonton chapter of the Imperial Order of the Daughters of the Empire (IODE) also organized a petition and sent it to Frank Oliver, the Minister of Immigration. The petition concluded by stating that "the experience of the United States should warn us to take action before the situation becomes complicated and before the inevitable racial antipathies shall have sprung up."[41]

White Canadians in most areas of the country feared that Black immigration would introduce "the Negro Problem" to Canada, which, for them, meant social upheaval and racial violence. The *Toronto Mail and Empire* articulated this view succinctly: "If negroes and white people cannot live in accord in the South, they cannot live in accord in the North."[42]

As these views indicate, many Canadians during this period held a racial stereotype that associated Blacks with crime, poverty and, perhaps worst of all, a threat to the safety and sexual innocence of white women. In their petition to the Minister of Immigration, the Edmonton branch of IODE expressed this sentiment clearly: "We do not wish that the fair fame of Western Canada would be sullied with the shadow of Lynch Law but we have no guarantee that our women will be safer in their scattered homesteads than white women in other countries with a Negro population."[43] This characterization of Blacks was deeply rooted in the history of slavery, and it formed part of a complex racial mythology that was central to southern segregationist ideology. The mythology builds on variety of slave personality types including the classic Sambo stereotype that regarded Blacks as being, docile, lazy, servile, untrustworthy and irresponsible. It was argued that by virtue of the inherent attributes of race and personality, Blacks would always need to be governed by a strict set of social controls.[44] In the post–Civil War south, the slave personality stereotype evolved into a more menacing image of emancipated Blacks that were uncontrolled, demanding and a threat to the social order. These traits combined with the long-held myth of Black promiscuity and heightened sexuality were a serious cause for concern among southern whites. During the 1920s, the Ku Klux Klan achieved national stature in the United States, and it was chiefly responsible for widely disseminating this racial stereotype of Blacks. In the United States, the Klan attracted over 4 million members nationally, and in 1924, it supported a presidential candidate who nearly won the nomination at the

Democratic National Convention.[45] Although the Klan never received anything close to this level of support in Canada, it had branches in nearly every province of the country. The Edmonton-based Klan newspaper, *The Liberator,* claimed to have a circulation of 250,000, and by 1925 there were as many as 8,000 Klan members in the city of Toronto alone.[46] That same year, there were hundreds of cross burnings in small towns across southern Ontario, and over the next several years, organized mobs of angry, hooded, Canadian KKK members engaged in acts of physical violence, and in a few instances, threated to lynch innocent victims.[47]

In spite of the Klan's radical racist ideology and acts of violence, in some regions of the country it was successful for a short period of time in appealing to mainstream popular opinion. In Saskatchewan during the 1920s, support for the Klan fed on popular reaction to large-scale immigration from central and southern Europe following the First World War. Although the Klan in Canada had limited appeal because of its American origins, in Saskatchewan it was successful in identifying with the popular nationalist (and imperialist) desire of the period to keep Canada British.[48]

Canadians who had few personal encounters with Blacks were particularly susceptible to the degrading racial stereotypes that were being fostered by the Klan as well as by a large number of home grown nativists. One of the most powerful negative portrayals of Blacks was visually dramatized in D.W. Griffith's epic silent film *The Birth of a Nation* that was shown repeatedly to audiences in packed movie houses across Canada from its release in 1915 to the end of the silent movie era in 1927. The movie was based on the novel *The Clansman* by Thomas Dixon Jr., and it dramatically enacted imagined scenes of chaos and violence throughout the war-torn south during the Reconstruction Era that occurred as a direct result of the emancipation of slaves. The movie depicted unruly mobs of Blacks running wild in the south, and the message it conveyed to its audience through a carefully contrived story line is that whites have everything to fear from the presence of free Blacks. The film tells the story of how the Ku Klux Klan was organized in order to help re-establish social order in the south. In one graphic and horrifying scene, the film depicts the brutal revenge killing by Klan members of a Black man by the name of Gus, played by a white actor in black face, who attempted to pursue an innocent white girl. One can only imagine the impact that *The Birth of the Nation* had on Canadian audiences in cities and in small towns across Canada.[49] It must be noted as well that the movie theatre provided a relatively new form of community entertainment, and it quickly developed as a centre for other forms of entertainment. It provided the venue for the ever-popular minstrel shows as well as productions like "Uncle Tom's Cabin" that used local actors who performed with blackened faces. All of these forms of entertainment helped to convey similar negative stereotypical portrayals of Blacks.

The Canadian Government was deeply concerned about the influx of Black immigrants to Canada. Through the Immigration Acts of 1906 and 1911 and the work of the Minister of Immigration, Frank Oliver, and the superintendent of immigration, William D. Scott, the Laurier Administration developed a multi-faceted strategy to ensure that Canada would remain a nation "for the white race only."[50] The Canadian Government regarded the "Negro Problem" as an immigration issue, and it deemed Blacks as undesirables on grounds that they were physically unfit for the harsh northern climate of Canada. In addition to giving extraordinary discretionary powers to border officials to exclude Blacks on fiscal and medical grounds, the Laurier Government engaged in a campaign to dissuade Blacks from immigrating to Canada. The government secretly commissioned articles published in American newspapers that described Canada's western environment as "desolate, frigid," and "unsettled."[51]

The election of Robert Borden and the Conservatives in 1911 did not substantially change Canada's racially restrictive immigration policy. Although Borden expressed a more tolerant stand on immigration during his campaign, when he took office, the only major change he effected was to allow a limited number of Blacks from the United States and the West Indies to immigrate in order to work in the service and entertainment industries. The majority of these immigrants worked for the railroads, especially as sleeping car porters. Here again racial stereotyping was very much at play as an influence on Canadian immigration policy. When the railway tycoon, William Van Horne, took up management of the Canadian Pacific Railway in 1881, he introduced the Pullman sleeping car and sleeping car porters to Canada. The Pullman sleeping car porter became a central feature of the service Canadians came to know and expect when they travelled on the CPR. Pullman founder, George Pullman, had astutely marketed an idealized racial image of Black male servants that incorporated much of the Sambo stereotype. According to Sarah-Jane Mathieu: "Pullman sleeping cars encapsulated a gendered and racialized mobile beau ideal in which rich, civilized white men were served by Black men doing women's work, thereby reinforcing Black manhood's incompleteness."[52] The sleeping car porter was a reminder of the race relations of the old south, which was based on the master and slave relationship. The Black man was expected to play the part of an emasculated male version of the slave "Mammy" that had served the master's household in antebellum south.[53] He "made beds, cleaned house, tended to white children, shined shoes, served food, and catered to passenger's caprices. Within Pullman's sleepers, Black manhood posed no threat to white civilization, since porters, uniformly called 'George,' [after Pullman car founder, George Pullman] were most often stripped of their individual identities."[54]

The Pullman model of southern comfort and service was eventually adopted by all the major railway companies in Canada. The demand for this service was so popular that Canadian railway companies aggressively recruited young Black males from several predominantly Black colleges in the United States to work as sleeping car porters in Canada. Mathieu notes that as a result of the efforts of the Canadian railway industry "young Black male workers — especially sleeping car porters — constituted the largest class of Black immigrants admitted into Canada between 1911 and the early 1960s."[55]

It is not known exactly how many Blacks immigrated to Canada during the early period of industrialization. Although the official census records indicate that the Black population grew only slightly by less than 1,000 from 1901 to 1921, the number of Black immigrants arriving to Canada over this same period was substantially greater. Despite the racially restrictive immigration policy, nearly 5,000 Black immigrants arrived to Canada from the United States and the West Indies from 1900 and 1916.[56] This figure does not reflect a significant number of "unofficial" immigrants who crossed the border by train or by ships arriving at Canadian port cities. In Nova Scotia, there was a continuous flow of undocumented immigrants from the West Indies who arrived by ship to Sydney, Glace Bay, Port Hawkesbury and Halifax during the first decade of the twentieth century.[57] Many of these immigrants found work in the coal and steel industries in Cape Breton and others made their way to cities like Montreal where they found work on the railroads or in the entertainment and other service industries.[58]

The demand for labour was fairly constant throughout the period before the end the World War I. The Dominion Iron and Steel Company (DISCO) in Sydney actively recruited immigrants as cheap labour from southern and eastern European countries as well as Blacks from the United States and the West Indies. In 1901, DISCO foreman, John H. Means, brought a large contingent of Black workers from steel making towns in Alabama, Pennsylvania and Colorado to work as "Coloured Furnace Men" in DISCO's new open hearth.[59] In October 1901, 250 Black workers and their families arrived by train in Sydney with the promise of a high wages and better way of life. Although these workers and their families experienced such severe hardships of climate, broken promises and racial discrimination that they eventually returned to the United States, their initial willingness to make the long trek north is evidence that for many American Blacks, Canada was part of their vision of the Great Migration.[60]

Canada's New Culture of Segregation

The practice of racial segregation had long been established in Canada. It existed *de facto* as part of the early Black settlement pattern in Canada, and it extended to major community institutions such as schools and churches. As we have seen, the Black Loyalists in Nova Scotia and the planned Black settlements such as Dawn and Buxton in southwestern Ontario developed voluntarily as racially segregated communities. The first legally imposed forms of racial segregation occurred in education, and this was sanctioned in Nova Scotia under the Education Acts of 1836 and 1865 and in Ontario under the *Common School Act* of 1850. In both provinces, the existence of racially segregated schools continued until the 1960s. In many instances, Blacks resisted the practice of racial segregation in education, especially in cases like the Halifax petition campaign of 1883, where the practice of school segregation severely limited the educational opportunities for the children of the Black middle-class families. Generally, however, the early voluntary pattern of racial segregation in Canada provided a strong sense of community and collective identity. This was the case in Africville and in the planned Black agricultural settlements in Ontario and in western Canada. In all these communities, the bonds of racial identity were reinforced in Black churches and in other community organizations. This was even the case in many of the Black segregated schools. Although often grossly unequal in terms of educational and material recourses, racially segregated schools did provide Black children with a supportive and caring environment. Many teachers in these schools were respected members of the Black community and they took pride in their efforts to educate their students. Like good teachers everywhere, the best of them left a lasting positive influence on their students.[61]

The process of early modernization brought a new and more blatant Jim Crow style of racial segregation to Canada. The seeds of this grew from ignorance and fear of the so-called Negro Problem, and it was nourished on the racial stereotypes that were based on Canadian nativist and Southern racial ideology. As we have seen, the first overt attempt by the Federal Government to institutionalize Jim Crow occurred in Canada's racial restrictive immigration policy. This culminated in an order-in-council initiated by Frank Oliver, the Minister of Immigration, which put into effect for one year the total exclusion "of any immigrants belonging to the Negro race, which race is deemed unsuitable to the climate and requirements of Canada."[62] On August 12, 1911, Prime Minister Wilfrid Laurier signed this order-in-council, and although the edict was never fully implemented, it was the first attempt by the government to nationally enact a Jim Crow law in Canada.[63]

The Department of Immigration was not the only branch of government to adopt a Jim Crow style of segregation. In the development of government policy in relation to industrial disputes, the Department of Labour sanctioned a similar practice of racial segregation within the Canadian labour movement, especially in its support of the unionization of railway workers. In 1908, the Canadian Brotherhood of Railway Employees and Other Transport Workers (CBRE) was created under the leadership of Aaron Mosher, a young charismatic freight handler who worked for the Inter Colonial Railway. Mosher was an unabashed Canadian union nationalist and white supremacist, and he succeeded in organizing, under the umbrella of a single national union, all the Canadian railway workers but with the deliberate exclusion of Black railway workers. In 1909 and in 1913, Mosher negotiated two landmark contracts with the government-owned Inter Colonial Railway that gave increased wages and benefits exclusively to white railroad workers. Under the provisions of the 1913 contract, a clearly defined line of colour separated workers with the same jobs. White workers received wage increases, ten-hour workdays, as well as vacations and other benefits while Black workers received no wage increases and only limited benefits.

Mosher lead the CBRE for several decades, and the contracts he helped put in place advanced the rights of white railway workers; however, his white supremacist views effectively denied Black railway workers the benefits of collective bargaining. According to Mathieu, the Inter Colonial Railway agreement of 1913 "Institutionalized separate and unequal promotion scales for railway workers, reserving well remunerated supervisory positions exclusively for white men and permanently locking Black railroaders into competition for lower-wage service positions."[64]

By the beginning of World War I, "White supremacy dictated employment policy on all Canadian railway lines."[65] Even with the creation of the Order of Sleeping Car Porters in 1917 that steadfastly fought for the rights of Black porters, the practice of Jim Crow in the Canadian railway industry did not finally end until the 1960s.

In the first two decades of the twentieth century, the policies of the Canadian Government reflected a developing culture of Jim Crow in Canada. Through the actions of the Laurier Government, Blacks were either excluded from Canada, or they were effectively denied equal employment rights. During World War I, the practice of Jim Crow extended to the military under the Borden Government. Initially, the Government regarded Blacks as entirely unfit for military service and did not allow Blacks the right to fight as patriotic citizens in the defence of their country. After sustained pressure from a growing chorus of protests, the Government relented, but instead of permitting Blacks to join integrated combat units, it created the No. 2 Construction Battalion, a racially segregated, non-combat unit lead by a white commander and officers. The battalion received official authorization on July 6, 1916, and drew nearly 900 Black volunteers from Nova Scotia and Ontario.[66]

The history of the first half of the twentieth century illustrates how deeply ingrained racism was in the Canadian national psyche. Like all forms of prejudice, racism is both systemic and personal; it is expressed in a specific set of policies and in the day-to-day interactions between people. The dynamic of racial prejudice, as a function of culture, is experienced and reinforced on the community level. When three train cars of skilled Black labourers and their families arrived in Sydney, Nova Scotia, in 1901 to work at DISCO's blast furnace, for example, they were immediately met with racial prejudice on all levels. Typical among the responses from local residents was the view that Black workers, like other foreigners, were taking jobs away from local able-bodied men. In one letter to the *Daily Record,* Blacks were referred to as "foul-mouthed n*****s" who came to Canada in order to replace hard working and "god-fearing" local men.[67]

The majority of this group of Black steel workers were from Alabama, and they came to Sydney because they believed they would be paid good wages and would be better off than they were in the south. Even though they were classified as skilled labourers, it was clear that "race superseded skill in determining the status accorded to Black workers."[68] This was immediately apparent in the accommodations they were given. Despite the fact that they were given "alluring promises of fine houses to live in," as one Black worker stated, the accommodations they received consisted of small "shacks" designed for single men and clustered together in a racially segregated area very close to the coke ovens. The Black community came to be known as "Cokeville" or "Cokovia" or sometimes simply as "Shackville," and it was regarded as the least desirable area for any skilled or unskilled foreign worker to live in.[69] The conditions of the "coloured shacks" were described at the time as "bad beyond description," and "the majority [were] exceedingly filthy. There [was] no sewage or water connection and ventilation [was] foul."[70]

As a community, the Black workers and their families were regarded as a threat to the white residents of Sydney and the community of Whitney Pier. Newspaper and police reports gave particular emphasis to their unruly behaviour, and Black women were singled out "for charges of drunkenness, vagrancy and prostitution."[71] Local accounts frequently described Blacks and their community in terms of "squalor, violence and sexual immorality."[72]

By 1902, the Black residential area of Cokeville became a coherent racially segregated community with its own African Methodist Episcopal Church as well as school for "coloured children."[73] The single-room school was called Cokovia School, and it had one Black Nova Scotia teacher and thirty-two pupils; it remained in operation until the Black workers returned to the United States in 1904.[74]

The experience of the Black steel workers and their families in Sydney was a reflection on the micro level of the new urban residential pattern of segregation that was developing in towns and cities across Canada and the United States. This was occurring more dramatically on a much larger scale in the major industrial cities like Chicago, New York and Detroit, and over a short span of time, each of these cities had developed sizable racial ghettos, like Chicago's "Black Belt." In Canada, the process of industrialization brought Black railway workers to cities where they created their own communities like Point Douglas in Winnipeg and St. Antoine in Montreal. In Nova Scotia, demand for labour in the steel and coal industries continued to bring Black immigrants not only from the United States but also from the West Indies, where they became part of expanded Black communities in Sydney, Whitney Pier, Glace Bay and Pictou.

Although the magnitude of Black migration and urban settlements differed greatly between the industrial centres of Canada and the United States, the dynamics of racial segregation were very similar. The growth of urban Black communities, like most other racial and ethnic and communities, involved a natural tendency of people of one particular group desiring to live together in the same community. However, unlike many other urban communities, including immigrant slums of most industrial cities, Black communities evolved into ghettoes because the residents had very few choices in determining where they could live. Chicago's Black residential distribution evolved into a single, racially segregated area called the Black Belt because Blacks were increasingly denied access to accommodation in other areas.[75] The borders of the Black Belt were commonly understood boundaries that formed an arbitrary but definitive line of colour, often dividing portions of the same street. On the northern boundary of the Black Belt, the demarcation extended as an imaginary but real line racially separating the beach area along Lake Michigan. In the summer of 1919, a group of Black boys accidentally drifted on their makeshift raft across the imaginary colour line to the waters off the whites' only beach. This incident sparked a reaction from the white beach goers that rapidly escalated into one of the worst race riots in American history. Before the riot ended, thirty-eight Blacks were killed and several thousand were left homeless.[76] Dubbed Chicago's "Red Summer," the riots were one of several dozen similar incidents of racial violence that occurred during the period immediately following World War I.

Canadian cities with Black residential populations did not experience anything like the race riots in the United States. However, there were similar racial tensions in some of the industrial areas of Nova Scotia. In 1918, the militia had to be marshalled to deal with a race riot that broke out in Glace Bay. The incident was sparked by a dispute involving an Italian immigrant who was a participant in a bicycle race at a local Sunday picnic event organized by Black residents of the town. The exact nature of the dispute is not certain, but as a result of the riot, one Black male was shot and killed, and the authorities had to impose a curfew in order to control racial tensions.[77]

In Pictou, Nova Scotia, there was racial incident described by Carrie M. Best that took place in 1919 in which "bands of roving white men armed with clubs stationed themselves at different intersections and allowing no Blacks to go beyond that point."[78]

Although the incidents of racial violence were far less prevalent and intense in Canada, they were nevertheless symptomatic of the developing pattern of Jim Crow racial segregation. In Canada, local businesses were allowed to discriminate on racial grounds under "freedom of commerce" laws. This principal of law stemmed from nineteenth century *laissez-faire* economics that influenced Canada's legal theory during the late Victorian era, and in Quebec, it was supported under the French principle of "la liberté du commerce."[79] In cases involving individuals who challenged the practice of Jim Crow in restaurants, bars, hotels and theaters, the courts sided in favour of the right of business owners to engage in freedom of commerce over the rights of individuals to be treated equally. When confronted with the charge of racial discrimination in local restaurants, a common defence under this principle was that in a democratic society like Canada "You can't force anyone to serve a Negro."[80]

By the 1940s, a culture of Jim Crow had developed in all urban areas of Canada with sizable Black populations. Pearleen Oliver, an early Nova Scotia civil rights activist, lived in Halifax during the 1940s, and she recalled that the colour line delineating the Black residential area of the city included parts of three main north end streets: Cornwallis, Creighton and Maynard. She noted that with the exception of a single Black woman, all inner-city Blacks resided in this area.

"[In] those days," she stated, "you couldn't get into any hotel [and] you couldn't eat at any restaurant."[81] The practice of Jim Crow superseded all other social distinctions including class, occupation and even country of origin. Oliver related an account of a wealthy Black doctor from New York City who arrived with his wife by car for a vacation in Halifax. Unaware of the local culture of Jim Crow, the doctor and his wife were shocked to discover that because they were Black, not a single Halifax hotel would give them accommodation. In their desperate attempt to seek lodging, the couple was eventually directed to the Black Baptist church on Cornwallis Street where Pearleen's husband, Rev. William Oliver, was the minister. Pearleen was able to find the couple a place to stay in the home of West Indian woman near Creighton Street.[82]

The practice of Jim Crow was also firmly entrenched in several of the small towns in southwestern Ontario. The case of Dresden is particularly noteworthy because its history is one of sharp contrast between a community based on racial tolerance and one divided by racial discrimination and segregation. Dresden was a terminus of the Underground Railroad and close to the home and gravesite of Josiah Henson. As mentioned in the previous chapter, Henson's autobiography inspired Harriet Beecher Stowe, who partially modelled her main character after Henson in her novel *Uncle Tom's Cabin*. In the 1940s, Henson's gravesite, known as Uncle Tom's grave, became a popular tourist attraction that drew visitors from other areas of Canada and the United States. In the era of the Underground Railroad, the rich farmland around Dresden was the location of the Dawn Settlement, founded by Henson and the British and North American Settlement Company (BNASC). Dawn was one of seven planned Black agricultural communities that was created for former slaves in the region of southwestern Ontario. Recent research by local historian Marie

Carter has revealed that Dawn, although a predominantly Black settlement, was a multi-racial community. There were several-mixed race marriages between Black residents and local First Nations people, and a number of local white children attended the Dawn settlement schools.[83] The community prospered for several decades, but at the end of the nineteenth century the area went into economic recession, and the BNASC was forced to sell off large tracks of land. As a result, the land was transferred to white owners and major portions of the Black agricultural settlement were incorporated into the developing town of Dresden. The town had grown from a small lumber-based community founded in 1825 under the name of Fairport to a picturesque rural agricultural town that reached a population of nearly 2,000 by the early twentieth century.[84]

By the 1940s, Dresden had developed its own culture of racial segregation. Although the majority of the town's 300 Blacks resided on a two-block section of Main Street, others lived in other predominantly white areas of the town. Racial segregation, however, was strictly enforced in other areas of social contact, and by the end of the decade Dresden became infamous as one of Canada's most visibly racist communities. In 1949, journalist Sidney Katz visited the town and wrote an expose for Maclean's entitled "Jim Crow Lives in Dresden." He wrote in the opening section of his article that "although Dresden citizens do not like to talk about it, Negroes cannot eat at the town's three restaurants serving regular meals, cannot get a haircut in the four regular barbershops, cannot send their wives to the only beauty parlour."[85] He also noted that local Black residents were barred from poolrooms, service clubs and from attending any of the several white churches in town. "The chances of even a trained young Negro getting a good non-manual job are almost nil." And Katz added that he "did not find a single Negro in Dresden working in an office or waiting on customers."[86]

Not all the white residents and business owners were in agreement with the practice of Jim Crow, but because of the assertive views of a few, they accepted the practice. In this regard, Dresden is a good case study into the dynamics of prejudice, and it illustrates how racial discrimination can take hold of an entire community. Perhaps the most vocal and unapologetic racist in Dresden was Morley McKay, owner of Kay's Grill, the largest of the town's three restaurants. McKay staunchly defended his right to bar Blacks from his place of business. "I've run it for 26 years myself" he told Katz, and he added: "Nobody is going to tell me how to run it now."[87] The other restaurant owners were less vocal in defending their refusal to serve Black customers and Katz noted that they feared they would lose business if they didn't follow McKay's lead in refusing to serve Blacks.

Racial segregation was not practiced uniformly throughout the town. In addition to the lack of any consistent pattern of residential segregation, the children of Black families attended white schools and younger children of both races played together and became friends throughout the early years of their lives. Katz commented that it was not uncommon "to see colored and white children walking the streets arm and arm."[88] It is apparent from these kinds of behaviours that racial segregation in Dresden was primarily the product of the adult white population. No doubt it was driven, in part, out of fear among the adult white citizens that their sons or daughters might date and marry a Black person. For this reason, social activities and venues that might bring young and older people of both races into contact were severely restricted. There were "no tennis courts, golf courses, bowling alleys or swimming pools; no home and school club, dramatic society, town hall or community centre."[89]

The town of Dresden and the surrounding agricultural region was, in the matter of race relations, a story of contrasting opposites. Katz observed that on one farm near the town he "watched a group of white and colored farmers passing a pitcher of cold water from mouth to mouth during a breather in a tobacco field."[90] Bill Carter, a prominent member of Dresden's Black community, explained this paradox: "We work for each other, visit back and forth, eat at the same table. But if we should happen into town together, something happens. We can't eat at the same restaurant."[91]

The Struggle to End Racial Segregation in Canada

The struggle for racial equality and human rights is an integral part of the broader narrative of Canadian history. From the institution of slavery under the French and British regimes during the seventeenth and eighteenth centuries to the abolitionist movement and the Underground Railroad in the nineteenth century to the civil rights movement of the twentieth century, Canadian history chronicles the ongoing tension between racial prejudice and discrimination and the ideals of freedom, equality and human rights.

In twentieth century Canada, resistance to Jim Crow took many forms, and it involved a diversity of individuals and organizations. Unlike the dramatic events associated with the American civil rights movement that culminated in the landmark Supreme Court *Brown* decision in 1954 and the *Civil Rights Act* of 1964, the struggle for racial equality in Canada occurred in a piecemeal manner on a province-by-province basis.

In Ontario, the *Racial Discrimination Act* was passed in 1944, prohibiting the public display in any form of signage that showed discrimination based on race, ethnic origin, or religion. This limited piece of anti-discrimination legislation was followed by a more comprehensive legislative initiative under the *Conveyance and Law of Property Act* of 1950 that prohibited restrictive covenants in the sale or transfer of property based on race, ethnic origin and religion. A year later, the Ontario legislature passed

Kay's Café, Dresden, Ontario, 1949, Maclean's, 1 November 1949

the *Fair Employment Practices Act* and the *Female Employment Practices Act*. Both these pieces of legislation were inspired in part by the United Nations *Declaration of Human Rights* of 1948, and they prohibited discrimination in hiring practices and established the principle of equal pay for equal work. In 1954, the *Fair Accommodation Practices Act* was passed, which declared that "no one can deny any person or class of persons the accommodations, services or facilities usually available to members of the public."[92] With the exception of the province of Saskatchewan, which under the leadership of Tommy Douglas passed a comprehensive bill of rights in 1947, all other provinces followed a similar piecemeal process in adopting civil rights legislation. Nova Scotia, like Ontario, passed the *Fair Employments Act* in 1953 followed by the *Equal Pay Act* of 1956 and the *Fair Accommodations Act* of 1959. In 1963, Nova Scotia passed a more sweeping and inclusive civil rights act under the *Human Rights Act*. Similar comprehensive civil rights legislation was passed in Ontario (1962), Alberta (1966), New Brunswick (1967), Prince Edward Island (1968), British Columbia (1969), Newfoundland (1969), Manitoba (1970) and Quebec (1975). Finally, the consolidation of civil rights occurred on the national level in 1982 under the *Charter of Rights and Freedoms*.[93]

The fight to end racial segregation involved the coordinated efforts of provincial legislatures, the courts and successive generations of activists and their supporters. This struggle has been well documented in relation to the Canadian railway industry in several important publications.[94] These studies have described in detail the extent of racist attitudes and policies within the CBRE and within the Canadian railway industry as a whole. Jenny Carson notes that "it was not until the 1960s that Blacks in Canada and the U.S. gained access to higher-paying skilled jobs such as engineering and conducting."[95] These gains were the result of the sustained and courageous efforts of a number of extraordinary individuals such as John A. Robinson, Arthur R. Blanchette and Stanley Grizzle, all of whom fought to organize the American-based Brotherhood of Sleeping Car Porters in Canada, and they sought to link union militancy with the fight for civil rights.[96] Grizzle, who had worked as a porter with the CPR for twenty years, became a well-known spokesperson for human rights in Ontario and later became the first Black judge on the court of Canadian citizenship. Grizzle was active in the effort to change Canada's immigration policy, and he joined a delegation to Ottawa, lead by Donald Wilfred Moore, that on April 27, 1954, presented a landmark brief to Walter Harris, the Minister of Immigration. The following year, the Federal Government began to loosen restrictions to immigration from the West Indies, and this eventually led to the passage of the *Immigration Act* of 1962 that replaced the racially restrictive *Immigration Act* of 1923.[97]

The struggle to end the practice of Jim Crow in Dresden began with the efforts of Hugh Burnett, a Black World War II veteran, local carpenter and business owner. In 1943, Burnett wrote a letter to the Federal Government protesting the practice of racial discrimination at Kay's Café. He was informed that the government could do nothing to change the business practices in the town of Dresden.[98] In 1948, Burnett co-founded the National Unity Association (NUA), which spearheaded a coordinated effort to end racial discrimination in Dresden. Burnett brought together in the NUA a group of other Black residents of Dresden, some of whom were close friends and fellow war veterans, and others, like Burnett's uncle, Bill Carter, were prominent members of Dresden's Black community. In the fall of 1948, the NUA appeared before the all-white Dresden town council and lobbied to have a non-discrimination agreement as a requirement for new business licenses. The town council resoundingly rejected their request, and this forced the NUA to develop a much broader provincial-wide strategy to end racial discrimination. In 1949, Burnett and the NUA found a natural ally with Kalmen Kaplansky, the president of the Jewish Labour Committee. Kaplansky was a skilled labour union leader and human rights activist, and through his pioneering work he was able to marshal the power of the organized labour movement in the struggle to end racial discrimination in Ontario.[99]

Kaplansky and Burnett helped organize a delegation of thirty-six activists representing Ontario's human rights organizations that met with Leslie Frost, the newly elected Premier of Ontario. The delegation sought to strengthen the

Ontario *Racial Discrimination Act,* and they advocated for new legislation to end discrimination in employment, housing and public places. The Frost Government eventually agreed to amending the *Racial Discrimination Act,* and in 1951 the Frost Government created new legislation under the *Fair Employment Practices Act* and the *Female Employees Fair Remuneration Act.*[100]

The passage of anti-discrimination legislation did not immediately end the practice of Jim Crow in Dresden. Morley McKay remained defiant of all attempts to require his restaurant to serve Blacks. In 1954, the Frost Government passed the *Fair Accommodation Practices Act,* and after appealing his earlier convictions of racial discrimination, Morley MacKay was eventually found guilty and fined under the new legislation. On November 16, 1956, two members of the NUA entered Kay's Café and they, like all the white patrons of the restaurant, were served without incident.[101]

In Nova Scotia, the fight to end racial discrimination during the era of Jim Crow involved the actions of a number of dedicated and courageous individuals. In the early 1940s, Pearleen Oliver began a campaign to raise public awareness about the extent of racial discrimination in the province. She was the first Black woman to cross the colour line that existed at hotels in Halifax in order to address white businessmen and service clubs. Oliver was a founding member of the Nova Scotia Association for the Advancement of Colored People, and she was largely responsible for ending the practice of barring Black girls from training and practicing the profession of nursing in Canada. Her tenacity and persistence in fighting for racial equality distinguishes her as one of Canada's most important Black civil rights activists in the twentieth century.[102]

Carrie M. Best was also a pioneer in the struggle to end racial discrimination in Nova Scotia. In 1941, she challenged the practice of racial segregated seating at the Roseland Theatre in her hometown of New Glasgow. Her legal challenge, like the many similar challenges to racial segregation in theatres and other public placed across Canada, was unsuccessful.[103] Best, however, continued with her fight for racial equality, and in 1946 she established *The Clarion,* one of the first Black community newspapers in Nova Scotia. *The Clarion* ran for three years until it was expanded into a national newspaper under the title *The Negro Citizen,* which ran until 1956.

The struggle for justice in ending the practice of Jim Crow in Nova Scotia and in Canada as a whole has involved a sustained effort over several generations. The work of activists like Pearleen Oliver and Carrie M. Best exemplify the dedication and courage needed in the effort to raise public awareness in order to ultimately change attitudes and behaviour. This struggle has also involved the actions of other remarkable individuals who acted spontaneously when confronted with injustice. Their singular acts of courage have been and continue to be an essential part of

THE CLARION

Published in the Interest of Colored Nova Scotians

VOL. 1., NO. 1.   NEW GLASGOW, N. S.   DECEMBER 31, 1946.

Locals

The Season's Greetings to
All Our Readers

Mr. and Mrs. James MacPhee have moved into their new home on South Albert Street.

Calbert Best, student at King's College, Halifax, will spend the Christmas recess with his parents, Mr. and Mrs. A. T. Best.

Congratulations are being extended to Rev. and Mrs. Thomas for their Christmas Calendar. It is a lovely job!

Miss Evelyn Williams, daughter of Mr. Norman Williams, stenographer with the Pay Roll Department at Ottawa, will be home on Dec. 20th to spend the Christmas holidays with her family.

Friends will be interested to know that Miss Thelma Parris, formerly of this town, has become an American citizen. She is making her home in Cambridge, where her mother, Mrs. Douglas Gordon, resides.

The Ladies' Auxiliary of Second Baptist Church held a successful sale and tea in the Church Hall on Dec. 10th. A lovely display of fancy work was noted.

Mr. and Mrs. Lemuel Mills left Saturday, Dec. 14, for Boston, where they will spend Christmas with their daughters, Mrs. Thornton Harper and Mrs. Bennie Shepherd.

Johnnie Mills met a deer—DEER, that is, recently, while driving his mother to Halifax. The deer darted out on the highway near Elmsdale and hit the side of the car. Not seriously injured, the deer soon scampered off, none the worse of the impact.

Word has been received that Miss Irma Halfkenney will be a participant in the St. John Music Festival in May. A student at Mount Allison School of Music, Miss Halfkenney is a soprano of promise, and that she will make a creditable showing goes without saying.

The Senior B. Y. P. U. of Second Baptist Church motored a bus and motored to Riverton where they held a service for the inmates of the Pictou County Home. Among those who took part were Rev. H. D. Thomas, Howard Lawrence, Miss Althea Lawrence and Mrs. Gordon Clark. About twenty-five persons made the trip.

The Ladies' Auxiliary of the Second Baptist Church had a surprise party early in December for Rev. and Mrs. Thomas, at the Parsonage, Washington St. The gifts included china, linen, etc., and each gift was accompanied by an original verse. Typical of the verses was the one accompanying the crocheted doily gift of President Mrs. L. Mills:

"I may be small, but my mission is great, I'm here to decorate your cake plate. Your cakes I know are a treat to eat, So use me when next your guests you treat."

MRS. VIOLA DESMOND

Takes Action

Mrs. Viola Desmond, 32-year-old Negro Halifax beautician, arrested and fined $20 and costs by Magistrate Rod G. MacKay, of this town, for sitting downstairs in the Roseland Theatre while holding an upstairs ticket.

Mrs. Desmond was fined for defrauding the Federal Government of one cent, the difference in the Amusement tax on an upstairs ticket of two cents and a downstairs ticket of three cents.

Counsel for Mrs. Desmond, F. W. Bisset of Halifax, has served a writ against Henry MacNeil, manager of the theatre, charging false arrest, false imprisonment, assault and malicious persecution.

E. M. Macdonald, K.C., of New Glasgow, is acting for Mr. MacNeil.

Mrs. Desmond, the former Viola Davis, daughter of Mr. and Mrs. James Davis, of Halifax, is well known throughout the Province. She is a graduate of the Halifax High School, and is also a graduate in Beauty Culture from a leading Beauty College in New York. She is a niece of John Davis, Civil Service employee (Post Office Division), Halifax.

◆

Viola Desmond's Appeal

Just as we go to press w. are in receipt of a letter from Mrs. Bernice Williams, Sec'y N. S. A. A. C. P., informing us that an appeal trial of the Viola Desmond case will be held in Halifax on Dec. 27th, also a Viola Desmond Court Fund has been established by the Association soliciting contributions. A public meeting will be held by the Association on Dec. 22nd in Halifax asking everyone to attend and give their donation.

◆

The N. S. A. A. C. P. is the Ladder to Advancement. STEP ON IT! JOIN TODAY!

Did You Know?

(a) That Adult education in rural communities is being sponsored by the N. S. A. A. C. P.

(b) That the Educational Department of the Province of Nova Scotia is supporting the movement.

(c) That a class has already started in Hammonds Plains and is progressing favourably.

(d) That the C.G. I. T. group of Cornwallis Street Baptist Church, Halifax, raised the sum of $35.00 at their Christmas Sale. Mrs. Oliver is leader and all girls are under 16 years.

(e) That the money will be used for the work of the Summer Camp at Fall River.

(f) That Mr. Horborn, of Fall River, gave the use of an island near the Cornwallis Street Church camp site for the promotion of the Young People's work of that Church.

(g) That two Colored girls are enrolled as student nurses in two Halifax hospitals. They are Miss Gwendolyn Barton of Halifax and Miss Ruth Bailley of Toronto.

(h) That J. Calbert Best of King's College, Halifax, will write for the Afro-American, one of the largest weekly Negro newspapers in the U. S. A. Mr. Best has been asked to prepare a 700-word article on Canada. The weekly circulation of the Afro is 200,000.

The N. S. A. A· C. P.

The Nova Scotia Association for the Advancement of the Colored People was organized in 1945:

(a) To improve and further the interest of the Colored people of the Province.

(b) To provide an organization to encourage and promote a spirit of fraternity among its members.

(c) To co-operate with Governmental and private agencies for the promotion of the interest and the welfare of the Province or any community therein, wherein Colored People are resident, and particularly in reference to said Colored people.

(d) To improve the educational opportunities of Colored youth and to raise the standard of the Colored people of the Province or any community therein.

The following people comprise the charter members of the Association:

Arnold P. Smith, Richard Symonds, William Carter, Bernice A. Williams, Carl W. Oliver, Walter Johnson, Pearleen Oliver, William P. Oliver and Ernest Grosse.

----◆----

Join the N. S. A. A. C. P.

Write BERNICE A. WILLIAMS, Sec'y
166 Maynard Street.
Halifax, N. S.

WANDA ROBSON
17 VIEW ST
NORTH SYDNEY NOVA SCOTIA
B2A 1E9

The Clarion, Vol. 1, No. 1, December 1946

the struggle for social justice in Canada and in every part of the world where there is injustice.

In Nova Scotia, Viola Desmond, a Halifax beautician and businesswoman, was one such individual. Viola was raised in a large close knit and supportive middle-class family and developed a strong independent character. Like Carrie M. Best and Pearleen Oliver, and many other Black women of her generation, including her younger sisters, Viola did not see her future solely within the traditional role as wife, mother and homemaker. Nor did she see that her employment opportunities were limited to the area of domestic service, as did many other Black women of her generation. As an educated and independent woman, Viola began her career as a beautician who specialized in providing services and beauty products to Black women. She quickly expanded her business into the Desmond School of Beauty Culture, one of the first of its kind in Canada. She attracted students from all the eastern Canadian provinces as well as Quebec, and Viola hoped to continue to expand her business and to eventually establish a franchise of Black beauty parlours across Canada.[104]

In November 1946, Viola set out on a business trip from Halifax to Sydney, Nova Scotia, but was forced to stop in New Glasgow due to car problems. She was informed that her car would not be ready until the next day and she would have to spend the night in New Glasgow. Viola was not accustomed to having large amounts of free time, so she decided to take in a movie at the local Roseland Theatre. Unlike, Carrie M. Best, Viola was not entirely familiar with the local culture of Jim Crow. In purchasing her movie ticket, she was told that she was required to sit upstairs because the balcony section of the theatre was reserved for Blacks. Interestingly, had Viola decided to attend the Academy, New Glasgow's second movie theatre, she would have been told to sit downstairs because the balcony was reserved for whites only.[105]

Viola made a spontaneous decision to sit in the downstairs section of the theatre. After being asked by the ticket agent and theatre manager to leave the white's-only section, Viola was forcefully removed by the manager with the assistance of a local police officer. She was arrested and taken to the county jail where she remained overnight. The next day, Viola was brought before a local judge and found guilty of defrauding the Provincial Government of the amusement tax on her purchase her theatre ticket. There was a difference in the price of a ticket for the balcony and downstairs seats, and because she sat downstairs, she was found guilty of not paying the one-cent difference in the tax between the seats in the two sections of the theatre.

Viola's decision to sit in the white's-only section of the Roseland Theatre and her persistent refusal to leave her seat reflects her strength of character and her sense of the injustice of the situation. As an independent and respectable Black business-woman, Viola was not accustomed to experiencing personal and abusive acts of racial discrimination. After receiving advice from her family and members of the Halifax Black community including Pearleen Oliver and her husband Rev. William Oliver, both of whom were executive members of the newly formed Nova Scotia Association for the Advancement of Colored People (NSAACP), Viola appealed her conviction. With support from the NSAACP, her case was eventually brought before

The Clarion, Vol. 2, No. 5, 15 March, 1947

the four judges of the Nova Scotia Supreme Court where, like so many other cases involving racial discrimination in Canada during this period, she lost her appeal.[106]

The Viola Desmond incident raised awareness about racial discrimination in Nova Scotia; however, following the initial publicity and reaction among the Black community, the event was quickly forgotten by most citizens in Nova Scotia. The NSAACP continued its fight for civil rights in the province, and partly through its efforts the Nova Scotia Government passed the *Fair Employment Practices Act* in 1955 and the *Fair Accommodations Act* in 1959.

In April 2010, sixty-four years after her guilty verdict, the Nova Scotia legislature granted Viola a mercy free pardon, which is the first such pardon of its kind in Canada. Viola's pardon is mercy free because, as the record now shows, she never did anything wrong to begin with. Her pardon acknowledges the accountability of the Nova Scotia Government for its complicity in supporting the practice of Jim Crow in Nova Scotia.

Notes

1. W.E.B. Du Bois, *The Soul of Black Folk* (New York: Washington Square Press, 1970), p. 11.
2. W.T. Lhamon Jr., *Raising Cain: Blackface Performance from Jim Crow to Hip Hop* (Cambridge: Harvard University Press, 2000). The practice of blackfaced performances became popular in Canada, as well. During the twentieth century, local movie houses became popular venues for minstrel shows. Although minstrel shows generally declined in popularity by the 1960s, the practice of blackfaced performances has continued until the present. Controversy over this practice has surfaced recently in two separate incidents, one involving a vice principle in the Peel District School Board in Ontario who appeared in a blackface character as a Halloween costume. The other incident involved a Liberal member of the Nova Scotia Legislature who was pictured as "Black Pete," a racist caricature popular in the Christmas tradition in the Netherlands. Black Pete was a servant to St. Nicholas, and is regarded by many as a throwback to the era of slavery. See "'I Didn't Sign Up for This': Nova Scotia Liberal Breaks Down Discussing 'Black Pete' Photo." *Globe and Mail* (December 2, 2013).
3. Wynn Craig Wade, *The Fiery Cross: The Ku Klux Klan in America* (London: Simon and Schuster, 1987), p. 252.
4. Edward L. Ayes, *The Promise of the New South: Life After Reconstruction* (New York: Oxford University Press, 1992), p. 136.
5. Bertram Doyle, *The Etiquette of Race Relations in the South: A Study in Social Control* (Chicago: University of Chicago Press, 1937), p. 147.
6. Leon F. Litwack, *Trouble in Mind: Black Southerners in the Age of Jim Crow* (New York: Alfred A. Knopf, 1998), p. 237.
7. William Archer, *Through Afro-America: English Reading of the Race Problem*, reprint of the 1910 edition (New York: Negro Universities Press, 1970) quoted in Leon Litwack, *Trouble in Mind*, p. 237.
8. Edward Ayes, *The Promise of the New South*, 1992, p. 137.
9. Edward Ayes, *The Promise of the New South*, 1992, p. 139.
10. Leon F. Litwack, *Trouble in Mind: Black Southerners in the Age of Jim Crow*, 1998, p. 231.
11. Leon F. Litwack, *Trouble in Mind: Black Southerners in the Age of Jim Crow*, 1998, p. 234.
12. Edward Ayes, *The Promise of the New South*, 1992, p. 146.
13. For a thorough discussion of the geographical distribution of Blacks in Canada, see Joseph Mensah, *Black Canadians, History, Experience, Social Conditions*, second edition (Black Point, NS: Fernwood Publishing, 2010). Mensah argues that the Black geographical distribution in Canada, like the Black experience generally, is not well understood.
14. Killian Crawford, *Go Do Some Great Thing: The Black Pioneers of British Columbia*, expanded edition (Vancouver: Commodore Books, 2008).

15. The first known Black in Canada was Mathieu Da Costa, an explorer and interpreter of African and Portuguese descent who travelled with the French to Port Royal in the early 1600s. See A.J.B. Johnston, "Mathieu Da Costa and Early Canada: Possibilities and Probabilities, Canada" (2011). Retrieved from <pc.gc.ca/ihn-hhs/ns/portroyaledu/edu1/edu1f.aspx>.

16. George Elliott Clarke, "'Indigenous Blacks': An Irreconcilable Identity?" in Ashol Mathur, Jonathan Dewar and Mike De Gagne, editors, *Cultivating Canada: Reconciliation Through the Lens of Cultural Diversity* (Ottawa: Aboriginal Healing Foundation, 2011), p. 399.

17. From the historical perspective, the tendency to regard the various groups of Black immigrants as distinct waves of temporary refugees is due, in part, to the emphasis on the part of historians to the outward migration of the Black Loyalists and Maroons to Sierra Leone. Harvey Armani Whitefield notes: "For most scholars the story ends here or continues in Sierra Leone." Whitefield's own research has done much to correct this view in support of the fact that "the story of Blacks, including slaves, continues in Nova Scotia." Harvey Armani Whitefield, *Blacks on the Border: The Black Refugees in British North America 1815–1860* (Burlington, VT: University of Vermont Press, 2006), p. 20.

18. Karolyn Smardz Frost, *I've Got a Home in Glory Land: A Lost Tale of the Underground Railroad* (New York: Farrar, Straus and Giroux, 2007).

19. George Elliott Clarke, "'Indigenous Blacks': An Irreconcilable Identity?" 2011, p. 400.

20. Robin Winks, *The Blacks in Canada,* 2nd edition (Montreal: McGill-Queen's University Press, 1997), pp. 150–53.

21. Loren Bridgen, "A Membership for Manhood: Masculine Cultures in Nineteenth Century African–Canadian Organizations." Paper presented to Claiming the Promise: A Retrospective on African Canadian History and Invitation to New Research, 5th Promised Land Project Symposium, Chatham, Ontario, June 14–16, 2012.

22. Judith Fingard, "Race and Respectability in Victorian Halifax," *Journal of Imperial and Commonwealth History* 20 (1992): p. 172.

23. Judith Fingard, "Race and Respectability in Victorian Halifax," 1992, p. 180.

24. Judith Fingard, "Race and Respectability in Victorian Halifax," 1992.

25. Judith Fingard, "Race and Respectability in Victorian Halifax," 1992, p. 172.

26. Robin Winks, *The Blacks in Canada,* 1992, pp. 376–79; Judith Fingard, "Race and Respectability in Victorian Halifax," 1992, pp. 169–95.

27. Donald H. Clairmont and Dennis William Magill, *Africville: The Life and Death of a Canadian Black Community,* third edition (Toronto: Canadian Scholars Press, 1999), pp. 30–31.

28. Donald Clairmont and Dennis Magill, *Africville,* 1999, pp. 44–45.

29. Donald Clairmont and Dennis Magill, *Africville,* 1999, p. 51.

30. Donald Clairmont and Dennis Magill, *Africville,* 1999, p. 48.

31. Isabel Wilkerson, *The Warmth of Other Suns: The Epic Story of America's Great Migration* (New York: Random House, 2010).

32. Pierre Berton, *The National Dream: The Great Railway, 1971–1885* (Toronto: Anchor, 2001); Pierre Berton, *The Last Spike: The Great Railway, 1881–1885* (Toronto: Anchor, 2001).

33. Sarah-Jane Mathieu, *North of the Color Line: Migration and Black Resistance in Canada, 1870–1955* (Chapel Hill: University of North Carolina Press, 2010), p. 12.
34. Sarah-Jane Mathieu, *North of the Color Line,* 2010, p. 164.
35. Ninette Kelly and Michael Trebilock, *The Making of the Mosaic: A History of Canadian Immigration,* second edition (Toronto: University of Toronto Press, 2010).
36. Sarah-Jane Mathieu, *North of the Color Line,* 2010, pp. 23–24, 30.
37. Sarah-Jane Mathieu, *North of the Color Line,* 2010, p. 22.
38. *Lethbridge Daily News,* 8 April 1911; *Lethrbridge Daily Herald,* 15 April 1911, quoted in Mathieu, pp. 51–52.
39. Edmonton Board of Trade to Sir Wilfred Laurier, 3 May 1911, quoted in Mathieu, p. 48.
40. Sarah-Jane Mathieu, *North of the Color Line,* 2010, p. 49.
41. Ada Knight, secretary, Edmonton IODE, to Frank Oliver, 31 March 1911, quoted in James W. St. G. Walker, *"Race," Rights and the Law in the Supreme Court of Canada* (Toronto: The Osgood Society for Canadian Legal History and Wilfred Laurier Press, 1997), p.127.
42. *Mail and Empire* (Toronto), 28 April 1911, quoted in James Walker, *"Race," Rights and the Law in the Supreme Court of Canada,* 1997, p. 126.
43. Ada Knight, quoted in James Walker, *"Race," Rights and the Law in the Supreme Court of Canada,* 1997, p. 127.
44. The Sambo stereotype was the subject of Stanley M. Elkin's classic study of slavery, and it generated a prolonged debate over the nature of institution of slavery and the slave personality. For a discussion of this controversy and Elkin's response, see Stanley M. Elkins, *Slavery: A Problem in American Institutional Life,* third edition (Chicago: University of Chicago Press, 1976).
45. Wyn Craig Wade, *The Fiery Cross: The Ku Klux Klan in America,* reprint edition (New York: Oxford University Press, 1998), pp. 197–98.
46. Tom M. Henson, "Ku Klux Klan in Western Canada," *Alberta History* 25, 4 (Autumn, 1977): Constance Backhouse, *Colour-Coded: A Legal History of Racism in Canada, 1900–1950* (Toronto: University of Toronto Press, 1999), p. 189.
47. Constance Backhouse, *Colour-Coded,* 1999, p. 187. The practice of cross burning among the KKK began with the revival of the Klan in 1915. The idea originated with Thomas Dixon Jr.'s fictional account of the Klan in his novel *The Clansman,* published in 1905. In 1915, D.W. Griffith added several graphic scenes of Klan cross burnings in his epic film *The Birth of a Nation.* For Dixon's account of the Klan's practice of cross burning see his novel, *The Clansman: A Historical Romance of the Ku Klux Klan* (New York: Grosset & Dunlap, 1905), pp. 317–27; for a fuller discussion of the influence of Griffith's *The Birth of a Nation* on the emergence of the Ku Klux Klan in Canada, see Chapter 6.
48. James Pitsula, *Keeping Canada British: The Ku Klux Klan in 1920s Saskatchewan,* (Vancouver: University of British Columbia Press, 2013).
49. Constance Backhouse, *Colour-Coded,* 1999, p. 226.
50. William D. Scott, *Immigration by Races,* Vol. 1, *Canada and its Provinces,* Adam Shortt and Arthur George Doughty (eds.), (Edinburgh: T. & A. Constable, 1914) p. 531; Sarah-Jane Mathieu, *North of the Color Line,* p. 24.

51. *Oklahoma Guide*, 6 July 1911, quoted in Sarah-Jane Mathieu, p. 45.
52. Sarah-Jane Mathieu, *North of the Color Line*, 2010, p. 70.
53. Deborah Gray White, *Ar'n't I a Women? Female Slaves in the Plantation South* (New York: Norton, 1999), pp. 27–61.
54. Sarah-Jane Mathieu, *North of the Color Line*, 2010, p. 11.
55. Sarah-Jane Mathieu, *North of the Color Line*, 2010, p. 58.
56. Sarah-Jane Mathieu, *North of the Color Line*, 2010, p. 43.
57. Immigration Branch Records, Government of Canada, Beaton Institute, MB66-MG16, Reel No.6 (RG 76, Volume 566, File 810666, pt.1). See the document section of the book.
58. Dorothy Williams, *The Road to Now: A History of Blacks in Montreal* (Montreal: Vehicule Press, 1997).
59. Elizabeth Beaton, "An African-American Community in Cape Breton, 1901–1904," *Acadiensis* xx, 1 (Spring 1995), p. 77.
60. Sarah-Jane Mathieu, *North of the Color Line*, 2010, p. 78.
61. From the perspective of many of the Black teachers who taught in racially segregated schools in Nova Scotia, see Doris Evans and Gertrude Tynes, *Telling the Truth. Reflections: Segregated Schools In Nova Scotia* (Hantsport, NS, 1995). For a history of racially segregated schools in Nova Scotia and Ontario see the documentary film produced by Sylvia Hamilton, *The Little Black Schoolhouse* (Halifax: Maroon Films, 2007). See also the Appendix (below) for Sylvia Hamilton's discussion of her documentary film in her presentation at the Promised Land Project Symposium.
62. *Orders in Council*, 1–2, Geo. 5, 1911, quoted in Mathieu, p. 57.
63. Sarah-Jane Mathieu, *North of the Color Line*, 2010, p. 57.
64. Sarah-Jane Mathieu, *North of the Color Line*, 2010, p. 83.
65. Sarah-Jane Mathieu, *North of the Color Line*, 2010, p. 83.
66. Robin Winks, *The Blacks in Canada*, 1997, p. 318.
67. Letter to the Editor by D.W.S., "Steel and Native Labour," *Daily Record*, 14 April 1902, quoted in Elizabeth Beaton, "An African-American Community in Cape Breton, 1901–1904," 1995, p. 70.
68. Elizabeth Beaton, "An African-American Community in Cape Breton, 1901–1904," 1995, p. 81.
69. Elizabeth Beaton, "An African-American Community in Cape Breton, 1901–1904," 1995, p. 81.
70. Elizabeth Beaton, "An African-American Community in Cape Breton, 1901–1904," 1995, p. 82.
71. Elizabeth Beaton, "An African-American Community in Cape Breton, 1901–1904," 1995, p. 83.
72. Elizabeth Beaton, "An African-American Community in Cape Breton, 1901–1904," 1995, p. 86.
73. Elizabeth Beaton, "An African-American Community in Cape Breton, 1901–1904," 1995, p. 88.
74. Elizabeth Beaton, "An African-American Community in Cape Breton, 1901–1904," 1995, p. 92.
75. Thomas Lee Philpot, *The Slum and the Ghetto: Immigrants, Blacks, and Reformers in*

Chicago, 1880–1930, second edition (New York: Wadsworth Publishing Company, 1991), pp. 116–62.

76. William M. Tuttle, Jr., *Race Riot: Chicago in the Red Summer of 1919* (Chicago: University of Illinois Press, 1976), pp. 3–9, 242.

77. *The Sydney Record,* 3–6 and 9 September 1918; Joan Weeks, *One God, One Aim, One Destiny: African Nova Scotians in Cape Breton* (Sydney, NS: Centre for Cape Breton Studies, 2007).

78. Carrie M. Best, *The Lonesome Road: The Autobiography of Carrie M. Best* (New Glasgow, NS: The Clarion Publishing Company, 1977), pp. 43–44.

79. Constance Backhouse, *Colour-Coded,* 1999, p. 256; James W. St. G Walker, *Races, Rights and the Law in the Supreme Court of Canada,* 1997, pp. 160–61.

80. Sidney Katz, "Jim Crow Lives in Dresden," *Maclean's,* 1 November 1949, p. 9.

81. Pearleen Oliver interviewed by Catherine Arseneau, 8 November 1992, Beaton Institute.

82. Marie Carter, "Reimaging the Dawn Settlement," in Boulou Ebanda de B'beri, Nina Reid-Maroney, and Handel Kashope Wright, ed., *The Promised Land: History and Historiography of the Black Experience in Chatham-Kent's Settlement and Beyond* (Toronto: University of Toronto Press, 2014), pp. 185–89.

83. Pearleen Oliver, 8 November 1992.

84. John Cooper, *Season of Rage: Hugh Burnett and the Struggle for Civil Rights* (Toronto: Tundra Books, 2007), pp. 13–16.

85. Sidney Katz, "Jim Crow Lives in Dresden," 1949, p. 8.

86. Sidney Katz, "Jim Crow Lives in Dresden," 1949, p. 9.

87. Sidney Katz, "Jim Crow Lives in Dresden," 1949, p. 9.

88. Sidney Katz, "Jim Crow Lives in Dresden," 1949, p. 52.

89. Sidney Katz, "Jim Crow Lives in Dresden," 1949, p. 9.

90. Sidney Katz, "Jim Crow Lives in Dresden," 1949, p. 9.

91. Sidney Katz, "Jim Crow Lives in Dresden," 1949, p. 9.

92. "Human Rights in Canada: A Historical Perspective," Canadian Human Rights Commission, retrieved from <chrc-ccdp.ca>.

93. "Human Rights in Canada: A Historical Perspective."

94. Stanley G. Grizzle, *My Name's Not George: The Story of the Brotherhood of Sleeping Car Porters in Canada* (Toronto: Umbrella Press, 1998); Eric Arnesen, *Brotherhoods of Color: Black Railroad Workers and the Struggle for Equality* (Cambridge: Harvard University Press, 2001); Beth Thompkins Bates, *Pullman Porters and the Rise of Protest Politics* (Chapel; Hill: University of North Carolina Press, 2001); Sarah-Jane Mathieu, *North of the Color Line: Migration and Black Resistance in Canada, 1870–1955* (Chapel Hill, University of North Carolina Press, 2010).

95. Jenny Carson, "Riding the Rails: Black Railroad Workers in Canada and the United States," *Labour/Le Travail,* 50 (Fall, 2002), p. 276.

96. Sarah-Jane Mathieu, *North of the Color Line,* 2010, p. 195.

97. The brief was presented by Donald Moore and the Negro Citizenship Association to the Prime Minister, the Minister of Citizenship and Immigration and other members of the Government of Canada. It singled out the "discriminatory and dangerous" provisions of the *Immigration Act* of 1923, which, as the brief stated, was "purposely written and

revised to deny equal immigration status to those areas of the Commonwealth where coloured peoples constitute a large part of the population. This is done by creating a rigid definition of British subject: 'British subjects by birth or naturalization in the United Kingdom, Australia, New Zealand or the Union of South Africa and citizens of Ireland'. This definition excludes from the category of 'British subject' those who are in all other senses British subjects, but who come from such areas as the British West Indies, Bermuda, British Guiana, Ceylon, India, Pakistan, Africa, etc." Memorandum Brief presented to the Prime Minister and Minister of Citizenship and Immigration by the Negro Citizenship Association, April 27, 1954. City of Toronto Archives, Fonds 431, file 1.

98. John Cooper, *Season of Rage*, 2007, p. 28.

99. Ross Lambertson, "'The Dresden Story': Racism, Human Rights, and the Jewish Labour Committee," *Labour/Le Travail* 47 (Spring 2001) p. 59.

100. Ross Lambertson, "'The Dresden Story': Racism, Human Rights, and the Jewish Labour Committee," pp. 64–66.

101. John Cooper, *Season of Rage*, 2007, p. 55.

102. Pearleen Oliver's fight for racial equality is the subject of Chapter 7.

103. Constance Backhouse, "'I Was Unable to Identify with Topsy,' Carrie M. Best's Struggle Against Racial Segregation in Nova Scotia, 1942," *Atlantis* 22, 2 (Spring/Summer 1998), pp. 16–26.

104. Constance Backhouse, *Colour-Coded*, 1999, pp. 250–52.

105. Constance Backhouse, *Colour-Coded*, 1999, p. 240.

106. Wanda Robson, personal communication to the author.

Chapter 3

My Early Memories
of Race, My Sister Viola and
My Journey of Self-Discovery

by Wanda Robson

I was born in Halifax on December 16, 1926, and I was the youngest of fifteen siblings. We were a respected, Black, middle-class family, and my father's side of the family had roots in Halifax going back several generations. We lived in a predominantly white neighbourhood on Swaine Street in the west end of Halifax. The house we lived in for the first six years of my life was one of several houses my parents had inherited from my maternal grandparents. My father, James Albert Davis, rented out several houses, and the family moved between these homes in the years before I was born.

My father, like his father and other male members of the family, was a barber by trade, and he worked at the Davis Barber Shop, a family owned business in the north end of Halifax. The barbering trade was racially segregated during this period because white barbers refused to cut the hair of Blacks. It was one of the few professions open to Blacks and one in which they could make a decent living. My father eventually left barbering in order to work as a shipwright in the Halifax Shipyards, and later he managed the family owned properties. As a result of the drop in the real-estate prices during the Depression, he eventually worked at a car dealership. Interestingly, his father also left the barbering trade, and he was one of the first Blacks in Halifax to take the public service exam in order to become a postal carrier. One of my father's brothers, John Alexander Davis, followed the lead of their father and became a postal clerk, a position he held for over forty years.

My mother, Gwendolyn Irene Johnson, was born in New Haven, Connecticut. Her father was a Baptist minister born in Richmond Virginia. He was the son of a plantation owner and a Black housekeeper.

My maternal grandmother, Susan Irene Smith, was white while my maternal

James and Gwendolyn Davis, by permission of Joe and Wanda Robson

grandfather, Henry Hatcher Johnson, was bi-racial. During this period of time in the United States, a person was considered coloured or negro if they had any mixture of African ancestry. This was called the "one drop rule" and it applied to the same extent in Halifax as in the United States.

My grandfather studied theology at Tuskegee Institute and became a Baptist minister. Upon graduation, he settled in New Haven Connecticut, and in 1881 he was invited to serve as the minister at the Cornwallis Street Baptist Church in Halifax. He had two terms as a minister at the Cornwallis Street Baptist Church. The first was from 1881 to1884, and the second was from 1892 to 1895. During his last term, his wife and their two young children — my mother and her brother, accompaniedhim.

During his last term at the Church in Halifax, his wife (my grandmother) died. He left the children in the care of a capable couple (mom's foster mother) in Halifax, and he took his wife's body to New Haven for burial. At that time, my mother was 5 years old, and her brother was 7.

When the family reunited in the early 1900s, my grandfather enrolled my mother in the Boston Ladies College. The lessons were varied — music, English, history, social graces, dancing and art. She was in her early teens when she graduated.

My mother vacationed at her foster mother's home in Halifax County, and it was there she met my Dad. They fell in love, and during her vacation in 1908 they secretly married at Trinity Anglican Church in Halifax.

My First Experiences of Racial Prejudice

My childhood years in Halifax were in many respects typical of most children in my neighbourhood. I don't remember the exact time I became racially aware, but later, as a young girl, my parents told me about an early incident that happened when I was 3 years old. I was playing outside our house on Swaine Street, and a boy from across the street came over and called me the "N" word. I had never heard this word before so I shouted it right back to him. My parents heard me and dragged me back into the house and tried to explain to me that I should never say that word. Because I was so young, I did not understand the connotation of the word.

My first clear memory of being different because of the colour of my skin occurred after my family moved to Gottingen Street in the north end of Halifax. I was 7 or 8 years old, and I had several close friends in my neighbourhood that I used to play with. One of my playmates, Marjory, lived across the street from me. She and another friend and I would play together in our back yard and we always got along well together.

Marjory's father was in the army, and whenever he returned home, she was not permitted to come over and play with me, nor could I go to her house to play. One day I asked her why, and she said, "My father won't let me and he told me I wasn't allowed to go over and play with you." But her mother let us play together. Even so, my father was very annoyed, and he told my mother that if the neighbours think our daughter is not good enough to play with Marjory, "We're not letting Wanda go over to their house to play." My mother was more understanding of the situation. "They are only children and thank goodness they don't see colour," she said. "They're friends and they don't understand it, so let them play as little girls." She also told my father, "You'd want to bar that little girl like our daughter's barred from going over there. We don't retaliate that way."

The episode with my childhood friend Marjory was my first memory of racial discrimination. This was followed by another incident that happened to me when I enrolled at Alexandra Elementary School in the north end of Halifax. I was in grade two, and I was so eager to start at my new school. As a child, I loved books, reading, learning and the entire school atmosphere. This was something that my whole family shared in common; we were all encouraged to read at home and my mother taught us the importance of education.

On the first day in my new school, I remember arriving at my grade two homeroom and being told by my teacher, Ms. Reid, to sit at the back of the class with all the other coloured children. Our teacher all but completely ignored us, and the only time we knew we existed in her eyes was when we made a noise and Ms. Reid told us to be quiet. Some of the Black children didn't mind being ignored, but others of us did.

Ms. Reid's seating arrangement was based on how well we performed on monthly tests. The best students sat at the front of the class. So, if a student got the highest grade on the test, the student sat in the first seat in the first row, followed by the student with the next highest test result, and so on. Ms. Reid gave us a test at the end of the first month of class, and I received the highest score. Begrudgingly, she followed her own rule for class seating, and she told me to go to the front row of the class and sit in the first seat. I could feel that she was angry with me, but I had no idea what I had done wrong. Ms. Reid stayed angry the entire day and she seemed to take it out on the other Black students in the class. I continued to do well on the tests and stayed at the front of the class. This went on until one day Ms. Reid called me out for talking in class before the bell rang. I said something to the girl behind me and the teacher said, "Wanda Davis, were you talking?" I told her that I was just asking the girl behind me a question. Ms. Reid replied: "No, you were talking…. Pick up your things and go to the back of the room." So, this was my punishment for talking. I stayed there until the next test and once again Ms. Reid put me in the front row; however, this time, she could not control her anger. Later she asked the class a question, and when I raised my hand saying eagerly, "I know," she mocked me by saying: "Oh, look, we have a genius in our class; a girl that knows everything. So, what do we do with people who are too smart for this class? We put them in the next class." So, Ms. Reid moved me to the next grade class, and I heard her tell the teacher: "This is Wanda Davis, she's in our class and she is to go at the back of your room. Don't give her anything to do, just make her sit there and think about how she's showing off in class." Fortunately, the teacher was kind to me and seemed to understand the situation. She told me to sit down since by now I was crying because I was scared and didn't know what I had done wrong. The teacher, Ms. Gleason, explained to me that if I told her where I was in my textbook, I could continue with my lessons while I was in her class.

In a few weeks, Ms. Reid returned me to her class and put me at the back, again, with the other Black children. The following day was Parent's Day, and I became very upset because I hadn't told my mother about what had happened. She was under the impression that I was still sitting at the front of the class. My mother and my older sister Viola were coming to school for Parent's Day. Viola took time off work to accompany my mother because she was always interested in knowing how her younger siblings were doing in school. The night before Parent's Day, I was so upset that my mother asked me what was wrong and I told her everything. The next day at school, just before noon, Ms. Reid told me to pick up my things and sit in the front of the class. I was very confused, and as a young child, I had no idea why I was being moved again to the front of the class. My mother and Viola never said a word to me about what happened at my school on Parent's Day, and to this day I do not know what they might have said to my teacher.

I remember another racial incident that happened at Alexandra Elementary School. Every year a photographer would come to our school to take our class picture. The photographer had an old fashioned stand up camera with a cloth hood that covered his head and part of the camera. Posing for pictures was quite an effort and it required everyone to remain completely still while the photographer positioned us in order to take his pictures. He seemed to put all the Black children in the back row. As a reward for us, he would tell us a story, and every year it was the same one — the story of "Little Black Sambo." He never stopped telling it, and I would cringe because all the children would laugh. I would come home very upset not only because of the story but also because of the way the photographer would mimic the characters. This instilled in the minds of the children the idea that Blacks were nothing but ignorant, comedic buffoons. I knew that a few years later Pearleen Oliver (the wife of the Reverend William Oliver, the minister at Cornwallis Baptist Church), successfully waged a campaign to remove this book from the schools in Nova Scotia, and eventually the book was banned from all the schools in Canada.

By the time I reached junior high, I was fully aware I was Black. Perhaps a strange statement, but I grew up in a home with loving parents and a gentle mother who only saw the good in everyone and never allowed colour to enter her world. In junior high, there was a mixture of Black and white students, and it wasn't too bad to be in your own group. In high school, racism was very evident. The girls formed into tight cliques, and the only Black girls who got noticed were those who were athletic. I didn't excel at sports, so I wasn't noticed and wasn't popular. It was apparent to me that I was being left out because I was Black, or coloured, because that was the term used at that time. I remember talking to my mom about this and telling her how much I wanted to be white. She said to me: "You can't be white." My Mother sat me down and quietly told me that I should be content and proud of who I was. "Be the best person you can be" she said, "colour has nothing to do with who you are inside." I understood what she was saying, but I was (and still am) a very social person and wanted to join in the social activities.[1]

As a student at Queen Elizabeth High School, I did well in most of my courses, and I particularly liked English. I remember one day in grade 11 when the drama teacher was organizing a play for the entire school and I read a notice on the bulletin board announcing there would be casting for the play after school. My mom encouraged me to try out for a role in the play, knowing that I liked English and acting. I went to the casting session, and I put my hand up for every part imaginable, from an old woman to an old man. I knew I could take on any of these parts, so I kept putting up my hand. But it was as if I wasn't even in the room. There were only two-dozen students and lots of parts to audition for, but the drama teacher never even asked me my name or if I had acting experience, which I had in performing in church plays. I was so discouraged after that incident that my grades began to fall. For a time, my mom was very worried about me and she gave me a great deal of support. I had several good teachers at school, especially in English and History, which were subjects I liked. I took the provincial exams, and I made the highest grade in English in the province. I still have the prize book presented to me. My English teacher made me feel proud because she pointed this out in class. This helped me to do better in school, and it gave me the self-confidence and strength to cope with the effects of racial prejudice.

I experienced a number of other racial incidents over the years. I can recall an incident that happened in 1962 when I was living as a single parent in Halifax. On Sundays, I taught Sunday school and attended service with my three boys at Trinity Anglican Church. While I was seated in church one Sunday, a woman in the row in front of me turned around to me and said: "I see you are here every Sunday. Wouldn't you rather go to your own Church than come here?"

Another incident occurred a few years later when I was living with my children on Brunswick Street. I was washing clothes one Saturday and the washing machine broke, so I sent my three boys to the local laundromat with our laundry and change for the washing machines. I told them to start the wash and said I would join them as soon as I could. A short while later, as I was leaving the house on my way to the laundromat, I was approached by a policeman who had my three boys with him. I could see that my boys were very upset. The policeman explained that the attendant at the laundromat had money stolen from her purse, and she was convinced my boys were guilty of this crime. She was so convinced of this that she told all the white patrons to leave the premises while she locked the doors of the Laundromat and called the police. She had the police strip search my boys, and of course, they found nothing. Even after they found no evidence connecting my boys to the crime, the policeman behaved as though they were in fact guilty. When the policeman left the boys at our house, he uttered the sarcastic warning to them: "Watch your step!" My boys never forgot this incident.

I can recall many other subtle and not so subtle experiences of racial prejudice over the years. In 1960, I was renting a house owned by Dalhousie University and was given notice to leave because the house was being demolished in order to make a parking lot. I had a very difficult time finding an apartment for myself and my three children. I was given every excuse under the sun why apartments I was trying to rent were not available to me. In one instance, I arrived at an apartment less than an hour after I had phoned and asked to see it and was told the apartment had already been rented. In another instance, I approached an apartment for rent and was told: "Go away or I'll call the police!" On one occasion, an owner didn't even have the courtesy of opening the door but with the chain still holding the door partially shut and told me abruptly, "It's gone!" On another occasion I was told: "You people never pay your rent! Go!"

One more incident I would like to mention happened in 1970. I was visiting Sydney, Nova Scotia, and staying in a local hotel. On the day I was returning to Halifax, I went to the hotel dining room for breakfast, sat down and began reading the newspaper. The waitress approached me, and without speaking to me, she immediately returned to the back of the dining room. I noticed she began talking to the manager. The discussion ended abruptly when the waitress dropped her apron on the floor and stormed out of the dining room. I didn't make much of this at first and thought that the waitress was just having a bad day. However, when the manager came to me and apologized for her behaviour, I knew that the waitress left because she did not want to serve me.

My Sister Viola and the Incident at the Roseland Theatre

After all these years, I think I have only now come to fully understand the personal as well as the historical significance of these incidents together with what happened to my sister Viola. In the culture of the 1940s, I can see how much courage my sister had in order to stand up against the practice of racial segregation. She was an extraordinary individual, and although many of us now know her story, it is worth telling it again from my perspective as her youngest sister.

Viola Irene (Davis) Desmond was born in Halifax July 6, 1914. She was a successful businesswoman and beautician, the only Black one in Nova Scotia at the time. This is a remarkable achievement because there were very few careers open to Blacks at the time, and Black women were not admitted into the nursing profession or to schools of beauty. Viola was an excellent student in high school and she wanted to be a teacher. When she graduated in 1930, Blacks were not admitted to the teacher's education program in Truro, so her only option to become a teacher was to obtain a teaching certificate by passing a provincial test. The teaching certificate was available to Black students who had a grade 12 pass, but it only allowed them to teach in the Black schools. Viola was successful in getting her certificate, and she started teaching at a segregated school in the Black community of Upper Hammonds Plains, on the outskirts of Halifax. At about this same time, Viola read an article about Madam C.J. Walker who was a pioneer in

Viola Desmond,
by permission of Joe and Wanda Robson

Viola's Culture of Beauty School Graduation, Class of 1947,
by permission of Joe and Wanda Robson

developing beauty products for Black women.

Madam Walker was a successful businesswoman, and in the early 1900s she developed and manufactured a line of beauty products for Blacks that she promoted and sold. She also established beauty schools to train beauticians to work on Black women throughout the United States. Madame Walker was the first self-made female millionaire in North America.

The success of Madam Walker inspired Viola, and she began saving her teaching salary so she could pay for the training she needed to become a beautician. Because Blacks were restricted from attending beautician training schools in Halifax, Viola went to Montreal in 1936 and enrolled at the Field Beauty Culture School. A year later she graduated and returned to Halifax and opened Vi's Studio of Beauty Culture on Gottingen Street. Before leaving Montreal she married John "Jack" Desmond, a fellow Nova Scotian who became the first Black registered barber in Nova Scotia. Vi's was the only business of its kind in Halifax, and it offered a variety of products and services for Black women.

Viola was an ambitious and hard-working professional, and she constantly strove to improve and expand her business. In 1939, she went to Atlantic City and attended the famous Apex College of Beauty Culture and Hair Dressing. She studied cosmology and wig making, and after graduating a year later, she returned to Halifax.

By the mid-1940s, Viola had established a very successful business serving Black women in Halifax. Her clientele included the renowned Black opera singer Portia White and Gwen Jenkins, the first Black nurse in Nova Scotia. Viola expanded her business by setting up the Desmond School of Beauty Culture in order to train Black women as beauticians. Her first class of five students graduated in 1945. By this time, she was receiving orders for her products from all over the province, and in order to serve her customers she bought a car (a 1940 Dodge sedan). At the time, it was quite extraordinary and unique for a Black woman, or any women for that matter, to obtain a driving license, buy a car and take business trips by herself on the back roads of Nova Scotia. This is testimony to Viola's independence and self-confidence.

On November 8, 1946, with a packed lunch from mom, Viola set out from Halifax on a sales trip to the city of Sydney on Cape Breton Island and would travel through Eastern Nova Scotia on the way. It was a grey, sleety November day when she left and everything was going well until she got to New Glasgow and heard a troubling noise coming from the engine of her car. Viola stopped at a service station in New Glasgow and was told by the mechanic that he needed to send for a part in Halifax and that her car wouldn't be ready until the next day.

Viola was not accustomed to having a lot of free time, so she decided to take in a movie, which is something she rarely did. She walked down the main street of New Glasgow and noticed on the marquis that the movie *Dark Mirror* was playing at the Roseland Theatre. Viola was a great fan of Olivia De Havilland who starred in this movie along with Lew Ayers. She entered the theatre and said to the cashier: "I'll have a ticket for downstairs, please." The girl in the booth looked at her and

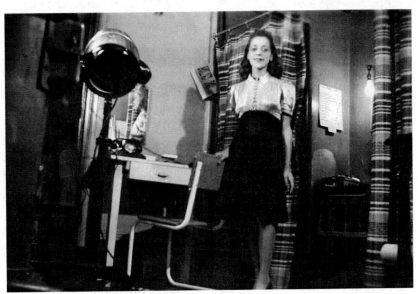

Viola in her studio, by permission of Joe and Wanda Robson

gave her a ticket and change. Viola entered the theatre and sat downstairs. Within a few minutes the usher came and tapped on Viola's shoulder and said: "Miss, you can't sit here because your ticket is for the upstairs balcony." My sister said that she would change it and she got up and went back to the cashier and told her, "I would like this exchanged for a downstairs ticket." The cashier replied: "We are not allowed to sell downstairs tickets to you people." Viola immediately realized that she was being discriminated against, but she tried to explain that when she went to the theatres in Halifax she always sat downstairs because she had poor eyesight and needed to sit close to the screen. She tried to pay the extra ten cents for the downstairs ticket, but the girl refused to accept her money. So Viola went back inside the theatre and returned to her seat. The usher approached her again and said "I'm sorry, but I'm going to have to call the manger if you don't move." Viola said that she wasn't causing any trouble and she was not going to change her seat. By this time, Viola fully realized that she was confronting the practice of racial segregation, and I believe she made a spontaneous decision to resist what she felt was wrong.

Initially, my sister did not know that she had entered a racially segregated theatre. The practice of racial segregation varied a great deal from place to place across Nova Scotia, and it wasn't even consistent within a particular community. If my sister had crossed the main street of New Glasgow, for example, and gone to the Academy theatre, my understanding is that she would have found that the pattern of segregated seating was the opposite to the Roseland theatre: Black patrons were required to sit downstairs while whites sat upstairs. Since Viola lived in Halifax, she was not fully aware of the local practice of segregation in New Glasgow. However, it is possible that she may have known about the seating arrangement at the Roseland theatre because Carrie M. Best, a Black civil rights activist and resident of New Glasgow, had unsuccessfully challenged the practice of racial segregation at the Roseland theatre four years earlier. Carrie was a regular client of Viola's, and I think it is likely that, at some point in time, they would have discussed the subject of racial segregation in New Glasgow. But given the sudden and unexpected change in Viola's business trip plans and because she was so used to sitting on the lower floor and close to the screen when she attended theatres in Halifax, Viola most likely lost sight of the particular practice of racial segregation before she entered the Roseland theatre.[2]

Viola's courageous refusal to leave her seat eventually provoked the theatre manager to call the police. When a police officer arrived, he took one of Viola's arms and the manager took the other arm and they forcefully dragged my sister out of the theatre. Viola said she didn't go quietly and she tried to hold on to the door jamb of the theatre entrance as they forced her into the street. Roughed up and bruised, Viola was taken to the local jail and placed alone in a small cell. She sat on the cell cot, upright, all night long. I asked her later what she did while she

The Roseland Theatre, New Glasgow, Nova Scotia (c. 1950),
The Times of African Nova Scotians, Vol. 1, p. 5

sat alone in the cell for nearly twelve hours. "Well," she said, "I took my purse out and dumped it out on the cot, and sorted the items and I worked on my appointment book. I tried to kill time by keeping myself busy. During the night, a few drunks were brought into the jail, and when they realized that a woman was there, they started making obscene calls to me." But she said she was able to block these words and was determined to keep her composure as long as she was in jail. The next morning she was brought before a local judge and charged with a violation of the provincial amusement tax law. The theatre manager, Mr. MacNeil, claimed Viola had purchased a ticket for a balcony seat but sat in a downstairs seat. There was ten cents difference in the price of the two tickets and one-cent difference in the amusement tax. Viola had no council and argued on her own behalf that she offered to pay for a downstairs ticket but that this offer was refused by the cashier. The judge found her guilty of not paying the additional one cent in tax, and she had to pay a fine of twenty dollars plus six dollars in court costs or spend thirty days in jail. Viola later told me that she wanted to take the thirty-day sentence but she felt a responsibility to the students enrolled in her School of Beauty Culture and could not afford to take time away from her business.

Viola was too physically and emotionally shaken to continue with her trip and she returned home immediately following her ordeal. The next day, I remember how angry my father was. He was naturally very protective of Viola, and he was absolutely livid because she had been so abused and man handled. He insisted that Viola see our family doctor so he could examine her injuries.

She went to Dr. Waddell who was a West Indian Doctor practicing in Halifax.

Because Dr. Waddell was Black, he had no medical privileges at the Victoria General Hospital, even though he was an excellent, fully licensed doctor. Dr. Waddell was appalled by what had happened to Viola and told her she should see a lawyer. I only recently learned that after this incident Dr. Waddell was so incensed by the injustice and injuries to Viola that he wrote several letters to the Federal Government in Ottawa. Nothing ever came from these letters, but his action was indicative of the level of concern and support Viola received from members of the Black community. She sought the advice of family and friends, including Pearleen Oliver and her husband the Reverend William Oliver. The couple were both founding members of the Nova Scotia Association for the Advancement of Colored People, a branch of the National Association for the Advancement of Colored People that fought for racial equality and civil rights in the United States. The Association took up Viola's cause and provided the funds for Viola to hire a lawyer and appeal her case to the Nova Scotia Supreme Court. Ultimately, Viola lost her case on a technicality. Although no direct mention was made in the legal arguments about the practice of racial segregation, one of the four Supreme Court judges, Justice William Lorimer Hall, acknowledged in his comments that the case had everything to do about race. Justice Hall stated: "One wonders if the manager of the theatre who laid the complaint was so zealous because of the bona fide belief that an attempt to defraud the Province of Nova Scotia of the sum of one cent, or was it a surreptitious endeavor to enforce Jim Crow rule by misuse of a public statute."[3] Viola's case did have the effect of raising awareness in the community about the injustice of the practice of racial segregation. Carrie M. Best wrote several articles about the incident and the legal proceedings in her newspaper *The Clarion*, and after Viola's appeal, she and others continued the struggle to end racial discrimination in Nova Scotia.

I was only 19 years old at the time of the incident at the Roseland theatre, and I didn't fully understand its significance in the larger context of the struggle for human rights and social justice. I was, of course, upset with what happened to my sister, but I was also embarrassed by the fact she had been sent to jail. I think I, like a lot of other members of the Black community, didn't want to call attention to myself and to my family. It was the custom among respectable middle-class Blacks that, in matters of race, it was best to remain silent. I was also working at the time as a lab assistant at a Federal Government research station, and as the only Black employee, I just wanted to be like everyone else. I tried to keep the incident out of my mind, but that was difficult because Viola's case was so much in the news. One of my co-workers brought it up one day and asked, "Viola is your sister?" I answered, "Yes," and turned away with no further comment. I was not prepared to deal with all the attention Viola was getting, and I certainly didn't want to be in the limelight because of the fact she had been in jail. I missed the point that Viola had done nothing wrong, and instead, I continued my childhood pattern of not

Wanda and Viola at the Hi Hat Club, Boston, by permission of Joe and Wanda Robson

wanting to appear Black. I was very immature at the time, and I didn't have the awareness and courage to publicly defend my sister. Knowing what I know now, I would have acted very differently, and I would have been proud of my racial heritage and would not have been embarrassed about the action of my sister.

My Personal Journey of Self-Discovery through Education and Raising Public Awareness

My current state of awareness is the result of a very long journey of self-discovery and education. I didn't begin this journey in earnest until the year 2000, when I was 73 years old. Some of my children had completed university education and were working, and the others were in the final stages of their education. I had just finished two terms with the Nova Scotia Advisory Council for the Status of Women, and my husband Joe was now a retired teacher. I noticed an ad in our local newspaper, the *Cape Breton Post*, stating that a course was being taught at Cape Breton University by Dr. Graham Reynolds entitled The History of Race Relations in North America. I had always wanted to complete a university degree. My mother believed very strongly in the importance of education, and this stayed with me all my life. As a mother, I also stressed the importance of education with my children.

With the encouragement of my husband Joe, I started university, first by auditing Dr. Reynolds' course and later as a full time student in the Bachelor of Arts Program at Cape Breton University. From the very beginning, I was comfortable being a student, and I felt that I fit in well with the younger university students. During one of our classes, Dr. Reynolds discussed racial incidents that had occurred in Nova Scotia and he mentioned Viola Desmond and the incident at the Roseland Theatre in New Glasgow. The professor and I immediately bonded when I told him that the late Viola Desmond was my sister.

After I graduated from Cape Breton University in 2004, I began speaking about my experiences and the incident involving Viola to Dr. Reynolds' university classes and then to elementary and secondary school classes, women's groups and other community organizations. In 2006, Adrian Harewood, a CBC reporter from Toronto, interviewed me at my home in North Sydney. He was gathering information about Viola for a radio play commemorating the 60th anniversary of my sister's arrest and conviction. Before he left, he suggested that I contact the mayor of New Glasgow. Adrian thought that the town should acknowledge the incident involving Viola at the Roseland theatre with some kind of commemorative plaque. He interviewed Mayor Anne MacLean of New Glasgow on his way back to Toronto, and he later wrote to me to say that the Mayor was interested in creating some kind of permanent commemorative marking the event and said that the Major thought the council would be open to this idea.

I wrote to mayor MacLean in 2007 and learned that she was retiring. This meant that any initiative to create a memorial in honor of Viola would have to wait until the next mayor and town council took office. In the meantime, I was interviewed for an article for the *Beaver* (now published under the title *Canada's History Magazine*), and when this issue appeared in the spring of 2009, it prompted me to write again to the Mayor of New Glasgow.[4] It was now sixty-three years since the incident had occurred, and I thought that very few people would remember the incident nor care enough to do anything about it. I wrote to the new mayor, Barrie MacMillan, in July 2009 and was surprised to receive a very quick response. Mayor MacMillan indicated that he would raise the issue with the town council, and within a short period of time I was told that the council had agreed to acknowledge the event with a commemorative bench to be placed in the African Heritage Memorial Park on Vale Road in New Glasgow.

In the summer of 2007, Tony Colaiacovo, the owner of Effective Publishing in Halifax, visited me in my home in North Sydney. He was doing research on Viola and our family for his history journal, *The Times of African Nova Scotians,* and he intended to cover historical aspects of Black History in Nova Scotia from the early

1600s to the present.[5] The cover page of his journal was about Viola and the incident at the Roseland Theatre. Tony also introduced the Student Challenge Program in schools throughout the province. This initiative involved students at any grade level submitting a presentation, either individually or as a group. The presentation was intended to exemplify the contributions that African Nova Scotians have made to the history and culture of our province, and bursaries totaling $3,000 together with gifts and classroom resources were presented at a ceremony in Halifax in the spring.

In February 2010, Tony brought me to Halifax in order to help present the awards in the Student Challenge Program, and afterwards he arranged an interview with Sherri Borden Colley from the *Chronicle Herald*. She interviewed me at Tony's for a two-part feature article that appeared on March 6, 2010.[6] Sherri also interviewed retired Pictou County Provincial Court Judge, Clyde F. Macdonald of New Glasgow who was familiar with the case. The former judge stated that given the circumstances and the way Viola had been treated, he felt that she should be pardoned. Since it was a provincial statute that was used to convict Viola, Judge Macdonald suggested that the province should be the one to grant her the pardon. The day after the article appeared in the *Chronicle Herald,* Premier Darrell Dexter announced that the government was looking into the possibility of issuing a pardon for my sister.

On April 15, 2010, I was asked to attend Province House in Halifax where Premier Dexter, speaking on behalf of the Nova Scotia Government, offered an official apology to my family and to all African-Nova Scotians for the racial discrimination my sister was subjected to. Using the Royal Prerogative invested under the authority of Lieutenant Governor of Nova Scotia, the Honourable Mayann Francis, he announced that the Government of Nova Scotia had granted a mercy free Pardon to Viola Desmond. A free pardon is based on innocence, and it recognizes that the conviction was in error. In Viola's case, the pardon was issued to right a wrong because, in simple terms, she was not given a fair trial. The granting of a pardon usually erases the conviction from court records; however, in this instance, Viola's court record was left in place for the purpose of historical documentation.

Stuart Murray, President and CEO of the Canadian Museum for Human Rights in Winnipeg contacted me in April 2010 and offered congratulations on Viola's pardon, and he indicated that the Museum was creating a permanent display in honour of Viola. The museum opened to the public in 2014, and the Viola Desmond exhibit highlights the incident at the Roseland theatre as an important and uniquely Canadian story of courage.

Shortly after the ceremony in Halifax, President John Harker of Cape Breton University announced the creation of the Viola Desmond Chair in Social Justice, and he appointed Dr. Graham Reynolds to serve as the first holder of the chair. President Harker and his wife Eunice had attended the ceremony in Halifax, and

Grant of Free Pardon
VIOLA IRENE DAVIS DESMOND

Viola Irene Davis Desmond

Mrs. Viola Irene Davis Desmond was born on July 6, 1914 in Halifax, Nova Scotia, to James and Gwendolyn Davis. Mrs. Desmond was one of 15 siblings who went on to be a successful entrepreneur. She operated her own beauty parlour and beauty college in Halifax.

On Nov. 8, 1946, Viola Desmond became a victim of racism. While travelling to Sydney as part of a business trip, Viola stopped in New Glasgow at a local repair shop due to car troubles. While waiting for her car to be repaired, Mrs. Desmond decided to watch a movie at the Roseland Theatre.

At that time, the theatre had a policy that prohibited people of African ancestry from sitting on the main level of the theatre. African Nova Scotians were required to sit in the balcony where seating cost one cent less than the main level. Mrs. Desmond attempted to buy the more expensive main level ticket but was refused because she was African Nova Scotian.

Mrs. Desmond purchased a ticket which she thought was for the main level and proceeded to sit there. Her ticket was actually for the balcony. Mrs. Desmond was then removed from the theatre by the manager and police. After spending a night in jail, Mrs. Desmond was tried and convicted for an offence under the Theatres, Cinematographs and Amusements Act for failing to pay an extra cent in tax to the Province. She was given the option to pay a fine of $20 plus costs associated with the trial, or to go to jail for 30 days. Due to her business commitments, Mrs. Desmond chose to pay the fine.

In the early 1950s, Mrs. Desmond closed her business and moved to Montreal, Quebec, where she enrolled in business college. She eventually settled in New York where she passed away at the age of 50.

Granting of Official Apology and Free Pardon

On April 15, 2010, the province of Nova Scotia granted an official apology and free pardon to the late Mrs. Viola Desmond who was wrongfully fined and jailed for sitting in the white peoples' section of a New Glasgow movie theatre in 1946.

On the advice of the Executive Council, the lieutenant governor exercised the Royal Prerogative of Mercy to grant a free pardon. A free pardon is based on innocence and recognizes that a conviction was in error. A free pardon is an extraordinary remedy and is considered only in the rarest of circumstances.

A Royal Prerogative of Mercy Free Pardon is meant to right a wrong. In this case, the free pardon is meant to right the wrong done to Mrs. Desmond.

NOVA SCOTIA

Granting of Official Apology and Free Pardon, 15 April, 2010

they were deeply touched by the event as well as my praise for the role Cape University played in my personal journey of education and self-awareness.

On August 15, 2010, I was invited by the town of New Glasgow to take part in celebrations honouring Viola that coincided with the annual Black Homecoming Gala. Earlier that month my book *Sister to Courage: Stories from the World of Viola Desmond, Canada's Rosa Parks* was published, and my editor, Ron Caplan, of Breton

Books, arranged to use the occasion in New Glasgow as part of the official launch of my book. The celebration began with a dedication of a commemorative bench in the African Heritage Memorial Park followed later with the unveiling of an interpretive panel at Laurie Park by Lieutenant Governor Mayann Francis, Defence Minister Peter MacKay and mayor Barrie MacMillan. Later that same day in the town hall, Mayann Francis unveiled a portrait of Viola painted by artist Davis Macintosh. Viola's portrait is now on permanent display in Province House in Halifax.

NOTES

1. Much has been written on the subject of black self-identity in predominantly white societies. Frantz Fanon wrote about this in his classic study *Black Skin, White Masks*, revised edition (New York: Grove Press, 2008). This subject was raised recently by African-Canadian writer and poet Orville Lloyd Douglas in a provocative article published in the online edition of *The Guardian*. Douglas writes that as an African-Canadian male living in Toronto, he finds it difficult to feel positive about his black self-identity because there are such fear and negative attitudes expressed toward black males, particularly in public spaces. He states: "Every time I sit on a crowded street car, bus, or subway train in Toronto, I know I will have an empty seat next to me." See Orville Lloyd Douglas, "Why I Hate Being a Black Man," *The Guardian* (online edition, November 9, 2013). Retrieved from <theguardian.com/commentisfree/2013/nov/09/i-hate-being-a-black-man>.

2. For a full discussion of this earlier incident at the Roseland Theatre, see Constance Backhouse, "I Was Unable to Identify with Topsy: Carrie M. Best's Struggle Against Racial Segregation in Nova Scotia, 1942," *Atlantis* 22, 2 (Spring/Summer 1998), pp. 16–26.

3. Constance Backhouse, *Colour Coded, A Legal History of Racism in Canada 1900–1950* (Toronto: University of Toronto Press, 1999), p. 266.

4. Dean Jobb, "Ticket to Freedom," *The Beaver* (April–May, 2009), pp. 24–29.

5. Prior to the events that lead to Viola Desmond's free pardon in April of 2010, Tony Colaiacovo printed and distributed 35,000 copies of his *The Times of African Nova Scotians*, and this undoubtedly helped to raise public awareness regarding the Viola Desmond incident. *The Times of African Nova Scotians*, in book form, has been adopted for use in all schools in the Nova Scotia in the grade 11 African Studies Program.

6. Sherri Borden Colley, "Unintentional Activist; By All Accounts, Viola Desmond Was Ahead of Her Time, Making Inroads as a Woman and as a Black. A Sister Remembers Canada's Rosa Parks," *Chronicle Herald* (March 6, 2010), F1; Sherri Borden Colley, "Desmond Should Be Pardoned; Case Helped Eliminate Segregation in Province, Says Retired Judge," *Chronicle Herald* (March 6, 2010), F2.

PART II

A DOCUMENTARY HISTORY

Chapter 4

Marie Marguerite Rose

What Her Inventory of Material Possessions Tells Us About Slavery and Freedom in Eighteenth Century New France

By any standard of measure, Marie Marguerite Rose was a remarkable woman. Despite spending most of her adult life as a slave, she became a successful and respected innkeeper and woman of business in eighteenth-century Ile Royale. As we will see in this commentary, her inventory of final material possessions offers a unique window into her life as well as the practice of slavery in New France.[1] Before addressing Marie Marguerite Rose's inventory, however, it is first necessary to discuss some of the features that distinguished slavery in Canada and Ile Royale from that of other French colonies.

The institution of slavery in most French colonies was regulated under the *Code Noir*. Established by an edict under Louis XIV in 1685, it applied to the French West Indies and was later revised in 1724 for the practice of slavery in Louisiana. The *Code Noir* was an expressly French (Catholic) document, and the original sixty articles were a blend of paternalistic, religious and harshly punitive regulations for the treatment and subsistence of slaves. Slave masters, for example, were required to baptize and instruct their slaves in the Catholic faith, and all those who held positions of authority over slaves had to be practicing Roman Catholics.[2]

Written for the French colonies that had large slave populations, the *Code Noir* regulated the interaction between slaves and colonists. It was designed to protect the property of slave owners and to help prevent slaves from escaping their bondage as well as to guard against mass rebellion by limiting any large gatherings of slaves. Slaves who ran away were punished by having their ears cut off and being branded on their shoulder with a *fleur-de-lys*. If a slave ran away for a second time, their hamstring would be cut; a third escape attempt resulted in a death sentence.

In addition to the harsh provisions of the *Code Noir,* the document set minimum standards for the material well-being of slaves, including provisions for food and clothing. In accordance with the mores and thought of late seventeenth and early eighteenth century France, slaves were regarded as property to be bought and sold like animals; however, the French also afforded them some measure of humanity. Unlike the treatment of slaves in the British colonies and later in the American slave holding states, for example, the *Code Noir* attempted to maintain the integrity of the slave family by allowing for marriage among slaves and keeping children under the age of 14 with their parents. Also, if slaves achieved their freedom, they were given the same rights and privileges of free persons.

The conditions of slavery in Canada under the French were very different than in the French West Indies and Louisiana. There were far fewer slaves in comparison to the colonies with economies based on plantations requiring slave labor, and there was no threat of slave insurrections. Most African slaves that were brought to Canada were an expensive luxury reserved for the elite and bourgeoisie, and because they were in such close proximity to their owners, serving either as domestic servants or in the urban workforce, they did not require an extensive system of social controls.[3] The *Code Noir* was never legally implemented in Canada; however, most slave owners complied with selected provisions of the code regarding baptism, marriage and burial.[4] The *Code Noir* illustrates the difficulties of creating and enforcing any single, uniform system for regulating the practice of slavery in an imperial or colonial context. In Canada, as in other French colonies, slavery varied greatly according to local and individual circumstances.

Nearly half a century ago, Marcel Trudel wrote his now classic history of slavery in Canada and he observed that under French rule, slaves had a certain degree of autonomy and legal advantages they would not have had in other slave holding regions. In Quebec, for example, slaves could bring a civil suit against their masters, and in criminal courts "there was no [legal] distinction, between slaves and persons of free condition."[5] There were relatively few criminal cases involving slaves over the two hundred year history of slavery in New France, and in the overall administration of justice, slaves and free persons were treated in a similar manner.

There is, however, one famous criminal case involving a slave that reveals the underlying brutality of the judicial system and the conditions of slavery in eighteenth century New France. The slave was a young 24-year-old woman of African and Portuguese descent by the name of Angelique (short for Marie-Joseph-Angelique).[6]

Like Marie Marguerite Rose and most Black female slaves in New France, Angelique was a domestic slave. She was brought to Montreal in 1725 in order to serve as a servant in the household of Thérèse de Couagne and her husband, François Poulin de Francheville, a wealthy Montreal businessman and merchant. Angelique shared the domestic chores in the Francheville household with several other servants including a white maid and a male, Claude Thibault, a

French-Canadian servant. Angelique never fully accepted her situation as a slave in the Francheville household and was often in conflict with the white maid and frequently quarreled with her mistress, Madam Francheville, who was at times abusive toward her. Although some of the details of the story are unclear, it is likely that Angelique and the male servant, Claude, were lovers. In 1734, they escaped their bondage together but were quickly recaptured and returned to the Francheville household. Following this abortive escape, Angelique feared that her mistress was planning to sell her to a plantation in the West Indies, so on the evening of April 10, 1734, she allegedly set fire to the Francheville house as a diversion allowing her and Claude to escape again. The fire quickly spread to the adjacent houses, and before it was extinguished, a hospital and forty-six other buildings were consumed, making it one of the worst fires in the history of Montreal.[7]

Angelique was apprehended the next day and immediately imprisoned. Because of her deliberate intentions and the serious consequences of her actions, the judges in her case gave her the harshest sentence imaginable. In his account of the incident, Marcel Trudel wrote: "In the minds of the victims, [the] sentence was in proportion to the magnitude of the crime: [Angelique] would first be subjected to the most exacting and detailed interrogation under torture, then paraded in a refuse cart, compelled to make amends before the parish church, have her hand cut off, then burned alive."[8]

Exercising her limited judicial rights, Angelique appealed her verdict to the Conseil Supérieur — a higher court. On June 12, 1734, the Conseil upheld her death sentence; however, it amended her initial sentence and ruled that she would be hanged before being burned. Under the Conseil's ruling Angelique also had to endure the initial sentence of "interrogation under torture" in order to force her to reveal the name of her accomplice, which was, in all likelihood, Claude Thibault. Angelique did not give up her lover even under the pain of torture and went to her death in silence. Although the authorities spent a considerable amount of time and effort trying to apprehend Claude, he managed to elude capture.

We will likely never know the exact cause and all the circumstances surrounding the disastrous fire of 1734, but the testimony at Angeligue's trial tells us a great deal about her life and the conditions of slavery in New France. As a domestic slave in the Francheville household Angeligue had a considerable measure of autonomy in her day-to-day duties. Afua Cooper notes, "Even though Angelique engaged in a routine of hard and constant toil, she had some free time."[9] Her court testimony reveals that she often walked the streets of Montreal alone on errands, talked to soldiers, supervised children at play, drank and socialized with neighbors and visited patients at a local hospital.

Angeligue also struck up a close friendship with a *panisse* slave girl, Marie, in a neighbor's household, and they frequently met in each other's kitchens to share with the chores and tell jokes. It was also noted in the testimony that Angeligue had several relationships: one with a Black slave, Cesar, and, as mentioned, another with the white servant, Claude. By 1732, two years before her first attempt to escape with Claude, she had three children, all fathered by Cesar.[10]

Despite Angeligue's relative autonomy, she lived a hard life and was never far removed from the demanding authority of Madam Francheville. The tragic account of Angelique's life reveals a great deal about slavery and the social structure of eighteenth century New France. Historian Allan Greer observes that the practice of slavery during this period does not fit the image most Canadians have of slavery, which is derived largely from the system that developed in southern United States during the nineteenth-century. Greer states: "In New France, there was no simple dichotomy with free and white, on one side, unfree and Black, on the other." There was instead "degrees and varieties of unfreedom, with many French people ... subject to the authority of a master in almost the same way that a slave was. At this level of society, barriers of race and legal status were minimal."[11] Angelique's life was dramatic and brutal, and it captures the oppressive nature of slavery. However, her story is not in all respects typical of the life of slaves in Canada under French rule. Most slaves were domestic servants and there were relatively few incidents of slaves escaping their masters.[12] In this context, the life of Marie Marguerite Rose in Ile Royale offers an important counter weight to that of Angelique, and it further highlights the complex relationship between freedom and slavery within the evolving social structure of eighteenth century New France. Although there are similarities between Angelique and Marie, there are stark differences in their circumstances and lives. Both were sold into slavery at an early age and brought to Canada in order to serve as domestic servants in upper middle-class (bourgeoisie) households. As female domestic slaves, both experienced some degree of sexual exploitation. Both women gave birth to one or more children out of wedlock, and their children immediately became slaves and the property of their owners. However, the course and final outcome of the lives of these two important histori-cal figures were very different. Angelique met an untimely death on the gallows at age 24 and Marie served most of her adult life as a domestic slave until, at age 38, she gained her freedom, married and became co-owner of a tavern. Although she died suddenly of natural causes at the age of 40, she lived well past the average life expectancy for a female slave in New France.[13]

Marie's life as a slave began like that of countless other African women who were enslaved by the French. As a young girl, Marie was kidnapped from her homeland of Guiana on the west coast of Africa. In 1736, at the age of 19, she was purchased by Jean-Chrysostome Loppinot, a military officer stationed at Louisbourg. In September of that year, she was baptized and began serving as a domestic slave in the Loppinot household. Two years later, Marie gave birth to a son, Jean Francois, who, because of his mother's status, immediately became a slave. Jean grew up in the Loppinot home and helped his mother in the daily household chores. He became ill and died in 1751 at the age of 13.

Marie continued as a domestic slave in the Loppinot household, and over her nineteen years of service, she helped raise the Loppinot's twelve children. In 1755, Marie was freed, and a few months later she married, Jean Baptiste Laurent, a Mi'kmaq.[14]

We do not know the exact circumstances of Marie's release from bondage and marriage, but it is possible that the Loppinot's did not want to assume the responsibility of caring for an aging slave in the final years of her life. Marie was one of only three women at Louisbourg to become free and later marry, and it is possible that the Loppinot's freed her in an act of generosity so she could marry and begin a new life with her husband.

Whatever the particular circumstances, it is clear that Marie's freedom not only allowed her to marry but also enabled her to enter into a business partnership with her husband.

Together, Marie and Jean Baptiste rented a small house next to the Loppinot's residence and began operating a tavern offering patrons respectable and good quality cuisine that included a choice of wine, brandy, rum, coffee and home-cooked meals with salt beef, cod and a variety of fresh vegetables Marie grew from a garden adjacent to their new home.[15]

Marie's life as a tavern owner and free married women, as it has already been noted, lasted less than two years and ended in her unexpected death on August 27, 1757.

Immediately following her death, Louisbourg authorities entered her residence and began a legally required inventory of all her material possessions, including movable items such as furniture, cooking utensils, tavern supplies, clothing as well as business receipts and other written documents. This was a standard practice at Louisbourg, and it was mandated under French law. The inventory began in the evening of August 27, 1757. Several court authorities entered Marie's residence and immediately sealed the window and door of her room as well as a chest containing her personal belongings with strips of cloth affixed at each end to wax seals. After securing the room, the court authorities took an inventory of the moveable items in Marie's room, which included a buffet, dresser, chairs, a long table with benches, two empty chests, several plates and a brass candlestick. The court authorities were not able to complete the inventory of Marie's personal possessions during their initial visit that evening, so they placed the sealed contents of the home in the custody of two local residents who were likely friends of Marie.[16]

On September 2, the court authorities returned to the house and continued their inventory. After removing the seals, they examined the contents of Marie's chest, which included part of her personal wardrobe, a meager sum of 86 livres, 15 sols, two necklaces, one of pearls and the other of garnets, as well as other items belonging to her husband, including a three-piece vest, a waistcoat and seven shirts. The chest also contained a new man's shirt that Marie was likely making for her husband that had only one sleeve attached with a pin. Marie's wardrobe consisted of a modest assortment of worn items including four petticoats, a waistcoat, several mantelets (a women's short mantel), a white cotton gown, five shirts, a variety of coloured and muslin handkerchiefs, a new pair of black shoes, five pairs of woolen stockings and pair of Segovia and a pair of cotton stockings, two pairs of silk stockings, one white and the other grey, twelve cloths, a vest of white striped wool, five soap balls, a pair of shoe buckles and a pair of garter buckles of yellow pinchbeck, a ball of white and a ball of brown wool, three small balls of cotton, twelve coifs (caps) and fifteen coif bonnets, and two brown hooded cloaks. The chest also contained a small writing case and a wooden tobacco box. It is important to note that although Marie was not able to write, she did place her mark on official documents. Having a writing case would have been convenient in conducting her business because it would allow her clients to write or sign receipts and other documents.

The court authorities continued their inventory of Marie's material possessions and they proceeded systematically room by room. Marie and Jean Baptiste's rented house had four small rooms, two on each floor, with the tavern taking up space on the first floor. The kitchen and dining area were combined, and the inventory indicates there were enough seats, plates and utensils to accommodate thirteen guests. The bedroom downstairs contained a small table and a feather bed with straw mattress and a sheet with a woolen blanket. There were two rooms upstairs. One room was used for storage and the other as a guest bedroom. Marie offered her patrons room and board and the records show that at least one individual, Thomas Gallien, a sailor, stayed at the tavern for thirty-two days over part of February and March 1756.[17]

In addition to providing an inventory of Marie's material possessions, including receipts, bills and promissory notes, the court authorities conducted a public auction for the sale of Marie's property. Following the standard practice of the time, bidders to the auction were "summoned by a drummer" followed by the reading aloud of the conditions of the sale.

Estate auctions of this kind were common events at Louisbourg, and Marie's estate was sold to the highest bidders for a sum of 274 livres. Marie's estate was very modest in relationship to her status as member of the Louisbourg's lower bourgeoisie. There are several other inventories of bourgeoisie women who lived at Louisbourg during this period and their material possessions were substantially greater than Marie's.[18]

From a historical perspective, one the most interesting items in Marie's inventory was her pair of necklaces. Jewelry was not a common adornment among most of the women at Louisbourg, and it was usually reserved for women of upper class and bourgeoisie status. Marie also had a number of coloured handkerchiefs, a small quantity of blue starch or dye and two coloured petticoats, one red and the other blue with a cloth mantelet.

Former Parks Canada historian Ken Donovan speculates that these items may have reflected Marie's African roots. He notes that by the early sixteenth century, brightly coloured cloth had become fashionable along the coast of Africa and was imported to that region by slave traders. Jewelry was also a valued item of trade and in some areas along the African coast it served as a form of currency.[19]

Another particularly noteworthy item in Marie's inventory was a cookbook entitled *Le Cuisinier Royal*. Even though Marie was illiterate, the book, as Ken Donovan notes, was a highly valued possession and likely a gift from her previous owners.[20] It no doubt reflects Marie's ability to cook as well as the many years she spent helping to prepare the meals in the Loppinot household.

The tavern records that were included in Marie's inventory reveal that she and her husband were equals in relation to all major legal transactions. Under French law in force at Louisbourg, a married woman could not enter into legal agreements alone or without the expressed permission of her husband. However, in some of the business transactions, especially in the larger purchases of goods such as wine, Marie appears to be the one in charge of conducting the business. The inventory contains several agreements with men relating to the holding and lending of money in which Marie's name appears alone as "Marie Rose negress," or, as in one case, "Marie Rose negress libre." Although Marie was a tavern co-owner for less than two years, the inventory and the sale of her estate indicates that she managed her business well and had built trust among the people she knew and conducted business with. Her former owner, Jean Loppinot supported her business, and as a military officer and merchant, he was able to supply the tavern with meat and rum. Marie had established a sizable account with him in the amount of 226 livres.[21]

Marie's inventory offers valuable insight into the lives of slaves in New France, and it shows that the practice of slavery varied greatly according to individual circumstance and life experience. The extent of trust Marie had with merchants and members of the Louisbourg bourgeoisie extended beyond the operations of running a tavern. In 1757, Marie received a letter from Pierre Lapouble, a French merchant and patron, that illustrates not only the high personal regard and trust others had in her and her husband but also that Marie was in full control of the business.[22] The letter was addressed to Marie and was written by Pierre Lapouble, who was writing from France. Pierre describes the harrowing experience he had on his return to France from Louisbourg in 1757. He informs Marie that he was captured by an English frigate off the coast of Louisbourg and was kept prisoner for two months. The ship eventually made its way to Lisbon, where Pierre and other captives were put ashore. Pierre then walked 200 leagues (966 kilometers) to his home in France. The letter indicates that Pierre had assigned Marie power of attorney to conduct affairs on his behalf while he was away. The power of attorney was left in a trunk with certain unspecified items that Pierre wanted Marie to sell. Marie was instructed to keep a portion of the sale of these items as payment for money he owed her and to send him, through a letter of exchange, the remaining portion. Pierre also asked Marie to talk to Monsieur Imbert, a prominent Basque merchant in Louisbourg, about money owed to him as a result of a business transaction with another merchant, Monsieur Joseph Barret.[23]

The letter clearly indicates the high regard and trust he had in Marie to conduct business on his behalf, and it assumes that she would be able to successfully engage with other merchants in the conduct of his business.

This letter, together with the inventory of Marie's remaining effects, provides a picture of an extraordinary woman with a wide array of talents. In addition to being a successful tavern owner and businesswomen, Marie was an accomplished cook and gardener and, like many women of eighteenth century Louisbourg, she was skilled at making and mending clothes. Although Marie's freedom lasted less than two years and ended with her sudden death in August of 1757, her life as a slave and as a free women was extraordinary and shows that in spite of her African roots and her former status of being a slave, she achieved a relative degree of autonomy. Given her demonstrated management skills as well as the trust she gained with Louisbourg merchants, we have to assume that she had been well prepared to start a business long before she gained her freedom. Her former owner Jean Loppinot fully supported Marie's business venture and it is likely that she had demonstrated some of her management acumen during her nineteen years of service as a domestic slave in the Loppinot family.[24]

The following documents include the inventory of Marie's estate and the letter sent to her from the merchant Pierre Lapouble. These documents provide a number of insights into the conditions of slavery and the structure of society in eighteenth century Louisbourg, and it is hoped that they will stimulate new areas of research leading to a deeper understanding of the history of slavery in Canada. The documents allow for some interesting speculations regarding Marie's self-identity and status in Louisbourg society. Her inventory supports the possibility that Marie identified with her African heritage.

There were over 200 slaves of African descent in Louisbourg, as well as a small number of freed slaves, and given the similarities of circumstance and culture, it is possible that Marie may have formed some kind of association with others of African heritage. Slaves in Canada under French rule, as already noted, had some degree of autonomy, and Marie, like Angelique and other domestic slaves, would have been able to conduct her daily tasks unaccompanied, and she would have had some degree of freedom to come and go from the Loppinot home. The extent to which Louisbourg had a slave community is uncertain. Although the work of a slave did not allow much free time, Marie and other enslaved Africans had some limited opportunities to meet in public and to gather together in small groups, especially at official occasions such as baptisms.[25]

It also possible that Marie self-identified with her gender as a woman of status within French colonial society. Eighteenth century Louisbourg was an evolving multicultural society, and like other regions of New France, the role of women was changing in order to reflect the new realities of life.[26] The documents clearly indicate that in spite of Marie's former status as a slave, she became an independent woman

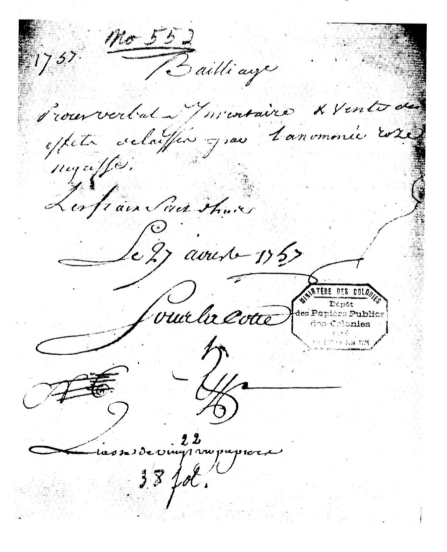

of business and gained the respect of her customers and business associates. As a domestic slave in the Loppinot household for nineteen years, Marie no doubt learned how to navigate the complex and changing social landscape of eighteenth century Louisbourg. Judging from what we know about her remarkable but brief life as a free woman, we can surmise that Marie gained access to Louisbourg's bourgeoisie. Her success and independence are testimony to her ability to overcome personal hardships as well as the many legal and social barriers that existed in eighteenth century Ile Royale.

THE INVENTORY AND SALE
OF EFFECTS LEFT BY MARIE MARGUERITE ROSE

Proces-Verbal de l'inventoire et vente des effets delaisser par la nomme Roze Negresse 27 aout 1757 (Report of the inventory and sale of the effects left by one Roze, a Negress, 27 August 1757), G2, vol 212, dossier 552, Archives Nationales, Outre-Mer.

In the year one thousand seven hundred fifty-seven, on the twenty-seventh day of August, at about nine o'clock in the evening, we, Laurent Domingue Meyracq, King's Councillor, Bailli, Civil and Criminal Magistrate in the Royal Bailliage of Louisbourg, Isle Royale, upon notice we received of the death of the one Roze, a Negrees, the wife of one Baptiste, an Indian, an inhabitant of this city, residing in the house belonging to Sieur Bernard Paris, a ship's captain, situated on Rue St. Louis in this city, went with the King's Procurer, accompanied by the Clerk and attended by the Process Sever of the Court, to the apartments which the said Roze occupied in the said house, for the purpose of apposing seals and taking an inventory of the effects found therein belonging to the said Roze, deceased, for the protection of the rights of those concerned; where being, we found the body of Roze; and speaking to one Jean Brion, a companion fisherman, and to Jenevieve Harnoy, the wife of Mathurin Chenot, whom we found in the room where the said body was, we informed them of the purpose of our coming, which was to appose seals over the openings and to take an inventory of the movables and effects which were in evidence; whereto we proceeded as follows:

First, we caused a strip of cloth to be placed and apposed over a small chest which was in the room which looks out over the courtyard of the said house and adjoins the one in which we found the body of the said Roze, at each end of which strip we caused the seal of the Court to be apposed, the key to the said chest remaining in the custody of the said Clerk.

Item, we caused a strip of cloth to be placed and apposed over the frame of the window looking out over the said courtyard, over each end of which we likewise caused the seal of the said Court to be apposed.

Item, another strip of cloth was apposed over the door of the said room, over each end of the which we also caused the seal of the said Court to be apposed, and the key to the same was given to the said Clerk. And there being no other openings over which seals could be apposed, we proceeded to a brief inventory and description of the movables which were evidence, as follows:

Movable Items Found in Marie Marguerite Rose's Residence,
25 August 1757

Item	Description
Buffet	Poor Condition
Dresser	
Six glass bottles	3 in the buffet and 3 on top of the buffet
Two earthenware plates	
Faience plate	
Long table with 2 benches	
Two empty chests	
Brass candlestick	
Four chairs	Poor Condition

And there being nothing else to inventory, we appointed and established for the custody and conservation both of the apposed seals and of the movables inventoried above the said Jean Brion and the said Jenevieve Harnoy, the wife of the said Mathurin Chenot who, being here present, undertook to show us the whole, and particularly the seals sound and entire, when required by us to do so; and neither the said Brion nor the said Jenevieve Harnoy, the wife of the said Mathurin Chenot, signed, because they did not know how when asked in accordance with the ordinance, on the said day of the month and year aforesaid.

Bascaud Meyracq cbc Lartique, Clerk

In the year one thousand seven hundred and fifty-seven, on the second day of September, at about two o'clock in the afternoon, before us, Laurent de Dominge Meyracq, Kings's Councillor, Bailli, Civil and Criminal Magistrate in the Royal Bailliage of Louisbourg, Isle Royale, appeared Maitre [Pascaud], Kings's Councillor and King's Procurer to the said Court, who told us that by our order placed at the bottom of his request presented by him on the morning of this day, we had been pleased to order that on this day and at this time we would remove the seals apposed over the openings in the apartments formerly occupied by the said Roze, a Negress, the wife of one Baptiste Laurent, and Indian, residing in the house belonging to Sieur Bernard Paris, a ship's captain in this city, situated on Rue St. Louis, who died on the twenty-seventh of August last, and take an inventory of the movables and effects under the said seals; and having gone there forthwith, along with the said King's Procurer and the Clerk of the Court, attended by the Process Server, we proceeded to remove the said seals and take an inventory of the said movables and effects as follows, after calling upon one Jean Brion, a companion fisherman, and on Jenevieve, the wife of Mathurin Chenot, appointed by us to have custody of the said seals and movables in evidence, in accordance with our report of the said day, the twenty-seventh of August last, to show us both the said seals, sound and entire, and the movables and effects which remained in evidence; which they promised to do; this done after acknowledging the seals apposed over the opening of the door of a room which looks out over the courtyard of the said house to be sound and entire, we caused them to be opened by the said Clerk, who was in possession of the key to the said door; and we found the following in the first room:

First, a chest over which we had a likewise caused seals to be apposed, and having found them sound and entire, we removed them; and after it had been opened by the Clerk, who was in possession of the key, we found a small locked chest; and having caused it to be opened, we found the following:

Items found in Marie Marguerite Rose's Locked Chest,
2 September 1757

Item	Description/Condition
The sum of eight-livres fifteen sols	
Two necklaces	One of pearls and the other of garnets
Three piece suit	Made of black ratteen
Worn-out waistcoat	Poor Condition
A cotton mantelet with a petticoat	Both made from embroidered cotton
A calico mantelet	Worn out
A petticoat	Made from striped cotton, in poor condition
A mantelet	Made from embroidered cotton, in poor condition
A gown	Made from white cotton

Item	Description/Condition
A petticoat	Made from embroidered cotton and half worn out
Five women's shirts	Poor Condition
Seven men's shirts	In both good and poor condition
One man's shirt	Only one sleeve and the other being attached with a pin, new
Man's waistcoat	Made from cotton, half worn out
Four women's handkerchiefs	Made from muslin
Six colored handkerchiefs	
One pair of women's shoes	Black and new
Give pairs of woolen stockings and one pair of Segovia	
Another pair of cotton, and a pair of thread	
Two pairs of silk stockings	One grey and one white
Twelve cloths	
One vest	Made of striped white wool
Five soap balls	
One pair of shoe buckles and a pair of garters buckles	Made of yellow pinchbeck
A muslin handkerchief	
A ball of white wool and a ball of brown	
Three small balls of cotton	
Twelve women's coifs	In poor condition
Fifteen coif bonnets	
A cloak with its hood and another cloak	All brown and in poor condition
A mall escritoire (writing case) of horn with a small wooden snuffbox	
The chest containing the above effects	

Inventory of Items found in Marie Marguerite Rose's Apartment,
2 September 1757

Item	Description/Condition
Two earthenware pots	
Eleven empty bottles	
A small tin box	

Item	Description/Condition
Four large crystal goblets and two small *idem*	
A faience teapot	
Eight coffee cups with their saucers	
Seven small earthenware goblets with a small candlestick	Reddish-brown in color
A small English pot or mug	
Two small glass vials of one quart each	
A quart and a demi-quart of pewter, with another quart *idem*	
Thirteen pewter spoons and thirteen iron forks	
Four faience pots	
A tin funnel	
Three to four livres of white sugar in a small bag	
A small cooking pot and a pot of earthenware	
Two pails hooped with iron	
Twelve livres of coffee in a small bag	
A quart in which there was a *tiers* of salted meat	
About six livres of leaf tobacco	
A barrel containing some raspberries	
A pair of sheets	Half worn out
A blue petticoat with a cloth mantelet	In poor condition
A flannel petticoat	
A bedstead	In poor condition
Two white woolen blankets	
A feather bed and a sheet	
A straw mattress	In poor condition
Two cooking pots	One pot contained a little sweet fat
Two men's coats	Made of whitish woolen cloth
A woolen blanket	
A gridiron and a fire shovel	
A frying pan, a shovel and pair of pincers	
An earthenware pot	

Item	Description/Condition
A bag in which there were some lead shot	
Four fusils and three powder horns	
A little wire and small necklace of pearls or garnets	
Seven pictures	
A quart containing twelve pots of brandy	
A straw-bottomed chair	
About seven to eight hundred walnuts	
A corselet	
A chest containing blue starch	
A calamanco petticoat	In poor condition
A pair of stockings	Woolen and in poor condition
A pair of panne trousers	In poor condition
A number of remnants of various stuffs	In poor condition
The chest containing the said effects	
An oil jug	

And there being nothing else to inventory in the said effects, we adjourned the session and postponed the inventory of some papers to another day; whereof a record was made, which we signed with the King's Procurer; which the said custodians did not do, because they did not know how when asked.

And on the fifth day of the said month of September in the said year one thousand seven hundred and fifty-seven, at about two o'clock in the afternoon, we, the aforesaid Bailli, at the request of the King's Procurer, went in the company of him and the Clerk, attended by the Process Server of the Court, to the dwelling and apartment which had been occupied by Roze, the wife of Baptiste Laurent, and Indian, residing in the house belonging to Sieur Bernard Paris, ships's captain in this city, situated on Rue St. Louis, to take an inventory of some papers which were in the said apartments; where being, we proceeded to do the same in the presence of the said Jean Brion and the said Jenevieve, as follows:

Inventory of Notes found in Marie Marguerite Rose's Apartment,
5 September 1757

Amount	Issued By	Issued To	Date	Notes
Sixty livres	Lessenne	Jean Baptiste, Indian	3 December 1756	Inventoried as one
Eighteen livres	Guillaume Fournier	Jean Baptiste, Indian	3 December 1756	On the back of which was a receipt from the said Jean Baptiste, Indian, for the sum of thirteen *livres* eleven *sols* three *deniers*. Inventoried as two.
Thirty-five livres five sols	J. Mendrel	Jean Pierre Laurent	25 March 1756	Inventoried as three
Fifty-one livres	Andre Marchand	Roze, Negress	8 June 1756	On the back was a receipt for the sum of twelve livres. Inventoried as four.
One hundred twenty-eight livres eighteen sols six deniers				An account provided by Sieur Tanguy Mervin to Roze. Roze owed Sieur Mervin the balance. Inventoried as five.
A receipt for six to seven hundred quintaux of cod[27]	L. Gautier	Joseph Bestieux and partners	3 May 1756	Given on account of the rent of a chaloupe which he had lent them for the autumn. Inventoried as six.

And there being nothing else to inventory, we adjourned the session and left the movables and effects inventoried by us on the second day of this month in the custody of the said Jean Brion and Jenevieve, the wife Mathurin Chenot, who voluntarily charged themselves therewith and promised to show them to us when required to do so, and caused the papers inventoried above to be taken to the office of the Clerk of our Court, given the absence of the said Jean Baptiste, Indian, to be deposited there until otherwise ordered by us; of all which we caused a record to be made, which we signed the King's Procurer; which neither the said Jean Brion nor the said Jenevieve did, because they did not know how, when asked in accordance with the ordinance.

Meyracq Lartigue, Clerk

In the year one thousand seven hundred and fifty-seven, on the third day of September at about two o'clock in the afternoon, in our house and before us, Laurent de Domingue Meyracq, King's Councillor, Bailli, Civil and Criminal Magistrate in the Royal Bailliage of Louisbourg, Isle Royale, appeared Maitre Jean Pascaud, King's Councillor and King's Procurer to the said Court, who told us that in execution of our order placed at the bottom of the request presented by him on the morning of this day, he had caused it to be published in the ordinary and customary places and locations in this city that on this day and at this time we would proceed to the auction, sale and award of movables and effects appertaining to the succession of the late Roze, a Negress, the wife of Baptiste Laurent, and Indian, in the house belonging to Sieur Bernard Paris, ship's captain in this city, situated on Rue St. Louis, and in the said apartment occupied in the same by the said Roze, deceased; wherefore he requested that we be pleased to go to the aforesaid apartment to proceed with the sale.

Wherefore we, the Bailli aforesaid, made and granted a record of the above appearance and request, and in consequence went with the said King's Procurer and the Clerk, attended by the Process Server of the Court, to the house of the said Sieur Paris, situated on Rue St. Louis in this city, and to the apartments which the said Roze, deceased, had occupied in the same; where being, and having seen our order of the morning of this day, we caused bidders to be summoned by a drummer, following the usage of the colony; and several persons having assembled, we caused to be read aloud to them the conditions of the said sale, which were that successful bidders should pay the price of their bids in cash to the Clerk of this Court, as depositary of Court monies, under penalty of imprisonment and seizure of their goods. This done, we caused the following effects of the exhibited and put up for sale:

Auction of Marie Marguerite Rose's Possessions, 3 September 1757

Lot	Bid	Bidder	Paid
Coffee cups and saucers, teapot and 1 mug	Four livres five sols	Sieur Droit	Promised to pay 4.5
Seven goblets of reddish-brown earthenware, a small candlestick idem, with a large goblet, a pot *idem*, together with a *demi- chopine*, a *quart* and *demi-quart*	Three livres	Sieur Droit	Promised to pay 3

Lot	Bid	Bidder	Paid
Thirteen pewter spoons and thirteen iron forks	Three livres	Sieur Ferret	Paid 3
A bag with 24 livres of coffee	Fourteen sols per livre, making the sum of sixteen livres sixteen sols	Madame LeLievre	Promised to pay 16.16
A bag in which there was some seed and mustard	Four livres five sols	Madame Deschamp	Paid 4.5
A jug and two pots of earthenware, together with two other pots in which there was a little fat	Eight livres	Sieur Clermont, soldier	Promised to pay 8
A dish and four plates of earthenware, with two faience pots	Four livres fifteen sols	Madame Deschamp	Promised to pay 4.15
Twelve dishes, both large and small, with four plates of earthenware and one of faience	Six livres five sols	Sieur Andelort	Promised to pay 6.5
A barrel in which there were some raspberries, together with a small bag in which there were about six *livres* of sugar	Six livres ten sols	Madame LeLievre	Promised to pay 6.10
A quart in which there was some salted beef	Nine livres ten sols	Sieur Silvain	Paid 9.10
A quart in which there were about twelve pots of brandy	Twenty-six livres five sols	Sieur Clermont, soldier	Paid 26.5
A feather bed, a bolster and a woolen blanket	Twenty-four livres	Sieur Clermont	Promised to pay 24
Two woolen blankets with a small pillow	Seven livres ten sols	Madame Lagrenade	Promised to pay 7.10
Two men's coats of whitish woolen cloth	Eighteen livres five sols	Sieur Clermont	Promised to pay 18.5
A shovel for digging, a gridiron and a frying pan	Nine livres	Sieur Dupont	Promised to pay 9
A chaloupe compass along with seventeen bottles	Seven Livres	Sieur Clermont	Promised to pay 7
Two Fusils	Eighteen livres ten sols	Sieur Clermont	Paid 18.10
Another Fusil	Six livres ten sols	Pierre Boy	Promised to pay 6.10

Lot	Bid	Bidder	Paid
A small pair of balances with a two-*livre* weight, two large goblets and two small ones of crystal, a funnel, two small vials, a tin box and four faience plates, along with a laundry iron, together with two small boxes	Eleven livres ten sols	Sieur DesRoche	Paid 11.10
Two pails hooped with iron, along with four earthenware pots	Six livres	Sieur Niel	Promised to pay 6
A small tobacco mill, a small chest, and two lines with the leads	Seven livres	Sieur Laron	Promised to pay 7
Two brass candlesticks and a basket containing a little wire, along with a little blue starch	Eight Livres	Sieur Roche	Paid 8
About six livres of leaf tobacco	Four livres	Sieur Clermont	Paid 4
A pile of walnuts	Three livres fifteen sols	Pierre	Paid 3.15
A pair of pincers, a pair of tongs and other small items of old iron, together with two lines in poor condition	Three livres fifteen sols	Sieur Clermont	Paid 3.15
A small table with two little drawers	Four livres	Louis Coustar	Promised to pay 4
An empty hogshead and three small barrels, empty, with a tap	Six livres	Sieur Paris	Paid 6
An empty chest without a lock	Five livres fifteen sols	Tourain	Promised to pay 5.15
Another empty chest	Four livres	Sieur Duchenne	Paid 4
A pair of pattens and a pair of woolen stockings, half made, along with two balls of wool of the same color, a pair of grapnels and other items of old iron	Forty Sols	Niaport	Promised to pay 2

249.1 livres

And it being five o'clock, we adjourned the session and postponed the continuation of the said sale to next Monday, at nine o'clock in the morning; whereof a record was made.

Meyracq Bascaud Lartigue, Clerk

And this day, the fifth of September one thousand seven hundred and fifty-seven, at about nine o'clock in the morning, we, the aforesaid Bailli, at the request of the said King's Procurer, went in the company of him and the Clerk, attended by the Process Server of the Court, to the house of the said Sieur Paris, situated on Rue St. Louis in this city, to the apartment which the said Roze, deceased, had occupied in the same; where being, and having seen our order of the third day of this month, we caused bidders to be summoned by a drummer, following the usage of the colony; and several persons having assembled, we caused the conditions of the said sale, as explained elsewhere, to be read aloud to them; this done, we caused the following movables and effects to be put and exhibited for sale:

Auction of Marie Marguerite Roses' Possessions, 5 September 1757

Lot	Bid	Bidder	Paid
A cloak, with its hood of brown camlet	Nine livres	Madame Mathurin	Promised to pay 9
Five men's shirts	Sixteen livres ten sols	Sieur Mouline	Promised to pay 16
Six shirts, four women's and two men's	Ten livres ten sols	Madame Lagrenade	Promised to pay 10.10
Two waistcoats and vest of dimity	Six livres	Sieur Leveille	Paid 6
A petticoat of striped cotton and two calico mantelets	Five livres	Madame Deschamp	Paid 5
A cotton gown with a petticoat of embroidered cotton	Nine livres	Madame Deschamp	Paid 9
A mantelet of striped cotton and a petticoat of embroidered cotton	Twenty-four livres	Madame Chauvin	Promised to pay 24
A small *Blanchet* or vest of blue cloth, with a mantelet of striped cotton together with a petticoat of striped cotton	Nine livres ten sols	Sieur Desroches	Paid 9.10
A cloak hood with a petticoat of embroidered cotton	Twelve livres	Sieur Leveille	Paid 12
A coat of brown woolen cloth	Ten livres five sols	Sieur Desroche	Promised to pay 10.5
Ten handkerchiefs, including five of muslin and five colored ones	Eleven livres ten sols	Madame Desroche	Promised to pay 11
Ten pairs of cotton, wool, and Segovia stockings, very old, with one pair of silk, together with a few balls of wool	Eight livres ten sols	Sieur Leveille	Paid 8.10
A new pair of women's shoes, black, a muslin handkerchief, and twenty-give coifs and bonnets	Thirteen livres	Fidelle	Promised to pay 13

Lot	Bid	Bidder	Paid
Five soap balls and a small ink vessel of horn	Four livres five sols	Fidelle	Promised to pay 4.5
Two old calamanco petticoats, one of them red, a pair of panne trousers, with several remnants of several stuffs, a pincer or *forcelet*, together with a book entitled *Le cuisinier royal*, and old chest	Ten Livres	Sieur Monfort	Promised to pay 10
A chest with its lock and key	Six livres	Marie Louis	Paid 6
Two pairs of shoe buckles and garters, which were awarded with two necklaces	Eight livres ten sols	Sieur Monfort	Paid 8.10
A pair of women's shoes, black	Three livres fifteen sols	Fidelle	Promised to pay 3.15
A fusil	Eight livres fifteen sols	Pierre Camino	Paid 8.15
A stovepipe	Five livres five sols	Sieur Desroche	Promised to pay 5.5
A table with five straw-bottomed chairs	Ten livres	Madame Deschamp	Promised to pay 10
A long table with two benches	Four livres five sols	Lavigne	Paid 4.5
A small armoire or buffet with a dresser, which was awarded, along with some items of old iron, after several bids, as well as a *demi-corde* of wood, which was in the courtyard	Sixteen livres	Sieur Lavigne	Paid 16
A bedstead with a straw mattress in poor condition	Thirty sols	Madame Deschamp	Paid 1.10
The vegtables in the garden	Forty-four livres fifteen sols	Sieur Paris	Promised to pay 44.15
Two hogshead in poor condition and an empty barrel	For sols	Pierre Camino	Paid 2
Ten cloths or napkins, very worn with two old shirts	Five livres	Fidelle	Promised to pay 5

274.15 livres

And there being nothing else to sell, we adjourned the session; whereof a record was made, which we signed, with the King's Procurer.

Meyracq Bascaud Lartigue, Clerk

Definitions[28]	
Faience	Tin glazed earthenware made in France
Livres	An old French monetary unit equal to 20 sols
Sols	An old French coin equal to 12 deniers
Ratteen	Coarse loosely woven cloth
Mantelet	A very short cape
Petticoat	A skirt worn as an outer skirt formerly worn by women and small children
Muslin	A thinly and loosely woven cotton cloth
Segovia	A province in North-Central Spain
Pinchbeck	An alloy of copper and zinc used especially to imitate gold in jewelry
Quart	A vessel or measure having a capacity of one quart
Bedstead	The framework of a bed
Fusil	A light flintlock musket
Corselet	A piece of armor covering the trunk or an undergarment combining girdle and brassiere
Calamanco	A glossy woolen fabric of satin weave with striped or checkered designs manufactured from the 16th to the 19th centuries
Panne	A silk or rayon velvet with lustrous pile flattened in one direction — called also *panne velvet* or a heavy silk or rayon satin with high luster and waxy smoothness
Quintaux	Quintal or quintaux (pl) — a unit of weight. 1 quintal is equal to 48.95 kilograms
Chaloupe	A small French boat (as a ship's boat or harbor craft)
Demi-Chopine	Half pint
Pattens	a clog, sandal, or overshoe often with a wooden sole or metal device to elevate the foot and increase the wearer's height or aid in walking in mud
Grapnels	a small anchor with usually four or five flukes used especially to recover a sunken object or to anchor a small boat

Madame Labatiste

LA LORANS NEGRESSE DEMURANT
PROCHE DE LA PLACE DE LUISBOURG A LUISBOURG

[letter is copied out of order, reordered in this transcription]

A St Jean de Luz
Le 26 fevrier 175[7]

Madame je vous ecris deux lignes pour vous marquer letat de ma Senter La quelle est en Bon Etat dieu Mersy — je souhete que La votre en Soient de meme aussy bien que celle de monsieur votre epoux, je suis été pris par ~~Les~~ une frigatte englesse qui croyset devan Luisbourg nous a gardes deus mois dans son bord dans lequel temps nous avons relâché dans Lille Serjent englese se la ditte frigatte d'avec un courselle ils ont convoyé quarante quatre Batimans marchans pour Lisbonne et la lon nous a mis a terre par la grâce du Seigneur il nous a falu faire deux cens Lieux par terre pour nous rendre chez nous

Vous ferez valoir La procurasion que je vous ai lesse pour ma coffre — et ce quy est dedans vous en ferez une vente Sil me revien quelle chose vous m'en ferez une lettre de change pour ce que je vous doies peje vous tout premierement, la premiere prise que monsieur josef barret at amené a Luisbourg jen fis la decouverte il me revien un demy lot vous en parlerez a monsieur imbert je vous prie de fere mes compliments a monsieur votre epous--------------

Je vous souhette une parfette sente et je rest atendan Loneur de vous voier votre tres humble serviteur
Pierre Lapouble-----
Mon adresse est chez monsieur Simon Casoraan a st. Jean de Luz

Madame, I write you these two lines to let you know of the state of my health which is good, thank god — I hope that yours is the same as well as that of monsieur your husband. I was captured by an English frigate that was cruising off Louisbourg [and] … kept … on board for two months during which time we were kept [as prisoners] in the hold and then the frigate with another privateer convoyed forty four merchant ships into Lisbon where they put us ashore thank god. We had to walk two hundred leagues [966 kilometers] to get home.

You will use the procuration [power of attorney] that I left you in my trunk — and you will make a sale of that which is inside. If this brings me anything you will make a letter of exchange for that which I owe you, pay yourself first. The first prize the Monsieur Joseph Barret brought to

Louisbourg, I discovered and he owes me a half share. You can discuss this with Monsieur Imbert. I make my compliments to you and Monsieur your husband---
I wish you perfect health and I remain awaiting the honour of seeing you your very humble servant
Pierre Lapouble
My address is at the home of ....

NOTES

1. Marie Marguerite Rose's inventory is part of the Fortress of Louisbourg Historic site collection of documents that is now housed at the Beaton Institute at Cape Breton University. It is available at Archives Canada: Proces-Verbal de l'inventoire et vente des delaisser par la nomme Roze Negresse 27 aout 1757 [Report of the inventory and sale of the effects left by one Roze, a Negress, 27 August 1757], G2 vol 212, dossier 552, Arcives Nationales, Outre-Mer. It is also available online. See <http://data2.archives.ca/e/e053/e001323648.jpg> through <http: data2.archives.ca/e/e053/e001323661.jpg>.
2. *Code Noir* (1685) at <https://directory.vancoucer.wsu.edu/site/directory.vancouver.wsu.edu/files/insert_/webintern02/code%20noir.pdf>; for a general discussion of the *Code Noir* in New France, see Marcel Trudel, *Canada's Forgotten Slaves: Two Centuries of Bondage*, translated by George Tombs (Montreal Vehicle Press, 2013), pp. 119ff.
3. Marcel Trudel, *Canada's Forgotten Slaves*, 1960, p. 151.
4. Marcel Trudel, *Canada's Forgotten Slaves*, 1960, p. 161; Ken Donovan, "Slaves and Their Owners in Ile Royale, 1713–1760," *Acadiensis* xxv, n1 (1995), p. 5.
5. Marcel Trudel, *Canada's Forgotten Slaves*, 1960, p. 190.
6. For a full discussion of Angelique and the burning of Old Montreal, see Afua Cooper, *The Hanging of Angelique: The Untold Story of Canadian Slavery and the Burning of Old Montreal* (Toronto: Harper Perennial, 2006); "Torture and Truth," Great Unsolved Mysteries in Canadian History <canadianmysteries.ca>.
7. Afua Cooper, *The Hanging of Angelique*, 2006, p. 201.
8. Marcel Trudel, *Canada's Forgotten Slaves*, 1960, p. 179. See also Afua Cooper, *The Hanging of Angelique*, 2006, pp. 14–22.
9. Afua Cooper, *The Hanging of Angelique*, 2006, p. 159.
10. Marcel Trudel, *Canada's Forgotten Slaves*, 1960, p. 174.
11. Allan Greer, *The People of New France* (Toronto: University of Toronto Press, 1997), pp. 87–88.
12. Marcel Trudel, *Canada's Forgotten Slaves*, 1960, pp. 174–78.
13. According to Marcel Trudel, the average age at death of a black slave in Canada was 25.2 years. Marcel Trudel, *Canada's Forgotten Slaves*, 1960, p. 136.
14. Ken Donovan, "Slaves and Their Owners in Ile Royale," 1995, p. 29.
15. Ken Donovan, "Marie Marguerite Rose and Slavery in Louisbourg, 1713–1768" (unpublished manuscript, Parks Canada, Fortress of Louisbourg, 2010), p. 3ff. Parks Canada Historian, Anne Marie Lane Jonah, has noted that the quality of goods in

Marie's inn was respectable. She offered her patrons brandy, wine, salt beef, mustard and coffee together with a variety of fresh vegetables grown in her garden (personal communication with the author, June 6, 2014).

16. Marie Marguerite Rose Inventory. See document, p. 97–98.
17. Ken Donovan, "Marie Marguerite Rose and Slavery in Louisbourg, 1713–1768," 2010, p. 1.
18. Anne Marie Lane Jonah and Elizabeth Tait, "Filles D'Acadie, Femmes De Louisbourg: Acadian Women and French Colonial Society in Eighteenth-Century Louisbourg," *French Colonial History* Vol. 8 (2007), pp. 23–52; for a discussion and references to other inventories of women in Eighteenth-Century Louisbourg, see note 7, p. 40.
19. Ken Donovan, "Marie Marguerite Rose and Slavery in Louisbourg, 1713–1768," 2010, p. 17.
20. Ken Donovan, "Marie Marguerite Rose and Slavery in Louisbourg, 1713–1768," 2010, p. 18.
21. Ken Donovan, "Slaves and Their Owners in Ile Royale," 1995, p. 28.
22. The National Archives of the United Kingdom (TNA) Public Record Office (PRO) High Court of the Admiralty (HCA) 30/264/ Letter 32, Pierre Lapouble to Madame Labatiste Laurens, negresse.
23. TNA PRO HCA 30/264/Letter 32.
24. This observation is provided in a personal communication to the author from Parks Canada historian, Anne Marie Lane Jonah (May 13, 2014). Lane Jonah states that the level of business activities and amount of goods that are sold to Marie and her husband Joseph Laurent indicate that she was "ready to launch into business before she was emancipated." Marie knew many of the merchants in Louisboug through the Lippinot's connections, and she had the opportunity to gain a good deal of knowledge about running a business. Lane Jonah also states that "the Laurents demonstrated an unusually equal relationship in running [their] business, and they both had the trust of their clients." Marie established a singular relationship of trust among those she and her husband had business with. In addition to serving as an agent with power of attorney for Pierre Lapouble, Marie was also entrusted with 200 livres from a seafarer by the name of Jean Norais. This money was placed into her care before Norais entered into a privateering venture. See item 21, ff37–38v of the complete inventory (not reproduced here).
25. Donovan, "Slaves and Their Owners in Ile Royale," 1995, p. 4, 7, and 31.
26. Anne Marie Lane Jonah, "Unequal Transitions: Two Metis Women in Eighteenth-Century Ile Royale," *French Colonial History* 11 (2010), pp. 109–29; Peter N. Moogk, *The Making of French Canada—A Cultural History* (East Lansing: Michigan State University Press, 2000), pp. 143–76. The fact that Marie married Jean Baptiste Laurent, a Mi'kmaw hunter and trader, suggests that the life choices available to her as a newly empowered free woman reflected the diversity and multicultural character of eighteenth-century Louisbourg. Although we know very little about Laurent, it is likely that he had some trade dealings with Jean Loppinot, and through this association, he would have had an opportunity to enter into a relationship with Marie. Interestingly, after Marie's death, there is no record of Laurent's presence either at the official inventory or the auction of her estate.

27. 1 quintal is equal to 48.95 kg. Harold Innis cites the British price of code for 1722 at 10 shillings for 1 quintal, which is the equivalent of 10 French livres. 500–600 quintaux of cod equals approximately 7000 livres. See Harold Adams Innis, *The Code Fisheries: The History of an international Economy* (Toronto: University of Toronto Press, 1954), p. 168, note 79.
28. Merriam-Webster Online: Dictionary and Thesaurus.

Chapter 5

West Indian Immigration to Canada, 1900–1920
What the Census Figures Don't Tell Us

In his comprehensive study, *Blacks in Canada: A History,* Robin Winks observed that the late nineteenth and early twentieth century witnessed a dramatic decline in the numbers of Blacks in Canada. In the decades following the American Civil War, as many as two-thirds of the African American population returned to the United States, and citing the census records, he indicated that the Black population declined from 21,394 in 1881 to 16,194 in 1911.[1] Winks accurately noted that during the first two decades of the twentieth century there was a concerted effort on the part of both Liberal and Conservative governments to restrict Black immigration to Canada on the belief that darker skinned immigrants were unsuitable to the climate and culture of Canada. These factors, together with increased racist sentiments in many regions of the country, led Winks to conclude that the period from 1865 to 1930 represented the low point, "the nadir" in his words, of the Black experience in Canada.[2]

It has been nearly half a century since Winks wrote his pioneering history of Blacks in Canada. Recently, some observers have re-examined the census figures and the patterns of Black immigration during the early years of the twentieth century and concluded that Canada's Black population has been seriously underestimated. James Walker argues that "official records, including the census, provide inadequate data on the numbers and location of African Canadians. Terminology has been imprecise, and there was sometimes a deliberate effort to underestimate the Black population."[3] Walker has determined that, based on independent and local estimates, the actual number of Blacks in Canada during this period was approximately double the official census total.[4]

As we have seen, Canada's immigration policy during the early twentieth century was racially restrictive. Under the direction of the superintendent of immigration,

William D. Scott, the government's most favored first line of defence against the so-called "Negro Problem" was to exclude Black immigrants from Canada altogether. Scott and other government bureaucrats carefully monitored Black immigration, and local border agents were ordered to inhibit entry into Canada by enforcing strict medical and monetary immigration requirements. Despite these efforts, however, it is estimated that nearly 5,000 African American and West Indians passed the scrutiny of border inspectors and officially entered Canada from 1900 to 1916.[5] Almost three-quarters of these immigrants were West Indians who came to Canada in search of work and a better way of life: often educated and skilled workers, they settled in the major industrial centres of Toronto, Montreal and Sydney. Although the census of 1911 lists a total of 1,878 people of West Indian origin in Canada, we know that the West Indian population was substantially greater than this figure.[6] In addition to the nearly 4,000 West Indians who passed through Canada's borders, there were a countless number of other undocumented West Indian immigrants who arrived by ship at various ports in Atlantic Canada.

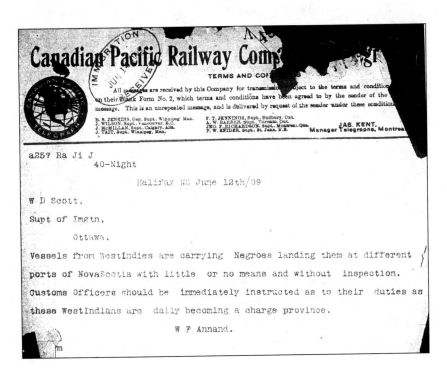

Reports of undocumented West Indian immigrants arriving on cargo vessels in port cities of Sydney, Glace Bay, Port Hawkesbury, Halifax and Saint John, New Brunswick, so alarmed William Scott that he appointed new immigration inspectors to monitor the situation and wrote letters to shipping agents, prospective employers and immigration inspectors, explaining the reasons for deeming Black immigrants undesirable to Canada. In a reply to a Brockville, Ontario, immigration inspector's inquiry about bringing domestic servants to Canada from British West Indies, Scott wrote: "After an experience of some years, both in Eastern and Western Canada, it was decided that coloured immigration was not an acquisition to this country, whether it be the immigration of domestics, farmers or persons of other occupations."[7] Scott went on to describe the efforts of his Department to deport Blacks who settled in Western Canada. He indicated that the same effort was being made to deport West Indian domestic immigration in eastern Canada. The primary reasons he gave in this letter for this deportation were "immorality and tuberculosis." In other correspondence, Scott argued that West Indians would become chronically unemployed and a public expense. For all these reasons, Scott viewed Black immigrants with racist distain and stated: "I think it is a distinct mistake to bring into Canada a class of people whose presence here constitutes a problem for all time."[8]

As a result of one investigation that Scott initiated, his agent in Nova Scotia, J.B. Williams, completed a report documenting the landing of West Indians by schooner over a three-month period from April to May 1909. The report named four schooners that arrived in Port Hawksbury bound for Sydney, Cape Breton, with a total of fifty-one undocumented West Indians. Scott and his Department of Immigration were particularly concerned that West Indian immigrants arriving by ship would not be able to find work and would become "a public charge." Williams made it clear in his report, however, that the West Indian immigrants who arrived in Port Hawkesbury "are of the better class, being well dressed and most of them following some trade." Williams indicated that "the men landing at Hawkesbury generally arrive in the morning, and take the afternoon train for Sydney where they endeavor to obtain work in the mines, or in the steel plant, or at various other occupations such as waiters in restaurants, carpenters, or in shoe-shine shops." A small proportion of the West Indians were young females, and Williams noted: "Negro girls have come over from time to time are in great demand as domestics, and those who have them in their employ speak highly of them."[9]

\05725

Yarmouth, N. S., June 29, 09.

W. D. Scott, Esq.,
   Supt. of Immigration,
      Ottawa, Ont.

Sir:-

Report re Landing of Negroes at Nova Scotia Ports.

As a result of information furnished me by Mr. Barnstad
I went to Port Hawksbury on Thursday June the 24th and met Mr.
Hennessey, the Collector of Customs at that port.

Since the first of April the total number of negroes from
the West Indies landed from schooners at Port Hawksbury bound for
Sydney, C. B. has been males 48 and females 3.

The names of the schooners and their captains and the
dates on which they arrived and the number of negroes are as follows:

Apr. 21   "Helen Stewart"   Capt. Miller   21 males 3 females
May 11   "Moravia"   Capt. Crooks   9 males
 "   18   " Annie Smith"   Capt. Lafuse   10 males
June 8   "Success"   Capt. Innis   8 males

Port Hawkesbury appears to be the principal port outside
of Halifax where the negroes have landed from the West Indies.   The
cost of the passage from Barbadoes to Hawkesbury is about $20 and
the negroes board themselves on the schooners whilst crossing.   I
understand the government of the Islands assists in the payment of
part of the passage to any of those wishing to leave, and the captains of the schooners receive the passage money, and not the owners
of the vessels.

Mr. Hennessey, who has himself visited the West Indies on

2.

many occasions, claims that the few negroes who have come to Hawkesbury, are of the better class, being well dressed and most of them following some trade.   The men landing at Hawkesbury generally arrive in the morning, and take the afternoon train for Sydney where they endeavor to obtain work in the mines, or in the steel plant, or at various other occupations such as waiters in restaurants, carpenters, or in shoe-shine shops.   Most of them appear to get work and the few that have returned have always taken the Plant Line of steamers from Hawkesbury to Boston.

I interviewed Mr. Crane the local agent of the Plant Line at Hawkesbury, and he informed me that so far as he was aware no objection was taken to the landing of these negroes in Boston, provided they paid the head tax of $4, and as far as he knew none of them had been returned for failing to fulfil that obligation.

The negro girls that have come over from time to time are in great demand as domestics, and those who have them in their employ speak highly of them.   Many of the families in Halifax have them engaged, and at Point Tupper just two miles from Hawkesbury, there are two of these girls working in the hotel, and are giving every satisfaction and appear to stand the winter weather all right, and many more could obtain employment in that district.

At NorthSydney I met Mr. Hickey the Dom. Immigration Agent, and he had no knowledge of any negroes becoming a public charge. He knew of several who are workin in the mines, some of them living in North Sydney.   He informed me that one captain had spoken about being over bringing over fifty negroes from Barbadoes to Sydney, but Mr. Hickey warned himthat if they did not get work and became a public charge he would have to take them back at his own expense.

3.

So far he has not attempted to bring them over.

In Sydney town I called on the Chief of the Police and he told me that no case had ever come under his notice of a negro from the West Indies becoming a public charge in that town. He was aware that there were some working in the mines and some in the town of Sydney following different trades. He spoke of them as always appearing on the streets well dressed, and as being very civil in their manner.

On my return to Halifax I called on Mr. Annand and he told me that he and his officers would watch the port of Halifax re the landing of these negroes.

Under these circumstances it appears to me that if Mr. Hennessey's appointment as Immigration Inspector at Hawkesbury which I have already recommended in a separate report meets with your approval, the chief port where these negroes have been landing will be watched.

I would recommend that extra copies of the Law and Regulations re Immigrants and also copies of the letter of June 4th sent to the various shipping companies be sent to:

John Hennessey, Collector of Customs, Port Hawkesbury,

Richard Hickey, Immigration Agent, North Sydney,

W. R. Cann, Customs Officer, Yarmouth,

These officers could then hand them personally to the captains of any schooners arriving at those ports from the West Indies with any further instructions you may deem necessary.

I remain,

Your obedient servant,

J. B. Williams.

The evidence from the records and first-hand observations indicate that, despite Scott's racist views and the efforts of his department to prevent Blacks from entering Canada and deporting those who were already in the country, there was, by land and by sea, a steady stream of Black immigration to Canada during the early years of the twentieth century. The demand for labour, especially during the war years of 1914–1918, served as a partial counterweight to Canada's racially restrictive immigration policy. Even superintendent Scott had to concede to the pressure from Canada's wartime industries. In a reply to an inquiry from the Inspector of Immigration Agencies in Annapolis Royal, Nova Scotia, Scott confirmed that his department had reluctantly granted the Dominion Steel and Coal Company in Sydney "the privilege of bringing in 1,000 coloured labourers from the West Indies. It was represented to the Government that it was absolutely necessary to bring in this coloured help as every effort had been made, without success, to get suitable labour from other sources." Scott stated that, given the need for the wartime production of steel, allowing West Indians to meet the high demand for labour was "the lesser evil." He concluded by stating: "You can readily understand how unwilling we would be here to make the concession under any but the strongest reasons."[10]

Notwithstanding the demand for labour during the war years, West Indian immigration to Canada during this period should be seen as part of a much larger movement of population from rural regions of the world to urban areas of North America. The urban industrial transformation in North America that began in the late nineteenth century attracted immigrants from Great Britain, Europe, the Middle East and the West Indies. It also provided the catalyst for the Great Migration that brought 6 million Blacks from the rural areas of the American south to the industrial cities of the north from 1910 until 1960.[11]

In cities like St. Louis, Detroit and Chicago, the presence of large numbers of Blacks was a source of racial tension, and the exclusion of Blacks from white urban neighbourhoods created ghettoes that became the hallmark of most industrial cities of the northern United States. Although these urban Black enclaves where the direct consequence of racial segregation, they also helped foster an emerging sense of racial pride and assertiveness among Blacks. Urban ghettos like Harlem in New York City became incubators for a racial awareness and self-identity called the "New Negro" as well as a Black cultural renaissance that lasted for several decades. The Harlem Renaissance inspired a similar revival of Black culture in Montreal, and during the nineteen thirties and forties, the city became renowned for its nightclubs that featured Black jazz and dancing. The Black entertainment industry in Montreal was also a major source of employment, and it attracted large numbers of West Indians from other regions of the country.[12]

In the United States, the assertiveness and aspirations of the "New Negro" translated into a collective action in support of civil rights. The older strategy of

LMF/IB.   810666 Imm.

Copy for Dr. Ellis,   23rd May, 1912.
       Mr. Lantalum.

Sirs,

   I understand that you were the consignees lately
of a vessel named the "Yolande" or"Yolando" which arrived
at St. John, N. B., on the 7th instant with 38 passengers.
I understand that the vessel is one of 172 tons register,
and that she is built for cargo carrying solely and has no
passenger accommodation and, with the exception of one state-
room certified for the master and the forecastle accommodation for the crew, the only available space is the hold of
the vessel, which was in this case partially filled with
rock ballast, and the passengers either lived on top of this
ballast or about the deck as the weather permitted.

   In this connection I wish to draw your attention
to the provisions of the immigration act and regulations

Enc. of Canada, a copy of which I send you herewith, and I may

SENT say that if your vessel proposes to engage in the passenger
P.R.V. traffic, it will be necessary to have the immigration regulations complied with in all respects.

   I would like to hear from you in this connection
at your earliest convenience.

     Your obedient servant,

        Superintendent of Immigration.

Messrs. The L. C. Prince Co., Ltd.,
  St. John, N. B.

Immigration Branch

Department of the Interior

Canada

St. John, N. B., July 25th 1912.

Sir,-

I beg to inform you that the Schooner Yolanda arrived today with 25 passengers, colored residents of Barbadoes coming to settle in Canada.

Earlier this season this schooner came here bringing a number of the same class of passengers for whom no provision was made for living accomodation in accordance with the requirements of the Immigration Act.

The matter was brought to the owner's attention at the time, the Department having written both owner and agents on the matter.

I called the Captain's attention to this matter again and he promises not to bring any more passengers here.

This schooner has been sold the new owner being B. Hope Ross, Barbadoes.

W. D. Scott, Esq.,
Superintendent of Immigration,
Ottawa.

Your Obedient Servant,

Dominion Immigration Agent.

32439

TELEGRAPH.

HBR/ER.   24126 Imm.

Department of the Interior,

Ottawa, 17th July, 1914.

881539

L. M. Fortier,
    Annapolis Royal,
        Nova Scotia.

Reported that natives of Barbados arriving
at Halifax and Dartmouth in large numbers. Proceed
to points immediately, impress upon our officers
necessity of strict enforcement of all regulations
to prevent influx of general labouring class. Report
action by wire.

W. D. Scott.

Sent 10.35 a.m. O'clock

By .... line

Per ....

Chg. Interior (Imm.)

B 20735

Woodstock, N.B. July 27th, 1914

The Superintendent of Immigration,

Ottawa, Canada.

Sir:--

Your telegram of the 20th inst.,
"In connection with the reported arrival of West Indian
Negroes,go to Glace Bay,and interview J.C.Douglas,M.P.P",
reached me at Halifax,and I proceeded without delay to
carry out these instructions. I had a talk with Mr.Douglas,
in his office at Glace Bay,on the 21st inst.,and satisfied
him that the Department was doing everything possible to meet
the situation. It is an undoubted fact that too many of these
West Indian Negroes are coming in. There are some hundreds of
them employed in the works of the Dominion Iron & Steel Co.,
and the Dominion Coal Co.,and scores of others hanging about
unemployed. Our Officers,both at Halifax and St.John,were under
the impression that they were bound to admit these people if
they passed the medical examination and had twenty-five dollars
in hand and ticket to destination,but in view of recent correspondence with the Department I have given instructions to let
no West Indian Negroes be admitted at all but that all are to be
rejected as l.p.c. I found plenty of evidence at Sydney that
the possession of twenty-five dollars on arrival was no proof
that the West Indian Negro would not become a public charge and
I trust this action will be approved and sustained by the
Department.

The Royal Mail Steam Packet Company.

(ROYAL CHARTER, DATED 26TH SEPTEMBER 1839.)

AGENTS,
W. THOMSON & C⁰

CABLE ADDRESS.
"ROYMAILPAC, ST. JOHN. N.B".

CODES.
WATKIN'S, SCOTT'S, LIEBER'S,
A.J. STANDARD.

Your reference

B 22139

St. John............. July 28th PM, 1914.
New Brunswick.

Reference

W. S. Scott, Esq.,
    Superintendent Immigration,
        Ottawa, Ont.

Dear Sir:-

We confirm our wire advising that the Royal Mail Steam Packet "CHALEUR" has arrived to-day from the West Indies and nine colored passengers have been detained. These passengers have full money requirements and have passed medical examination, and as they left points of embarkation before word of the recent regulations could be sent to the respective agents we trust you will issue instructions to Immigration Agent here, Mr. J. V. Lantalum, for their immediate release. As you are probably aware, the Immigration Buildings in this city are now closed and the passengers are having to be kept on the steamer at a great inconvenience and considerable expense.

                Yours truly,

                WILLIAM THOMSON

                Per

                    Agents.

IMMIGRATION
JUL 30 1914
RECEIVED.

WRL/JR   810666 Imm.

4 1 8 6 5

14th August, 1914.

Copy for Mr. E. J. Williams.

Sir,

I am in receipt of your letter of the 6th
instant in which you ask as to what procedure has to be
taken to obtain permission for the landing in Canada of
immigrants from the West Indies, and what conditions
have to be met by these people.

In reply I beg to inform you that owing to
the present labour conditions in Canada, persons of negro
origin from the West Indies are considered by the Department as persons likely to become a public charge. If
evidence can be produced to the effect that these immigrants
are going to assured employment and that such labour cannot
be obtained in Canada, immigrants of the above class would
not, of course come under the provisions of the above
section, provided they otherwise complied with the provisions
of the Act. In all such cases, however, I would ask you
to submit evidence before immigrants of the above class
are brought forward.

Your obedient servant,

W. D. Scott

Superintendent of Immigration.

Messrs. Young & Lorway,
181 Charlotte St.,
Sydney, N.S.

ADDRESS :
THE SUPERINTENDENT OF IMMIGRATION
OTTAWA

IN YOUR REPLY REFER TO NO. 886683 Imm

KINDLY DO NOT WRITE OF MORE THAN
ONE SUBJECT IN ANY ONE LETTER

FCB/LIC.

Ottawa, 7th November, 1914.

Copy for Mr. J.V. Lantalum.
　　File No.889473.
　　　　889421.
　　　　810666. /\

Sirs,

　　　　I duly received your wire of the 3rd instant
regarding the case of Arabella Edwards and Lillian Smith
ex "Caraquet" at St. John, N.B.　These two coloured
domestics were permitted to go forward to their respective
destinations.

　　　　I understand that on the same boat Joseph De
Pombo and wife, Portuguese Africans, applied for entry and
have been rejected as not being able to comply with our
Regulations.

　　　　On various occasions in the past I have called
attention to the fact that the Government does not encourage
the immigration of coloured people.　There are certain countries from which immigration is encouraged and certain races
of people considered as suited to this and its conditions, but
Africans, no matter where they come from are not among the races
sought, and, hence, Africans no matter from what country they
come are in common with the other uninvited races, not admitted
to Canada unless they comply fully with all the provisions of
the Immigration Act.

　　　　It is very essential that at the present time we
do not admit persons who are likely to add to the congestion
already keenly felt in many parts of the Dominion.　Our experience with coloured domestics is not reassuring as we have
had

Messrs. Pickford & Black,
　　Steamship Agents,
　　　　Halifax, Nova Scotia.

had to deport a large number on the ground of moral
and physical unfitness.

I think it is altogether in the interest
of Canada to discontinue this class of immigration and
I trust you will _issue_ appropriate instructions to your agents
in the West Indies and elsewhere.

Your obedient servant,

Superintendent of Immigration.

36172

FCB/IB.

810666 Imm.

16th September, 1915.

Sirs,

I have had referred to me by Sir Joseph Pope, a copy of your letter of the 8th instant, asking about the admission to Canada of two coloured women coming from Jamaica.

There is no head tax or landing tax demanded by the Dominion Government, but I may say to you frankly that we do not encourage the immigration of coloured people, as our climate and other conditions are not suitable. This decision was arrived at after years of experience, and our advice to steamship agencies is to refrain from encouraging any immigration of coloured people. There are plenty of white domestics to be had in Canada and, if the supply runs short, we can very easily get more from the British Isles or certain European countries. Such people would be a permanent asset to the country, and I trust that with this explanation you will endeavour to co-operate with us in our policy.

Your obedient servant,

W. D. Scott

Superintendent of Immigration.

Messrs. Thos. Cook & Son,
65 Yonge Street,
Toronto, Ont.

810666 Imm.

FCB/MBR   25th April, 1916.

Sir,

I am in receipt of your letter of the
11th instant, in which you make inquiries concerning
the bringing of domestic servants, coloured, from St.
Kitts, British West Indies.

In reply, I beg to state that, after an
experience of some years, both in Eastern and Western
Canada, it was decided that coloured immigration was
no acquisition to this country, whether it be the
immigration of domestics, farmers or persons of other
occupations. The movement to the West assumed con-
-siderable proportions and it was not long after it
started before we began to deport coloured people.
The same is true about coloured domestic immigration
to the East and the particular causes for deportation
have been immorality and tuberculosis.

I think it is a distinct mistake to bring
into Canada a class of people whose presence here
constitutes a problem for all time. Although just at
present it is difficult to obtain many European women,
this condition is but temporary and, after the close
of the war, I fancy that, with the smallest amount of
effort, we will be able to secure a plentiful supply

of splendid

F.C. Knight, Esq.,
     Immigration Inspector,
          Brockville, Ontario.

-2-

of splendid women who will be an asset to Canada.
Some like coloured domestics because they are
cheaper, but the Department never relaxes the
regulations to encourage that class of immigration
and any who apply to you should be encouraged to
employ white help.

Your obedient servant,

W. D. Scott

Superintendent of Immigration.

FCB/FS.

ADDRESS:
THE SUPERINTENDENT OF IMMIGRATION
OTTAWA

IN YOUR REPLY REFER TO No. 910890

KINDLY DO NOT WRITE OF MORE THAN
ONE SUBJECT IN ANY ONE LETTER

Ottawa, 10th August, 1916.

for General file re emig's of coloured people from West Indies 810666

Copy for the Dominion Steel and Coal Company to file.

Sir,

I beg to say in answer to your letter of the 31st ultimo, that the Dominion Steel and Coal Company got from the Department some weeks ago the privilege of bringing in 1,000 coloured labourers from the West Indies. It was represented to the Government that it was absolutely necessary to bring in this coloured help as every effort had been made, without success, to get suitable labour from other sources. The production of steel and coal must go on even at some expense to the country, and the concession is made on the principle of being the lesser evil. You can readily understand how unwilling we would be here to make the concession under any but the strongest reasons.

Your obedient servant,

Superintendent of Immigration.

L.M. Fortier, Esq.,
    Inspector of Immigration Agencies,
        Annapolis Royal,
            Nova Scotia.

A-61260

Government Immigration Agency.

Halifax, N.S., *May 26th* 19*10*

IMMIGRATION
MAY 28 1910
RECEIVED
30

Sir:

I learn on good authority, and beg to inform you that the Schr. *Marion* from Barbadoes landed at Port Hawkesbury twenty five Negros for point in Cape Breton. Of course these may have been properly examined by an officer, but as this is the time of year that quite a number of them come in schooners I thought it well to advise you.

Your Obedient Servant
W H Barnstead
Jr. Agent

W.D. Scott Esq,
Supt. of Imm
Ottawa

2 x 1 2 6
do
810967

patience, accommodation and gradual change that had been expressed by leaders like Brooker T. Washington gave way to the demand for immediate action and racial "uplift" through programs aimed at Black economic development. In 1909, Black intellectual W.E.B. Du Bois and a group of white sympathizers founded the National Association for the Advancement of Colored People (NAACP), and over the remaining course of the twentieth century, the organization led a sustained fight for racial equality and created numerous initiatives to improve the lives of African Americans.[13]

In Canada, there were similar expressions of racial pride and efforts to achieve "racial uplift."[14] In addition to the Black fraternal associations such as the Masonic Order, which included the Elks, Templers and Oddfellows, there were several self-protective organizations that were formed in order to actively promote racial equality. In 1917, the Colored Political and Protective Association was formed in Montreal, which sought to encourage its member to become politically involved and to support sympathetic candidates for elected office. During the same period, The Colored Protective Association was founded in Calgary that fought to resist racial segregation in housing. In 1923, the Canadian League for the Advancement of Colored People (CLACP) was established in Ontario, and like the NAACP, it developed a broad-based strategy to fight all forms of racial discrimination. The League also sponsored *Dawn of Tomorrow*, a Black national newspaper that served as the official voice of the CLACP for almost forty years.[15]

Most Black activist organizations during this period were created in order to address local and provincial concerns, and with the exception of the CLACP, they did not have a national presence. There was, however, one additional organization, the Universal Negro Improvement Association (UNIA), that had national as well as international appeal, especially among the West Indian population. Jamaican-born immigrant Marcus Garvey founded the Harlem-based UNIA in 1919. The organization is primarily known as an American and Caribbean Black nationalist movement that sought to establish an independent homeland for Blacks to return to in Africa. Recent scholarly research, however, indicates that the UNIA was also a distinctly Canadian movement with a significant presence in almost all regions of the country. During the first three years of its existence, the UNIA spread rapidly to West Indian and African Canadian communities from Sydney to Vancouver. By 1922, the Canadian UNIA had an estimated membership of 5000 and there were thirty-two separate divisions in Nova Scotia, New Brunswick, Quebec, Ontario, Manitoba, Saskatchewan, Alberta and British Columbia.[16] Until recently, the extent and influence of the UNIA in Canada has not been well understood, and this may partially explain why Winks regarded the early decades of the twentieth century as the "nadir" of the Black experience in Canada.

The success of the UNIA in Canada rested less on the adherence of its members to Marcus Garvey's pan-African nationalist ideology and more on the organization's ability to meet the needs and aspirations of local Black communities in Canada. James Walker notes: "In Canada the UNIA had its greatest appeal among West Indians, and, while the literal back-to-Africa message was effectively overlooked, a range of Black- consciousness activities was unleashed."[17] The UNIA sponsored a host of cultural, social and sporting events and created several auxiliary service organizations including the Black Cross Nurses, which provided first aid training for Black women who were denied access to the nursing profession in Canada during this period.

The Black Man

A MONTHLY MAGAZINE OF NEGRO THOUGHT AND OPINION

Edited by MARCUS GARVEY, D.C.L.,

Founder and President-General of the Universal Negro Improvement Association,
2, Beaumont Crescent, London, W.14, England.

SUBSCRIPTION RATES:

One Year	...	...	...	...	...	$1.50c.
Half-Year	...	...	...	...	...	75c.
In England	...	...	...	...	...	—

Payable in advance.

Vol. III.	JULY, 1938.	No. 10

EDITORIAL.

JOE LOUIS.

When Schmeling technically whipped Joe Louis in the first fight some time ago, Hitler and German people hurrahed. They had fixed up Schmeling to give Joe Louis the German blow of superiority, and true to his colours Schmeling rose to the occasion; but all this was done whilst Joe was not fully conscious of his responsibility to his race.

We wrote critically of the matter although we greatly admired Joe Louis, in that we regard him as being one of our messengers of goodwill throughout the world. The tables are now turned. Joe has had time for reflection and for the appreciation of the responsibility our race has placed upon his shoulders. Giant-like, he rose in the American stadium on the 22nd June and delivered the punches to Schmeling that are typical of our race in true action. In that knock out blow the hopes of the German people were shattered and a Negro rose triumphant in the great wilderness of prejudice.

We must pay homage to the American Negro for the grand place he occupies in the realm of sports. Not only in sports but in many other vocations the Negro of America stands out pre-eminently. He is our international leader and we take the greatest amount of pride in complimenting Joe Louis as the representative of the ring.

From the reports that have reached us, Joe's determination was buoyed by the fact that he was taken unawares as it was on the first occasion. He had in his mind the thought of revenge and why shouldn't he. The German people led by Hitler did their utmost to make him feel not only inferior but a worm. At the time he knew he could have whipped Schmeling, but he was off guard and so meeting him again has given him the opportunity to prove to the Germans and to the world that in every detail he is a worthier and abler man than the German Schmeling. We take pride in saluting the champion.

PASSING OF A GREAT MAN.

It is with the deepest regret we have learnt of the death of Arthur A. Schomburg, the celebrated Negro scholar and curator of the division of Negro literature, history and prints of the W. 135th Street Public Library of New York.

THE BLACK MAN. 7

It has been brought forcibly home to the British public that things are not well within the Empire and there is a growing need for Imperial readjustment. We feel that Jamaica, and not only Jamaica, the entire British West Indies, will benefit from the recent strikes in Jamaica. This is óur hundredth year of emancipation of the West Indies and outside of any other consideration the rise of the Jamaica labourer in the hundredth year of his freedom is about to mark an epical change in his condition.

There is one thing to be considered. The Jamaica labourer will not go back to the position he came out of in the strike. It is true that in the main he is ignorant, but nevertheless if proper attention were paid to his educational development he would have been able to act differently not only in strikes but in questions calling for his opinion. It is evident now that he is at any rate recognized as a man. As such a man he has expressed himself. The old leadership that has fooled him may well stop to think. By his determination he must go forward with better intelligence and better organization, and we do feel that such will be supplied him.

We wish for the Jamaicans all that is good and nothing less for the people of British Guiana.

MARCUS GARVEY SPEAKING IN MENELIK HALL, SYDNEY, NOVA SCOTIA.

THE WORK THAT HAS BEEN DONE.

The meeting started with a musical programme. Among those present on the platform were the Mayor of Sydney, the Rev. Ford the Chairman, the Hon. Mr. Morrison, M.L.C., Officers of the Divisions, and the Choir.

The Rev. Ford said: Your Hon. President-General, Your Worship, Ladies and Gentlemen: At this meeting, the first of a series that the Hon. Marcus Garvey is going to deliver, I stand before you expressing a peculiar and personal greeting to him this evening. We extend greetings to you from this City of Sydney and Cape Breton. In the person of the Hon. Marcus Garvey we have a man of the race who is conscious of his task. In him we have a captain at the helm. He has been called to administer to the people of African descent. He is a tried and true captain. We send our sons and daughters to college because they must cope with conditions. You must answer whether this race is ready for true leadership. We must hope for that time when every man of the race can say, "I am the master of my fate, I am the captain of my soul."

There was a musical programme, after which the Chairman called upon His Worship, Mayor Mather, to say a few words.

Mavor Mather: Rev. Mr. Chairman, Hon. Mr. Garvey, Ladies and Gentlemen: I think that this is the second time that it has been my pleasure and privilege to meet you in this hall. I was present at the opening of this hall and I was pleased to have been here. It was a pleasure just as it is now to be with you again. When the committee asked me to be here tonight to say a few words to your President-General I was glad in the first place because I have the opportunity of welcoming him and in the second because I would be allowed to be present to hear the stirring message which I am sure he will deliver to you tonight. On behalf of the citizens of the city of Sydney I extend to you a very cordial welcome to our city of Sydney and hope your stay will be a pleasant one and the message will be of such a nature as will induce you to gird your loins about you and accomplish greater things than they have done so far. The coloured colony in this city is one of which you may well be proud. All you have to do is to look around and see this hall that they have built for themselves, and it is theirs and theirs alone. This is a hall which any group of citizens in any community in Canada may well be proud. It shows what can be done with united effort on the part of any group. There is one great thing about your colony here. It is a minority colony. The object lesson to be drawn, therefore, is that while granting to the community the same rights, you should stick together in forwarding your own race. If

8   THE BLACK MAN.

you do that there is no limit to which you will not reach. If you bicker and are jealous of each other you cannot accomplish much. One of the first principles you must have is unity among yourselves because you are a minority group among other large groups. I am glad Mr. Garvey has come to this part of the country, and I am glad to be here to welcome him and to listen to his message. I thank you very much.

Mr. Ford : Your message has been a stimulant to each and every one of us this evening. (A piano solo was rendered.) I will now call on him who by the guidance of God will say much that will be uplifting and inspiring.

Mr. Garvey : Citizens of Sydney, Ladies and Gentlemen : This is the first time I have had the opportunity of visiting Nova Scotia. In my administrative capacity as President-General of the U.N.I.A. I have had to deal with communications and business matters going through the many Divisions or Branches of the Association in this section. Not having the privilege of knowing you personally and individually, I have had the privilege of knowing some of you by correspondence. I was very pleased at the hearty reception you gave me this morning, but tonight I am flattered with the genuine and spontaneous hospitality extended to me, evidenced by your large and truly representative gathering. I understand that the group of you who live in this section of Canada asked your Mayor to extend to me your goodwill, not only yours but those who could not find it possible to get here. Indeed I am flattered, indeed I am pleased, and I want to assure you I shall never forget this my first appearance in Sydney and in Nova Scotia.

I have come here to you from the Parent Organization with Headquarters in London as part of a tour I am making in the interest of the Organization. I came to Canada about six weeks ago direct to Toronto to preside over a regional Conference of the Organization of the American and Canadian Branches. I can only spend a short time in your midst. I am visiting two other Divisions — Glace Bay and New Waterford. On the 7th I sail for the West Indies to speak in those Islands of the Leeward and Windward group and British Guiana. The U.N.I.A. is engaged in presenting its programme for the next twenty years. We have just passed the first twenty years with glorious achievements. The first twenty years reveal that this Organization did more in this twenty years than any movement since we lost our imperial power in Africa. We brought a consciousness to the race that never existed before. We organized our race throughout the world without the exception of one spot. Africa, the West Indies, the United

States, South and Central America, wherever the Negro was to be found the U.N.I.A. reached him and took to him a consciousness of his race and of his responsibility. In the past twenty years we have given consciousness to the race professionally and otherwise. There are people who would not think of their success but for the inspiration they receive from the U.N.I.A. Thousands in the professions, in the Civil Service of the Colonial powers, who never would have had a chance but for the advocacy of the U.N.I.A. which we call the first epoch of the U.N.I.A.

I come to you with the best of fellowship, with the best of spirit, with the desire that you maintain that good relationship with the good Canadians with whom you live.

Mr. Mayor, I thank you very much, sir, for your welcome and for the way you have plainly stated the case of our group here. Indeed, they are a minority and a small minority at that. I hope we will all realize it. Minorities wherever they happen to find themselves should unite because they are in the midst of a majority. The temper of the majority cannot always be guaranteed even with the best Government. We have had evidence of that in Germany and in other continental countries. Minorities must be very thoughtful in living in the midst of majorities. Your conduct must be of such as to leave no loophole to constitute you an annoyance to the majority, as to give the majority the idea that you are not a people to be in their midst. Alien minorities are always at a disadvantage because they are not in their homeland. We have our homes and we have one principal home; and that home is Africa. That home is disturbed today —the peace of it—the intrusion of others. Our respective homes have been intruded upon. The result is that a large number of us are abroad because of those circumstances and conditions. But wherever we go as a race we have always maintained the peace. We have never been the aggressors in any society or any form of government. We have been always a peaceful people, sir, and I feel sure you will never find fault with those who live in Sydney. We are not Communists, we are not Reds of any kind. We are just working in co-operation with others. We are radicals though in connection with our country. We want to restore our country to its ancient glory. We are seeking to restore the land of our fathers. We came here not by our will—we were pulled here. We had a terrible time in those early days. We did our bit under difficult circumstances here to build up the glory of the race that enslaved us at the time. We contributed a lot to that civilization. If for

138 Viola Desmond's Canada

nothing else that race owes us a lot. We think there is no country more able to help us than Canada. Canada has always played a fair game. Canada is conscious of the wrong that was imposed upon us to help build up the civilization of which Canada is a part. We were brought to lay the prop of the present civilization. We toiled for it. We bore on our shoulders the heavy burden of this civilization. Cane, sugar, rum, cotton, were the industries on which the present civilization was built. We carried the load upon our shoulders. If a picture were to be shown as to how the present civilization was built you will find the Negro holding it up. We are glad that you are giving the Negro a chance in Sydney. The U.N.I.A. realizes that it has a responsibility not only to the group but to the world at large to place the Negro in his proper place. You, sir, and all, do realize that our world is undergoing changes now — very important changes—changes that are affecting all groups. The changes in the world today are affecting all groups of men. This has led to the particular group seeking its way out. The Jews are seeking the way out; the Japanese, the Chinese, the Hindu, the black man, is seeking his way out, but we are seeking our way out in a different way to other people. We believe in the law of reason and not in the law of the gun. We believe the gunsman is a dangerous man to society anywhere. We believe that nature never intended man to be a gunsman or the Creator would have given him a pistol in the Garden of Eden. The use of the pistol is contrary to the laws of nature, and we do not believe in going contrary to nature. We believe nature is a mighty power. She acts carefully and slowly but she grinds positively. We believe nature is on our side. If we keep within the laws of nature, that first cause and that Almighty Power will in time take care of the human situation. We are not using any pistols where we are. I do not know if in the whole of Sydney you will find five pistols among Negroes. I believe you will find more Bibles and Prayer Books than pistols. Whether with or without pistols, the Negro is looking up for his place in the world and I feel sure no self-respecting white man will blame him. We have been the most faithful servants, whether in the stable or in the mines. We have never been disagreeable workers anywhere. We have worked in this Western world to help others, and we feel that the conscience of others will cause them to help us. So long as Canada is Canada and the Negro lives here, he will be a good citizen. But like the Irish in Canada, he has to be thinking of that homeland across the seas. Not that he will think of going there, but he is helping to restore the land of

his fathers. The Irish Canadian has helped to restore Ireland, although he has not disturbed Canada. He thinks he should bestow some rights on Ireland. Although we have been away for three hundred years, yet we still have a feeling for the homeland.

In 1928 when I was at the League of Nations, among the many statesmen who gave encouragement to us was the then Prime Minister, the Hon. McKenzie King. He then assured me of his goodwill toward our cause, and he has ever been a good friend to our cause. *(A voice: He has to be elected next election.) So long as you have good men like the Hon. McKenzie King you will get your rights as citizens.

Scientists said once that the Negro was the missing link, but now they realize that the Negro is the oldest man in creation. He is so old that he is black, and everything darkens by age, therefore he could not be the missing link. Something must be missing from his link. That the Negro is old and that accounts for his colour there is a lot behind it. Because once upon a time we were a great people. We built the Pyramids and the Sphinx. When history is written in truth you will find that the first civilization was projected from the Nile on the Congo Basin. In the earliest dawn of civilization you found the Negro in Benin, in Timbuktoo, in Alexandria. Anthropologists will tell you that the Pharaohs were black men. When they dug up the mummy of Tutankhamen and saw he was a black man they would not tell the truth. Civilization went across the north to Europe to India, to China, all the way down and proved that the black man had circumnavigated the world. The North American Indian, the Australian Aboriginal, the Aztecs of South America were all people who became what they were through the contact of Africans who had travelled across the continents when they were carrying their civilization, just as how the great white man is travelling around the world to-day and planting the evidence of his race, but before modern history was written and produced in the different continents there were different shades of colour, each had their original civilization. I like all great people we fell. The present civilization is not the only one that existed, but before this we had Roman civilization, Greek civilization, Persian civlzation, Babylonian civilization and even medieval Egyptian civilization, but the Negro civilization anti-dated that. The African went down with his blundering civilization, the Persian, the Greek, the Roman all went down and we do not know how long this civilization will stand with its Mussolinis and its Hitlers. Civilization is a cycle. It changes. I should like to see black and white get on so well together that the black man will remember how

10   **THE BLACK MAN**

kind he was. It is the only way we are going to get along because man is man for that. The white man is no missing link, nor the black man, nor the yellow man either. Surely no animal could achieve what Marconi did, what Edison did, what the great engineers did, what the great scientists did. Surely no man could do what the Japanese are doing, no missing link could do what Carver is doing at Tuskegee. He is the greatest chemist to-day, who can bring out of one product so many chemicals. No monkey could do what the brown bomber did to the Welshman. If man will let a monkey beat him then he is lower than a monkey. We are men whether we are white, yellow or black, because we have one origin. We came from the same place and we are going back to the same place. The negro went to sleep for a long while, resting from his labours, but he slept too long, so everybody stole a march on him and therefore he is the only man without a country; and so the U.N.I.A. seeks to restore the Negro to his own vine and fig tree. Economically, for his own interest, the white man will not like it, but deep down in his heart he will say that the Negro is right. I would like to see Canada for the Canadians, England for the English, America for the Americans and in the same way I want to see Africa for the Africans, those at home and those abroad, so that when we are sick and tired and weary we may lay our heads in the lap of our mother and ask her to comfort us, bless us before we die. Every people should have a flag, a land of their own, and the U.N.I.A. points you to achieve something. A large number of you were and are members and I bring you the greetings of those in the other parts of the world.

We are going to emancipate ourselves from mental slavery because whilst others might free the body, none but ourselves can free the mind. Mind is your only ruler, sovereign. The man who is not able to develop and use his mind is bound to be the slave of the other man who uses his mind, because man is related to man under all circumstances for good or for ill. If man is not able to protect himself from the other man he should use his mind to good advantage. The fool will always pay the price. The fool will always carry the heavy burden. The fool will always be crushed without a tear from God or man because God Almighty never made a fool. God is all wise. When God Almighty made man in His own image and likeness, it wasn't the physical, it was the mind that was like God. Every man represents God in his unitary intelligence. When man abuses that intelligence he lowers himself. God has given you intelligence to take care of you. He hasn't repeated Himself yet. God was so thought-

ful of man and his progeny that he made a variety of things so as to pander to the taste of the Adams that would come after the first. When God made you He made you the masters of the world, not serfs and slaves, but your mind must be developed intelligently. It is your mind that rules the body. You cannot go further than that mind to seek truth and to know truth and to re-act to truth. That is the only way you will be able to protect your group. The white man is still doing research work with his mind. It has taken him to the bowels of the earth to extract what nature placed there for him. On that same intelligence he has gone into Heaven. What you see in Sydney, in Nova Scotia is only the fringe of the white man's intelligence. Everything that you see that is methodical is the product of the white man's mind. He visualises nations and kingdoms and he has them. There is nothing spiritual around his materialism. They are all objective things realised, dreamt and thought out. Sydney is only what men have visualised to a greater extent. The British Empire was the visualisation of men like Raleigh, and Drake, who, seeing things of value, attached them to the mother country. If places are not well protected then men take them and add them to their Empires. The U.N.I.A. is dreaming of a day when the Negro will possess himself of a homeland, when he will build for himself. The man who cannot build for himself is not only a poor fish in the sea, but ultimately will be a dead fish, plodding for himself. Nobody wants to die except the fool, because life is a worth-while thing. It is only people who are together can survive now-a-days. It is only by organising that we can get anywhere, as the Mayor told you. We are looking for the redemption and the freedom of our homeland. (We hope, sir, to invite you to Sydney, in Africa, because there we shall have different things than you have in Canada.)

Our obsession is like that of the Jews. They are working for Palestine. We are working for Africa, like the Irishman, he is working for Ireland, and the Canadian is working for a grand and noble Canada. We are helping to send on the great force of power of Canadian industry when the Canadians will realise that they too can help us to do some good as we have been helping them to do some good. We have been helping to build and up to now we are not dead, we have not fallen. The Negro has the power of resistance. He can do the job. I feel sure, as you have done in the past, you will continue in the future, whether I come here or not. Remember the primary purpose that has brought me here—goodwill, co-operation, unity from the rest of your fellows in the United States, Africa, the West

THE BLACK MAN 11

Indies. We have celebrated the happiness, the glory of our Organisation's accomplishments. We have had our ups and downs and failures, but that was only a drop in the bucket. If the Mayor were to tell you of the failures of his race, you would wonder at their patience. When the Liberals fail they go out of office and let the Conservatives go in, and the Government goes on. If you Negroes have a penny bank and it fails, you swear that you will never put another penny in it again. You should kick out the first dishonest man and put in an honest one. That is why you will have to swim it to Barbados, Trinidad and Demerara. You know how many times the Canadian Pacific failed until they now have their wonderful system? The only way you can be happy is to lay the foundation in one generation for the succeeding generation. If you do not build ships for the next generation you will always be walking. Take the white race, sometimes you see an old man president of the bank, knowing well that their grandchildren are coming after them and they are storing up for their generations to come after. Our disposition is to eat everything and let the boy work for his. We cannot treat our children as our fathers treated us, so do not eat up everything you get, for God's sake. Remember that the boy who is coming up is to carry on until God comes. Do not be here as serfs and slaves because God never made you anything else but men. Whatever that has happened to the man it is his own mind that puts him there. He has abused the force of power of that mind. Men can create the environment to suit himself. When you do not use your intelligence you fall and will be submerged. It is because we do not live up to the state of our intelligence why we suffer so much. Before I close, I want to appeal to you to use your intelligence to work out the real things of life. You have to apply that intelligence to the management of your own individual and collective racial affairs. Every race has to look after its own affairs. You have formulated no legal or moral claim. That is why people are taking away Africa to-day. Just how like Mussolini took away Ethiopia because he thought the Ethiopians had no use for it. One man used his intelligence and knocked out, while the other tried to pray.

The time you waste in levity, in non-essentials, if you use it properly you will be able to guarantee to your posterity a condition better than you inherited from your forefathers. The U.N.I.A. is carrying throughout the world the message of goodwill. This message is going on. It has reached you. It will go to others, so that we may have one outlook, one purpose in life. I do hope the friendship will continue, sir, economically, politically and that you will never have cause to believe that we are not what we seem. (Cheers.)

The Chairman, Rev. Ford: Speaking on behalf of the peoples of this community permit me to say that they have enjoyed this message of goodwill immensely. Please take back for us the message that we, in Cape Breton, shall stretch out the curtains of our habitation with this in view--one God, one aim, one destiny. I have spent over six years in college learning the various ologies, but to-night you have taught me one ology, and that is Negro ology. The Hon. Marcus Garvey told you to-night that the man who doesn't love his people cannot love his God. This is an epoch-making event. Let us bind ourselves together, not only when he is here, but when he is gone, so that we may be lifted up with wings as he goes.

(At this stage Mr. Pat Comeo rendered a violin solo.)

Hon. Mr. Morrison, M.L.C.: As the hour is growing late and your distinguished guest must need rest, I will not take up much of your time. My first impulse is to break out into politics. I have been wondering if this is a proper place for me to be—a clergyman on my right and a choir on the other. I begin to think that a sinner like me is out of place here. The splendid manner in which they rendered their numbers must be work indeed on the part of themselves and their choir master. I was telling His Worship the other day how a solicitor feels when he is examining his witness. No doubt His Worship and myself have found ourselves in worse places. I am a bachelor, and so is he. We will be glad to go to the Kingdom of Africa, but I will be satisfied to eat apples. I think Mr. Garvey made a mistake in not mentioning Eve. I met a gentleman who said that Canada was dis-united. As far as the City of Sydney is concerned we are a happy community of various sects, colours and religion and we get along admirably together. To-day, we welcomed to Sydney the Governor-General, who is over all Canadians, no matter what race, colour, or creed. The fact that we welcomed him and your leader shows that we can all be faithful to the one sovereign and adore that which is best in our particular races.

(After an anthem by the choir, Mr. Garvey said he thought is was time for the Sydney Division to commence moving on, as it used to do. It should be resurrected. I should like to meet those who are not at work on Monday.)

The centre of UNIA divisions in Canada was the community hall, which served as the focal point for all major activities and group gatherings. In 1925, the UNIA in Toronto had an estimated membership of 700, and it was able to purchase a permanent Hall at 355 Queen Street West. In a recent history of the UNIA in Canada, Carla Marano notes, "The UNIA Hall fostered an intimate community and social network among the West Indians."[18] A member of Toronto's UNIA division described the hall as "a place of refuge for 'colored' peoples, a place where racism and prejudice could not penetrate the front door. It was *the* meeting place for Toronto's Black peoples; 'every day of the week there was something going on up in the UNIA,' from recitals to dances, from dinners to socials."[19] Over the next ten years, the Toronto UNIA continued to grow in size and prominence as a leader among Garveyites in North America. In 1937, it hosted the International UNIA Convention, that attracting delegates from North America and overseas. The hall remained a community centre for Blacks in Toronto even after the decline of the UNIA following Garvey's death in 1940. It did not close its doors until 1982.

The UNIA in Montreal had perhaps the most active membership of any UNIA division in Canada. In 1919, the division opened its Liberty Hall, housed in the Canadian Pacific Railway Building on St. Antoine Street, and during its first year, the UNIA successfully recruited 400 members. The Montreal division became a mainstay for Montreal's Black community, which consisted mainly of West Indians and African Americans. Many African Americans during this period worked for the CPR and were not permanent residents of the city. This left West Indians as the largest permanent Black population in Montreal, and they provided the leadership for various social organizations within the Black community, including the UNIA.[20] The Montreal division maintained a wide range of social events and activities for the Black community including a literary club for teenagers and young adults.

Atlantic Canada had one of the largest concentrations of West Indians in Canada, and in Nova Scotia there were close to a dozen active UNIA divisions. There was an estimated 600 West Indians living in industrial Cape Breton, and there were active UNIA divisions in the industrial towns of Sydney, Glace Bay and New Waterford. The oldest of these was in the town of Glace Bay and was founded by Albert Francis, a native of Barbados, who worked as a miner for the Dominion Coal and Steel Corporation. The Glace Bay division attracted several hundred members, and by 1932, they had collected enough funds to erect their own hall, which still exists today as a UNIA cultural museum.[21]

Sydney had the largest UNIA division in eastern Canada with an active membership of approximately 250.[22] It also served as the central hub for the other two divisions in industrial Cape Breton, and it hosted a number of joint meetings and events, including a UNIA parade in 1921 with a marching brass band and a large contingent of Black Cross nurses. A picture of this UNIA parade appears below, and it was taken as it moved along Victoria Road in Whitney Pier. In addition to showing the Black Cross nurses, the photograph also documents the sizeable crowd of Black spectators that lined the parade route.

The UNIA in Atlantic Canada remained strong throughout the 1920s and 1930s. In 1937, Marcus Garvey attended the International UNIA Conference in Toronto, and afterward he visited Nova Scotia and addressed several UNIA gatherings in Halifax, Sydney and Glace Bay. His address before a large audience at the Menelik Hall in Sydney illustrates his effectiveness as an inspiring speaker with an ability to connect with Black audiences anywhere in the world. The speech articulated Garvey's Afrocentric views of history, which he traced back to the Ancient civilizations of Africa. "Once upon a time," he stated, "we were a great people [and] we built the Pyramids and the Sphinx. When history is written in truth you will find that the first civilization was projected from the Nile on the Congo Basin. In the earliest dawn of civilization you found the Negro in Benin, in Timbuctoo, in Alexandria."[23] Garvey's message was both uplifting and expressively non violent. "The use of the pistol" Garvey stated "is contrary to the laws of nature…. We are going to emancipate ourselves from mental slavery because whilst others might free the body, none but ourselves can free the mind."[24] Garvey's words gave inspiration to the UNIA audience in Sydney and they have resonated with Black nationalists over the years. In 1980, the British Rastafarian musician Bob Marley incorporated the words from Garvey's speech in Sydney in the release of his "Redemption Song" that remained popular throughout the 1980s and 1990s.

The first part of the twentieth century was a time of heightened racism in Canada, and the UNIA helped foster a sense of community among its members as well as ethnic and racial pride. In Nova Scotia, the process of urban industrialization resulted in an increase in racial tensions. In addition to several incidents involving racial violence that were discussed in Chapter 2, there was a widespread pattern of racism affecting many aspects of life including housing, education and employment. In Sydney, for example, West Indians experienced overt expressions of racial discrimination in attending church services. In one incident that occurred in 1910, the acting Anglican priest in the community of Whitney Pier refused to conduct burial rites to a Black man. In another incident that occurred a few years later, Blacks attending Sunday service at the Sydney Anglican church were told that they could no longer sit in the church unless they rented their own pews. They were also informed that no pews were available for rent. These incidents created the impetus for the establishment of the African Orthodox Church (AOC), an independent Black church founded in the United States by George Alexander McGuire in 1919. McGuire had been an executive member of the UNIA, but he eventually resigned this position in order to become the first Patriarch of the AOC. In 1921, at the request of members of the Whitney Pier West Indian community,

The U.N.I.A. Marching Band Whitney Pier, Nova Scotia, 1921, The Beaton Institute

the AOC granted them an "independent episcopal," and in 1928 the local congregation built St. Philip's Church that today still remains as the only AOC in Canada.[25]

The success of St. Philip's AOC stems from its ability to appeal to the spiritual
needs of the entire Black community. Although many of the West Indians who
joined the church were members of the UNIA, the AOC did not adhere to the radical
doctrines associated with Marcus Garvey. The theological and political roots of
the AOC were to be found in the American Episcopal Church, and in practice, they
incorporated elements of both the Anglican and Roman Catholic traditions.[26] In
spite of the racism that was evident in several of the established churches of area,
St. Philip's, in contrast, quickly evolved into a racially tolerant church that was open
to anyone who wanted to attend its services. By the early 1930s, St. Philip's became
the church of choice for nearly all Blacks living in the community.[27]

The increase and persistence of white supremacist views and widespread racial
discrimination during the post–World War I period created sustained hardships
for Canada's Black population. West Indians and African Canadians experienced
racial discrimination in all areas of their lives, and in response, they turned to their
own communities for support. The UNIA, CLACP and local churches and civil
rights organizations, together with the more traditional fraternal associations,

helped provide Blacks with a strong sense of racial-ethnic identity and pride. Viewed from the Black perspective, the period 1865 to 1930 that historian Robin Winks describes as the nadir of the Black experience in Canada may also be seen as a period of cultural awakening and solidarity, as illustrated by the growth and vitality of distinct Black communities in cities like, Toronto, Montreal and Sydney.

Canada's racially restrictive immigration policies remained in effect until the 1960s. In 1954, Black civil rights activist Donald Willard Moore led a protest delegation to Ottawa and presented a brief to Walter Harris, the Minister of Immigration. A year later, the Federal Government adopted changes to immigration restrictions and eventually it passed the *Immigration Act* of 1962. The new act introduced a merit-based system of immigration and it replaced the racially restrictive *Immigration Act* of 1923.

NOTES

1. Robin Winks, *The Blacks in Canada: A History,* 2nd. edition (Montreal: McGill-Queen's University Press, 1997), p. 287, 486.
2. Robin Winks, *The Blacks in Canada: A History,* 1997, pp. 313ff.
3. James W. St. G. Walker, "African Canadians," in *Encyclopedia of Canadian Peoples,* ed. Paul Robert Magocsi (Toronto: University of Toronto Press, 1999), p. 148. Walker states: "Most observers conclude that official census figures seriously underrepresent the number of West Indians in Canada," *The West Indians in Canada* (Ottawa: Canadian Historical Society, 1984), p. 10; Robin Winks also addresses the problem of estimating the size of Canada's Black population. See *Blacks in Canada,* pp. 484–96.
4. James Walker, "African Canadians," 1999, p. 148.
5. Sarah-Jane Mathieu, *North of the Color Line: Migration and Black Resistance in Canada, 1870–1955* (Chapel Hill: The University of North Carolina Press, 2010), p. 43.
6. James Walker, *The West Indians in Canada,* 1984, p. 10.
7. William D. Scott to F.C. Knight, 25 April 1916, Archives Canada, RG. 79, Vol. 566, File: 810666, pt. 2.
8. Scott to F.C. Knight; see also (below) Scott's letters of 17 November 1914 and 16 September 1915, Archives Canada, RC. Vol. 566, File: 81066, pt. 2.
9. J.B. Williams to William D. Scott, "Report of the Landing of Negroes at Nova Scotia Ports," 29 June 1909, Archives Canada, RG 76, Vol. 566, File: 810666, pt. 1.
10. William D. Scott to L.M. Fortier, 10 August 1916, Archives Canada, RG. 76, Vol. 566, File: 810666, pt. 2.
11. Isabel Wilkerson, *The Warmth of Other Suns: The Epic Story of America's Great Migration* (New York: Random House, 2010).
12. Sarah-Jane Mathieu, *North of the Color Line,* 2010, pp. 164–65.
13. William M. Tuttle, Jr., *Race Riot: Chicago in the Red Summer of 1919* (Chicago: University of Illinois Press, 1996), pp. 210–11.
14. Sarah-Jane Mathieu, *North of the Color Line,* 2010, pp. 141–84.
15. Sarah-Jane Mathieu, *North of the Color Line,* 2010, p. 152.

16. Carla Marano, "'Rising Strongly and Rapidly': The Universal Negro Improvement Association in Canada, 1919–1940," *The Canadian Historical Review* 91, 2 (June 2010), p. 248.
17. James Walker, "African Canadians," p. 155.
18. Carla Marano "'Rising Strongly and Rapidly': The Universal Negro Improvement Association in Canada, 1919–1940," 2010, p. 254.
19. Carla Marano "'Rising Strongly and Rapidly': The Universal Negro Improvement Association in Canada, 1919–1940," 2010, p. 253.
20. Carla Marano "'Rising Strongly and Rapidly': The Universal Negro Improvement Association in Canada, 1919–1940," 2010, p. 255.
21. Joan Weeks, *One God, One Aim, One Destiny: African Nova Scotians in Cape Breton* (Sydney, NS: Centre for Cape Breton Studies, Cape Breton University, 2007), p. 39.
22. Joan Weeks, *One God, One Aim, One Destiny*, 2007, p. 37.
23. Marcus Garvey, "The Work That Has Been Done," speech at Melnick Hall, Sydney Nova Scotia, *The Black Man: A Monthly Magazine of Negro Thoughts and Opinions* 3, 10 (July 1938), pp. 7–11.
24. Marcus Garvey, "The Work That Has Been Done." 1938, pp. 9–10.
25. Jennifer Reid, "A Toolshed from Gate #4: The Dominion Iron and Steel Company and the Formation of an African American Church," *Historical Papers 1999: Canadian Society of Church History*, ed. Bruce L. Guenther (Langley BC: Canadian Society of Church History, 1999), p. 90.
26. Kimberly L. Harding, "St. Philip's African Orthodox Church: A Case Study of a Unique Religious Institution," (unpublished Masters of Arts thesis in Sociology, Acadia University, 1998), p. 8.
27. Jennifer Reid, "A Toolshed from Gate #4," 1994, p. 90.

Chapter 6

The Culture of Racism in Canada
Burning Crosses, Blackened-Faced Actors and Minstrel Shows

The origin of Canada's racially restrictive immigration policy during the twentieth century should be seen in the context of the much larger debate over Canadian national identity that reached a peak following World War I. Superintendent of Immigration, William Scott, believed that Canada was a nation reserved for "the white race only" with the most desirable immigrants coming from Great Britain, United States, Europe and Scandinavia.[1] He believed that Asians and Blacks were undesirable because they were racially unsuited to the culture and climate of Canada. Scott was Canada's most significant gatekeeper on immigration for over two decades, and although his views were unequivocally racist, in many respects, he merely reflected the prevailing views of his time.[2]

Most Canadians of Scott's generation believed that Canada was an integral part of the British Empire, and like the other English speaking dominions, it was regarded as being a predominantly Protestant, Anglo-Saxon nation. The extent to which Canada was an independent nation, separate from Great Britain, was still a subject of debate. Before World War I, many Canadians were proud supporters of the British Empire and they sought to maintain imperial unity by strengthening the ties between the English speaking dominions and the mother country. After World War I, nationalist sentiments in support of a more independent Canada increased and some, like Liberal Prime Minister Mackenzie King, believed that Canada's sacrifices in support of the First World War earned the nation the right to establish a separate foreign policy, at least in the area of trade and commercial treaties.[3]

Running through all sides of the debate over national identity was the consensus that Canada shared the values, culture and racial character of Great Britain. Anglo-Canadians regarded Canada as a nation within an Empire and part of the vanguard in the march of Anglo-Saxon civilization throughout the world. Implicit within most expressions of nationalism and imperialism during this period was the tendency to equate nationality and race under the questionable assumption that nations, like individuals, possessed certain inherited traits. The so-called Anglo-Saxon race was almost universally regarded among English speaking people as being industrious, energetic, technologically skilled and capable of developing advanced democratic institutions. The darker skinned races, on the other hand, were generally seen as being overall less advanced and not capable of managing the institutions or practices of democracy.

There was a general belief among most educated Canadians that the future of the nation rested on maintaining the racial vitality of the population. It was hoped that all healthy "desirable" immigrants and their descendants would be assimilated into the dominant Anglo-Canadian society.[4] J.S. Woodsworth, a prominent member of the Social Gospel movement and first leader of the Co-operative Commonwealth Federation (CCF), spent nearly ten years working among the immigrant slum residents of Winnipeg. He expressed concern about the "quality" of immigrants to Canada, and he feared the consequences of unrestricted immigration that would allow "inferior stock" into the country. In 1909, Woodsworth published *Strangers Within Our Gates: or Coming Canadians* in which he presented views on immigration similar to those of William Scott. Woodsworth maintained that the white races of Great Britain and Europe were the most suited to the Canadian way of life and mixing large numbers of people of differing races was not in the best interests of the country. "We confess," he wrote, "that the idea of a homogeneous people seems to accord with our democratic institutions and conducive to the general welfare."[5]

Woodsworth eventually became involved in Canada's eugenics movement and served on the executive board of the Bureau of Social Research that conducted research on the "mental defective" in western Canada.[6] The eugenics movement was founded by Francis Galton, the cousin of Charles Darwin, who sought to apply the principles of genetics toward improving the human population. During the first half of the twentieth century, eugenics became popular in Canada, as it did in England and the United Sates. As a "new science," eugenics was the accepted practice in several provinces. The movement reflected the widespread fear among many Canadians that "alien and unfit" immigrant classes would lead to the "regression" of the entire population. In 1919, W.L. Lochhead, a leading Canadian eugenicist, stated:

> Many defects such as feeble-mindedness, epilepsy, deaf-mutation, and disposition to tuberculosis and other diseases are undoubtedly inherited, and to put no hindrance to breeding of the unfit and degenerate persons exposes our country to the gravest risk of regression, especially when it is recognized that the population is being largely recreated from inferior stock.[7]

Recent research on the eugenics movement in Alberta shows that it had a signifi-cant and lasting influence on the province's social and health policies. Jana Grekul states that the prairie-based Bureau of Social Research "actively campaigned for the segregation and sterilization of defectives." Woodsworth assisted the Bureau in developing a province-wide survey on mental hygiene in 1921. "The survey reported that mental abnormality and delinquency correlated with illegitimacy, prostitution, and dependency, thus setting the stage for increased activism towards eugenic legislation."[8]

The eugenics movement in North America is a glaring example of the unethi-cal use of science in attempt to prevent certain disadvantaged groups of people, who were arbitrarily defined as "defective" or "undesirable," from having children. It eventually led to the forced sterilization of thousands of individuals in North America and was a precursor to the even more ghastly misuse of science under Nazi Germany.

The popularity of the eugenics movement in Canada together with fears about unrestricted immigration was reflective of the desire to maintain the genetic vitality and racial purity of the nation. Concern about the future racial integrity of the nation was part the emerging Canadian nationalism that gained popularity following World War I. The convergence of nationalist and racist sentiments was a potent and appealing mix that drew widespread support from both major political parties and from a number of grassroots Canadian nationalist organizations that existed in many regions of the country. In 1921, the Native Sons of Canada was founded in Victoria, British Columbia, and over the next ten years, it expanded into a nationwide organization with a membership of well over 100,000.[9] The Native Son's brand of nationalism emphasized the idea of a distinct Canadian identity and the importance of building a nation with the "best stocks" of white immigrants and not those "tending to make Canadians a mixed or coloured race, or which tends to lower standards of living, education or morals, or which brings in the physically, mentally or morally unfit."[10] Similar racist sentiments were shared by virtually all Canadian nationalists organizations of the period.

In Ontario, there were several grassroots nationalist organizations. During the 1920s, the Association of Canadian Clubs attracted a large following, and from 1926 to 1928, it more than doubled in size from 53 to 115 clubs. The association was founded in Hamilton in 1896, and it promoted a more traditional brand of nationalism based on maintaining the imperial connection between Canada and Great Britain. Ontario was also home to an active and large Orange Order that pro-moted the white, Protestant links between Britain, Canada and Northern Ireland. The city of Toronto, often referred to as the "hub of the British Empire" was also considered the "Belfast of Canada," and in 1914, it had seventy-six Orange Lodges with a total active membership of 15,000.[11] Although Orangism was eventually eclipsed by a more distinctly Canadian form of nationalism, the Order "combined loyalty with evangelical Christianity," and in Toronto, especially, it " helped to shape the civic atmosphere ... and contributed to an emergent ... Anglo-Canadian national identity."[12]

So popular was the Order's message nearly a century ago that, on July 12, 1920, the day marking the historic Protestant victory in Ireland at the Battle of the Boyne in 1690, there were 8,500 marchers in Toronto's Orange Parade and over 20,000 spectators. At that time, Toronto only had a population of just over half a million people. Historian David Wilson observers: "Beyond the city, the Orange Order permeated the towns, villages, farms and frontier settlements of English–speaking Canada; one in three of the country's adult Protestant males passed through its ranks."[13] By the time Orangism reached its peak in Canada in 1920, it had an estimated membership of 100,000 people and 2,000 lodges. The steady stream of Irish Protestant immigrants to Canada and Newfoundland gave both regions the largest Orange Order membership in the world.[14]

Typical of popular thinking at the time, supporters of the Orange Order combined ideas about race, religion and politics in regarding themselves as respectable and loyal Canadians and as defenders of Britain's Protestant Anglo-Saxon Empire "against the machinations of Rome." Detractors viewed the Orange Order as an unwelcome presence of "Old World sectarian violence onto Canadian streets, who attempted to shut out Catholics from jobs at every opportunity, and who were a divisive and disruptive force in Canadian life."[15]

During this same period, Ontario and most other provinces also witnessed a sudden and dramatic growth of the Ku Klux Klan, which reached its peak during the late 1920s. Like the Orange Order, which was a movement imported from outside Canada, the Klan came to Canada from the United States shortly after its reemergence following the appearance in 1915 of D.W. Griffith's epic motion picture *The Birth of a Nation*. This monumental cinematic classic was based on the book, *The Clansman* by Thomas F. Dixon Jr., and its release marked the fiftieth anniversary of the ending of the American Civil War. As we have already seen, the Klan had a visible presence during the 1920s in Ontario, and it primarily targeted Blacks, Jews and Catholics. Although the Klan in Canada never engaged in the same degree of violence as its American counterpart, it practiced many of the same rituals including mass hooded gatherings and cross burnings. In Ontario, the Klan had its strongest support in Toronto and in the southeastern part of the province; however, its popularity was short lived partly due to internal conflicts involving leadership and organization.[16]

The Klan was most successful in Saskatchewan, where it avoided overt acts of violence in favour of a more respectable and mainstream strategy that stressed law and order, temperance and a host of other popular reform issues. Above all, the

Kingston, Ontario, 31 July 1927, National Archives of Canada/ PA-87848

Klan focused on keeping Canada white, British and Protestant. In his study of the Klan in Saskatchewan, James Pitsula argues that although the Klan in Canada never wavered from its white supremacist agenda, it was highly adaptable and "took on the colour of the community."[17] Klan organizers were sensitive to local concerns, and when they moved into a community "they listened to what was bothering people and worked on that." Unlike the more traditional Orange Order and other Canadian nationalist organizations, the Klan in western Canada was "a bottom-up, grassroots version of British Canadian nationalism that empowered lower middle-class and upper working-class individuals, who suddenly rose to prominence as Imperial Wizards, Grand Dragons, King Kleagles, and other such exalted offices."[18]

In Saskatchewan, the Klan succeeded where other nationalist organizations like the Orange Lodge did not because it offered a populist style of British Canadian nationalism. According to Pitsula, the Klan made its white supremacist message appealing by inspiring and entertaining its audiences: "The Klan went out to the people. It held public meetings and sent out charismatic lecturers, almost in a style of evangelical preachers. It created drama and excitement with a hint romance and danger. Crosses burned on dark hillsides, fiery spectacles visible for kilometers around."[19]

In eastern Canada, the Klan adopted a similar strategy of keeping Canada British, and although it never reached the size and popularity it achieved in Saskatchewan, it had a significant presence during the 1920s. There were seventeen active Klan lodges, or "klaverns," in New Brunswick from 1925 to 1930, and there were cross burnings in most major cities and towns in the province.[20] The letters that are

Ku Klux Klan, Vancouver 1925, City of Vancouver Archives/CVA-99-1946

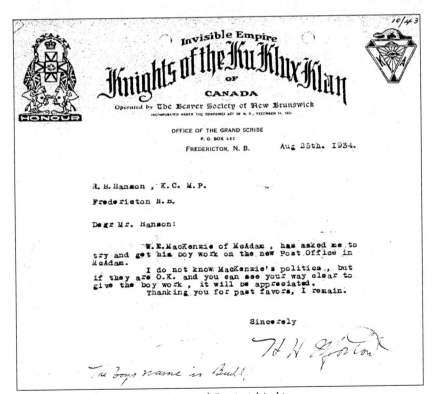

New Brunswick Provincial Archives

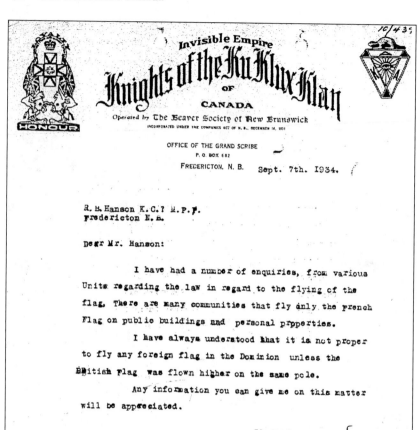

New Brunswick Provincial Archives

reproduced in this section reveal that the Klan in New Brunswick had an active participation in political life. The correspondence indicates that Klansman H.H. Morton was a friend of R.B. Hanson, the former mayor of Fredericton who was elected to Parliament in 1921. Hanson also had a number of important connections in the business world: he sat on the board of directors of the New Brunswick Telephone Company and served as a solicitor for the Royal Bank of Canada in Fredericton and for the Fraser Companies of Edmonton. The letters show how Klan members in Canada had, in certain instances, access to powerful public figures.

The Klan's proximity to party politics in New Brunswick began during the 1920s. In 1923, Peter Veniot became New Brunswick's first Acadian premier following the resignation of W.E. Foster. However, with the rise in Anglo-Canadian nationalism during the post-war era, French-speaking Catholics were frequently the target of

10/4/34

Fredericton, N.B.,
September 12th, 1934.

H. H. Horton, Esq.,
   P. O. Box 682,
   Fredericton, N.B.

Dear Mr. Horton:

        I have your letter of the 7th instant,
regarding the law in regard to the flying of flags,
other than the Union Jack, in communities in Canada.
So far as I am aware there is no law on the subject.
It is a matter of principle, however, that wherever
a foreign flag is flown the Union Jack should appear
above it. It is not proper to fly any foreign flag
on any public building in Canada.

        I am writing to Mr. E. H. Coleman, K.C.,
Under Secretary of State, at Ottawa, who should be
able to give me definite information on the subject,
and I will write you further after hearing from him.

                    Yours very truly,

RB::HVH

New Brunswick Provincial Archives

prejudice. Two years after Veniot was voted into office, the Klan played a significant role in the election campaign, and as a result, the Anglo-Protestant constituencies went "strongly in favour" of the Conservatives, and Klansman J.S. Lord was elected in Charlotte County. Similar to the situation in Saskatchewan, the Klan operated as part of the Conservative Party machine in New Brunswick. As for Hanson, he was appointed Minister of Trade in R.B. Bennett's Government in 1934 and served as interim leader of the federal Conservative Party in 1940.[21]

The popularity of the Klan as an organization in Canada declined dramatically during the 1930s; however, the Klan's particular brand of racism has left an enduring presence in Canada. From time to time, the hateful Klan rituals of cross burning and lynching, symbolized by the hangman's noose, appear from bellow the surface in communities in almost every region of the country. This was the case in Nova Scotia in 2010, when two brothers burned a cross on the lawn of a mixed racial couple in Hants County and in 2012 when a Black employee at Leon's furniture store in Dartmouth found a doll with a noose around its neck on his

10/43,

Fredericton, N.B.,
September 17th, 1934.

H.H.Morton, Esq.,
   P. O. Box 682,
   CITY.

Dear Sir:

        Since receipt of your recent letter
I have communicated with the Under Secretary of State
at Ottawa, Mr.Coleman, who has immediately replied,
and copy of his letter is herewith enclosed. He
states that there is no law on the subject and no
precise regulations, but that this is one of the
matters, such as the playing of the National Anthem,
which is governed by traditional custom.

                    Yours faithfully,

Encl.

RBM:HVH

New Brunswick Provincial Archives

desk.[22] Although these are rare incidents representing the most blatant expressions of racism, they nevertheless show how the Klan continues to affect the psyche of a small minority of Canadians.

In the broader context of the narrative of race in Canadian history, the Klan's influence in Canada is part of the Americanization of racial attitudes in Canada. This influence involved the Klan's limited presence in Canada as a popular organization as well as its more lasting impact through the dissemination of a particular set of racial stereotypes. These stereotypes are perhaps most vividly portrayed in G. W. Griffith's *The Birth of a Nation* that was shown repeatedly to packed movie houses in United States and Canada until the introduction of talking pictures in 1928.

During the fall of 1915, *The Birth of a Nation* premiered in Toronto, Ottawa and

Montreal. In Toronto, it opened initially for one week in September at the Royal Alexandra Theatre, but due to the unprecedented popular demand, the engagement was extended for an additional two weeks.[23] In December, the film returned again to Toronto for a special extended holiday season engagement at Massey Hall beginning on Christmas Day.[24] Without exception, the newspaper reviews in Canada were positive, and there was no mention made of Griffith's degrading portrayal of Blacks. At first, there were some efforts among Canada's Black communities to protest the film, and in Toronto, Rev. W. Hackley of the African Episcopal Methodist Church and his supporters petitioned the Government of Ontario in an effort to censor offensive scenes in the film.[25] Hackley's attempt to have the film censored was ultimately unsuccessful, as were similar attempts in other Canadian cities, and provincial censorship boards raised no objections to Griffith's depictions of Blacks.

After the premier engagements in 1915, *The Birth of a Nation* went on a series of roads shows across the United States and Canada. It toured the cities and small towns across Canada for an extended period of time, and as Hollywood's first blockbuster movie, it attracted large audiences wherever it was shown. One movie house in Alberta advertised round-the-clock showings, and at the Roseland Theatre in New Glasgow, Nova Scotia, the site of the Viola Desmond incident many years later, *The Birth of a Nation* was a popular favorite during the entire silent movie era. On its many return engagements, local musicians played in the thirty-member symphony that accompanied the film.[26]

The Birth of a Nation is testimony of the power of the new medium of cinema that, in the hands of a masterful filmmaker like Griffith, could shape the attitudes of audiences everywhere. The movie "argues for evil" in depicting Blacks in a degrading and inhuman light and invokes fear regarding the dangers of free Blacks in a white society.[27]

The racial stereotypes presented in *The Birth of a Nation* are drawn, in part, from southern racial mythology and, historically, were part of the southern defence of slavery. In the movie, slaves appear happy as they pick cotton in the fields; others are seen dancing with delight in the streets along side Confederate soldiers who are marching off to fight the Union army. In contrast, the movie portrays free Blacks in a far more negative and threatening manner. When groups of northern Black militia enter the southern town of Piedmont along side Union soldiers, they are depicted as marauding barbarians who seem intent on destroying everything in sight. The message from these and other scenes of the movie is clear: free Blacks are to be feared because of their inherent inferiority and violent (brutish) nature and, above all, because they pose a fundamental threat to the institutions of democracy and to the purity of the white race through miscegenation.

Griffith's sympathies were obviously with the south and the Ku Klux Klan, which is portrayed in the movie as a group of righteous vigilantes, guardians of

Toronto Daily Star, 18 September, 1915

white women and the southern way of life.

In the movie, white fears resulting from the emancipation of slaves are symbolized in the character Gus, played by the blackened faced white actor Walter
Long. Gus appears in several scenes throughout the movie as a freed slave and as
a solider in the Black militia that "invaded" the south along with the Union army.
Towards the end of the film and after the Civil War has ended, Gus lusts for a young
white girl, Flora, who is the youngest sister of one of the main characters in the
movie, Ben Cameron, a Colonel in the Confederate army and founder of the KKK.
Encouraged by the news that the Black majority of the South Carolina legislature
has passed an act allowing for inter-racial marriage, Gus stalks Flora as she goes into
the forest alone to fetch water, and after confronting her, he attempts to propose
marriage to her. After Flora rejects Gus' proposal, he chases her until, out of fear

The Birth of A Nation, G.W. Griffith, 1915

and desperation, she jumps off a cliff to her death. Gus is then pursued by Colonel Cameron and the KKK, and Gus is soon captured and killed. The movie ends with a biblical-like scene depicting the unification of southern and northern whites, and the message audiences take from this is that America is a nation for whites only.

The movie had a powerful effect on audiences everywhere. Film historian Donald Bogle notes that in the south it was advertised as a movie intended "to work audiences into a frenzy ... to make you hate."[28] The southern ad campaign may have been effective because there was a sudden increase in lynchings following the movie's release in 1915. As might be expected, the movie drew immediate protests from the NAACP, and over the next few years, the film stirred such public controversy and reaction among audiences that it was eventually banned in five states and nineteen cities in the United States.[29]

The racial stereotypes presented in *Birth of a Nation* have had a lasting influence on the way Blacks have been portrayed in Hollywood films. According to Bogle, Griffith used three distinct categories of racial stereotypes in his depiction of Blacks: the "faithful soul," such as the Black house servants Jake and Mammy; the "brutal Black buck," who, like Gus in the movie, acts out of brutish primeval instincts and the "light skinned mulatto," who hates whites and seeks power. The female mulatto was the only racial stereotype that was judged to be physically attractive to whites, and because of their potential sex appeal, light skinned Black actresses were sometimes given lead roles in Hollywood movies starting in the 1930s.[30]

Minstrel show cast, Sydney, circa 1950s, Abbass studio photo collection, Beaton Institute

Silent movies like *The Birth of a Nation* were part of the developing Hollywood film industry, and they ushered in a new form of community entertainment centred on movie houses and larger movie palaces that were built in cities and towns across North America. The movie house was a venue for a variety of forms of community entertainment including live theatrical and musical performances such as minstrel shows and vaudeville acts. In the nineteenth century, these performances were part of elaborate road shows that travelled throughout United States and Canada. With the advent of silent movies in the early twentieth century, movie houses became increasingly more common, and they were frequently used for minstrel shows, many of which were local productions sponsored by community organizations.

Minstrel shows were among the most popular forms of entertainment during the nineteenth and early twentieth century, and they usually involved a standard repertoire of shows, including performances by white actors wearing blackface.[31] Masonic lodges and local service organizations frequently sponsored both minstrel and vaudeville shows, and in addition to movies houses, these shows were also performed at many local churches. In 1922, the *Hamilton Spectator* reported a performance sponsored by the St. Thomas Church's Young Men's Club of the Tennessee Minstrels. The show was presented to a full-capacity Sunday school room at the church and "was one of the most successful entertainments" held there.[32] Canadian churches continued to be popular venues for minstrel shows, so much so, that in 1956 the Black civil rights activists Stanley Grizzle and Donald Moore

Roseland Theatre Minstrel Show Dalhousie Archives, Waldren Studios Collection

publically castigated the churches for promoting these performances, which, in their view, perpetuated degrading racial stereotypes.[33]

One of the most popular shows during this period was *Uncle Tom's Cabin*, which was adapted for stage from Herriot Beecher Stowe's famous abolitionist novel. In this enactment, the main characters of the novel were transformed into Black racial stereotypes performed by white actors wearing blackface. In addition to the shuffling and subservient house slave, Tom, there was Topsy, the little pickaninny slave girl, who delighted audiences with her carefree and uncultivated behavior. As historian Patricia Turner states: "Stage Topsys and other pickaninny characters ... were happy, mirthful characters who reveled in their misfortune. Their awkward speech, ragamuffin appearance, devilish habits, and butchered English were sources of humor in the minstrel and Tom shows that remained popular from the 1850s until well into the twentieth century."[34] The message these distorted representations of slave adults and children conveyed was, due to their inferior and uncultivated nature, they were not well suited for the responsibilities of freedom and they were better off and happiest living their lives under slavery.

Uncle Tom's Cabin was frequently performed in cities and in small towns in most regions of Canada. The show was so popular at the Roseland Theatre in New Glasgow that the owner, Norman Mason, brought it back almost every year.[35]

Mason built the Roseland theatre in 1913 as a silent movie house and refurbished it in 1929 to accommodate talking pictures as well as local performances of minstrel shows. In response to pressure from New Glasgow's white patrons, Mason imposed a racially segregated seating policy in 1941. In spite of protests from the Nova Scotia Black community, the theatre remained racially segregated until the province of Nova Scotia adopted the *Fair Accommodations Act* in 1959, which banned racial segregation in all public places.

The popularity of minstrel shows declined during the 1950s and 1960s, and as a main medium for the perpetuation of racial stereotypes, they were gradually replaced by more modern comedic incarnations, such as the all time popular show *Amos 'n' Andy*, which aired first on radio during the 1920s and later on television in the early 1950s.[36] With the advent of television, advertising also became a major vehicle for reinforcing racial stereotypes. Although the representation of Blacks on television has steadily increased over the years, subtle and persistent forms of racial stereotypes and deep-seated racial biases have continued to shape the attitudes of viewers in both in the United States and Canada.[37]

The culture of racism in Canada was, in many respects, similar to the attitudes and patterns of thought that existed in United States and Great Britain during most of the twentieth century. As in so many other areas, both the American and British spheres of influence played a central role in shaping racial attitudes in Canada as well as affecting the longstanding debate over Canadian national identity.

Today, the newest generations of Canadians enthusiastically embrace a national identity based on the *Charter of Rights and Freedoms*, and the majority of Canadians support the common goal of making Canada a culturally diverse and racially tolerant society. However, we should not forget that, in the not too distant past, the ideas about Anglo-Saxon racial superiority and cultural assimilation dominated Canadian public opinion as well as provincial and federal government policy.

NOTES

1. William D. Scott, "Immigration and Population," in *Canada and its Provinces: A History of the Canadian People and Their Institutions by One Hundred Associates,* Adam Shortt and Arthur G. Doughty, general editors (Toronto: Glasgow, Brook & Co., 1914), Vol. VII, p. 531; 578.

2. William D. Scott served as Superintendent of Immigration from 1903 until he retired from public office in 1924.

3. John Darwin, *The Empire Project: The Rise and Fall of the British World-System 1830–1970* (New York: Cambridge University Press, 2009), p. 395.

4. Assimilation and Anglo-conformity were the dominant views in Canada for the first half of the twentieth century. For a full discussion of these views, see Howard Palmer, "Reluctant Hosts: Anglo-Canadian Views of Multiculturalism in the Twentieth

Century," in R. Douglas Francis and Donald B. Smith, editors, *Readings in Canadian History: Post-Confederation* (Toronto: Harcourt Brace & Co., 1994), pp. 143–60.

5. James S. Woodsworth, *Strangers Within Our Gates or Coming Canadians* (Toronto: Stephenson, 1909), p. 277.

6. Jana Grekel, "The Right of Consent? Eugenics in Alberta, 1928–1972," in *A History of Human Rights in Canada*, Janet Miron, ed. (Toronto: Canadian Scholar's Press, 2009), p. 137.

7. W.L. Lochhead, quoted in Angus McLaren, *Our Own Master Race: Eugenics in Canada, 1885–1945* (Toronto: McClelland & Stewart Inc., 1990), p. 13.

8. Jana Gekul, "The Right of Consent? Eugenics in Alberta, 1928–1972," 2009, p. 137.

9. James M. Pitsula, *Keeping Canada British: The Ku Klux Klan in 1920's Saskatchewan* (Toronto: University of British Columbia Press, 2013), p. 6.

10. "Organization Believes Only Best Stock Should Be Brought to Canada," *Leader* (Regina), 31 July 1928, quoted in James Pitsula, *Keeping Canada British*, p. 7.

11. David A. Wilson, "Introduction: 'Who Are These People?'" in *The Orange Order in Canada*, David Wilson, ed. (Toronto: Four Courts Press, 2007), p. 10.

12. William Jenkins, "Views from 'the Hub of the Empire': Loyal Orange Lodges in Early Twentieth-Century Toronto," in *The Orange Order in Canada*, p. 144.

13. David Wilson, "Introduction: 'Who Are These People?'" 2007, p. 10.

14. David Wilson, "Introduction: 'Who Are These People?'" 2007, p. 21.

15. David Wilson, "Introduction: 'Who Are These People?'" 2007, p. 10.

16. Alan Bartley, "A Public Nuisance: The Ku Klux Klan in Ontario 1923–27, *Journal of Canadian Studies* 30, 3 (Fall 1995), pp. 156–74.

17. James Pitsula, *Keeping Canada British*, 2013, p. 17.

18. James Pitsula, *Keeping Canada British*, 2013, p. 18.

19. James Pitsula, *Keeping Canada British*, 2013, p. 109.

20. "Administrative History/Biographical Sketch: Ku Klux Klan of Kanada fonds," Provincial Archives of New Brunswick, MC 2604. Description retrieved from <http://www.archivescanada.ca/English/search/itemDisplay.asp?>; Constance Backhouse, *Colour Coded: A Legal History of Racism in Canada, 1900–1950* (Toronto: University of Toronto Press, 1999), pp. 186–87.

21. Information on the Klan in New Brunswick has been provided in a personal communication between the author and Don Nerbas. For a detailed description of the Klan and New Brunswick politics during the 1920s, see Don Nerbas, *Dominion of Capital: The Politics of Big Business and the Crisis of the Canadian Bourgeoisie 1914-1947* (Toronto: University of Toronto Press, 2013), pp. 42–47.

22. See "Introduction," note 16.

23. "Birth of a Nation Beyond Promises," *The Toronto World* (21 September, 1915).

24. "The Birth of a Nation," *The Toronto World* (18 December, 1915).

25. "Coloured People Protest," *The Toronto Daily Star* (17 September, 1915); for a fuller discussion of the immediate reception of *Birth of a Nation* in Canada, see Greg Marquis, "A War Within a War: Canadian Reactions to D.W. Griffith's *Birth of a Nation*," *Histoire Sociale/ Social History* 94 (June, 2014), pp. 421–42.

26. Sarah-Jane Mathieu, *North of the Color Line: Migration and Black Resistance in Canada, 1870–1955* (Chapel Hill: University of North Carolina Press, 2010), p. 168; Constance

Backhouse, *Colour Coded: A Legal History of Racism in Canada, 1900–1950*, 1999, p. 226.

27. Roger Ebert, "Great Movie: 'The Birth of a Nation.'" Retrieved at <http://www. Rogerebert.com/reviews/great-movie-the-birth-of-a-nation-1915>.

28. Donald Bogle, *Toms, Coons, Mulattoes, Mammies, and Bucks: An Interpretive History of Blacks in American Films*, 3rd edition (New York: Continuum Publishing Co., 1994), p. 15.

29. Donald Bogle, *Toms, Coons, Mulattoes, Mammies, and Bucks*, 1994, p. 15. Griffith's categories of racial stereotypes were based, in part, on those used by Thomas Dixon Jr. in his first novel, *The Leopard's Spots*. Dixon fashioned his racial stereotypes by deliberately distorting some of the main characters in Herriot Beecher Stowe's *Uncle Tom's Cabin*. See Melvyn Stokes, *D.W. Griffith's 'The Birth of a Nation': A History of the Most Controversial Motion Pictures of All Time* (New York: Oxford University Press, 2007), pp. 41ff.

30. Donald Bogle, *Toms, Coons, Mulattoes, Mammies, and Bucks*, 1994, pp. 15–16.

31. J. Stanley Lemons, "Black Stereotypes as Reflected in Popular Culture, 1880–1920," *American Quarterly* 29, 1 (Spring, 1977), p. 102.

32. *Hamilton Spectator*, 1 February 1922, quoted in Sarah-Jane Mathieu *North of the Color Line*, p. 168.

33. "Churches Rapped!!! Grizzle and More Speak Out Against Minstrel Shows," *Canadian Negro* 4, 1 (March 1956), p. 1.

34. Patricia A. Turner, *Ceramic Uncles & Celluloid Mammies: Black Image and Their influence on Culture* (New York: Anchor Books, 1994), p. 13.

35. Constance Backhouse, "'I Was Unable to Identify with Topsy': Carrie M. Best's Struggle Against Racial Segregation in Nova Scotia, 1942" *Atlantis* 22, 2 (Spring/Summer, 1998), p. 18.

36. Melvin Patrick Ely, *The Adventures of Amos 'n' Andy: A Social History of an American Phenomenon* (New York: Free Press, 1991).

37. Julia M. Bristor, Renee Gravois Lee and Michelle R. Hunt, "Race and Ideology: African-American Images in Television Advertising," *Journal of Public Policy & Marketing* 14, 1 (Spring 1995), pp. 48–59. The presence of racial stereotypes in Canadian television advertising is the subject of a major recent study. See Shyon Baumann and Loretta Ho, "Cultural Schemes for Racial Identity in Canadian Television Advertising," *Canadian Review of Sociology/Revue canadienne de sociologie* 51, 2 (May 2014), pp. 152–69.

Chapter 7

Pearleen Oliver
Pioneer in the Fight
to End Racial Discrimination

Many Canadians are not aware of the Viola Desmond story and the widespread existence of racial segregation in Canada during the first half of the twentieth-century. This lack of awareness also extends to the struggle among civil rights activists who fought to overcome the barriers of racial discrimination in Canada in order to extend equal rights and opportunities to all Canadians. Although little known to most Canadians, Pearleen Oliver (1917–2008) was one of several leading Black activists of Viola's generation who devoted her entire adult life to fighting for racial equality and improving the life of the Black community in Nova Scotia.[1]

Pearleen was the first Black graduate of the New Glasgow High School in Nova Scotia. After graduating in 1936, she married Reverend William Pearly Oliver, who became a well-known educator and social activist and served as minster of the Cornwallis Street Baptist Church from 1937 to 1962 and later at the Beechville Baptist Church until his death in 1989. Pearleen and the Rev. William Oliver formed a life-long spiritual bond that guided them in their relationship and in their service to their church and the community. Throughout their lives together, Pearleen maintained a supportive role to her husband's ministry. She learned to type and to take shorthand in order to help manage the administrative duties of the church, and she learned to play the piano in order to perform at church prayer services and at other functions. Pearleen also distinguished herself as religious leader in her own right. In addition to her involvement in numerous church-related and community organizations, Pearleen wrote several important church histories, and in 1976, she became the first female moderator of the African United Baptist Association of Nova Scotia.

As a civil rights activist and community leader, Pearleen helped establish the Nova Scotia Association for the Advancement of Colored People (NSAACP) in 1945, and she was an active member of the executive board during the association's formative years. Pearleen took a lead in support of Viola Desmond's court appeal

Fight Nova Scotia "Jim Crow" Restrictions — Mrs. Viola Desmond, who was carried bodily out of a New Glasgow, N.S., theatre after she refused to occupy a balcony seat, is seen at left. Supporting her fight against the "color line" rule is Mrs. W. P. Oliver (right), a member of the executive of the Nova Scotia Association for the Advancement of Colored People. She is the wife of the only Negro chaplain in the Canadian Army.

Globe and Mail, 3 December, 1946

and in the fight to end the practice of racial segregation in theatres and in other public places.[2] She was also devoted to the cause of education, especially for young disadvantaged girls. She was a long-time board member of the Maritime Religious Education Council and the Nova Scotia Training School for Girls. One of Pearleen's most significant achievements involved her successful struggle to allow Black girls admission to nursing schools so they could become practicing nurses in Canadian hospitals. As a young girl, she wanted to pursue a career in nursing but she knew that this profession was not open to her and other Black girls in Canada. In the early 1940s, she was personally touched by an account of a young Black girl who tried unsuccessfully to seek admission to a nursing school in Halifax. This incident served as a catalyst for her to begin a concerted public and private campaign to draw attention to this and other forms of racial discrimination in Canada.[3]

In 1946, her efforts paid off when two Black girls, Ruth Bailey of Toronto and Gwyneth Barton of Halifax, were admitted to the nursing program at the Halifax Children's Hospital. In 1948, they became the first two Black graduates of a Canadian nursing school to pursue careers in nursing in Canada.[4]

The Canadian nursing profession is an example of the nature and extent of the culture of racism in Canada during the first half of the twentieth century. Nursing in Canada during this period represented the Victorian ideal of white femininity and respectability.[5] The profession was exclusively reserved for white middle-class "ladies," and, almost without exception, nursing schools refused to admit women of colour and other visible minorities until after World War II. The only exception was in British Columbia where nursing schools began allowing a small number of Chinese and Japanese-Canadian women to train during the 1930s. A decade later, a small number of Haitian and Caribbean women were also admitted to Canadian nursing schools, but this exception was based on the requirement these students would return to their home countries after graduation.[6]

In the following interview, Pearleen tells the story of a young Black girl from Guysborough, Nova Scotia, who wanted to become a nurse. She met all the requirements for nursing school, and in 1940, she applied to the nursing program at the Victoria General Hospital in Halifax. The girl was very light skinned and did not raise any concern about her race when she arrived at the Hospital. However, in filling out the registration form, she indicated her racial identity as "coloured," and when a hospital staff member asked her if she had made a mistake, she said, "No." The reply she heard, according to Pearleen's account, was: "Oh well, then we can't take you here."

A similar incident occurred the same year at the Toronto General Hospital. A young girl wrote the Hospital for a nursing school application and she mentioned in her letter that she was coloured. The hospital staff wrote her back and told her that there we no vacancies in the nursing program. The girl knew that this was not likely the case since there was a high demand for nurses at home and overseas with the outbreak of World War II. Using a fictitious Spanish sounding name, the girl wrote for another application and was promptly instructed to appear for an interview at the hospital in order to be admitted to the nursing program.[7]

Perhaps the most telling account of racial discrimination in barring Black girls' admission to Canadian nursing schools is the one told by Ruth Bailey's father, Joe. In an interview with *The Toronto Star*, published in 1947, he recounted the efforts of both his two daughters to attend Canadian nursing schools.[8] Joe took a personal interest in his daughter's plans to pursue careers in nursing, and when his oldest daughter, Doris, received several rejections, he made inquiries on her behalf. "At one hospital," Joe stated, "I was told they were not taking Negro girls because they would not be able to live with the rest of the girls." Doris then applied to the Women's College Hospital in Toronto and was told that she would be notified by letter regarding a personal interview. After waiting a week with no reply, Joe called the head of the board of directors at the hospital and was told that "the door is closed as far as Negro girls are concerned because they couldn't live with other students and the patients would not accept them at their bedside." Joe concluded from these comments that "there was no use trying anymore." Doris applied to a nursing program in Nashville, Tennessee, and was accepted.[9]

Joe's youngest daughter Ruth also applied to a number of nursing programs in Ontario and British Columbia and received a similar series of rejections. Even though she met all the educational requirements for admission to nursing school, she was told by one hospital that she did not have enough high school credits. Several schools informed Ruth that their program was full and they weren't taking any more applicants. In December 1944, Joe said his daughter received a letter from the director of nursing at the Belleville General Hospital in Ontario that stated the following: "I regret to inform you that we do not consider applicants of the coloured race. There are such schools in certain parts of the U.S.A."[10] Ruth eventually corresponded with Pearleen Oliver, and through her efforts, she was accepted into the nursing program at the Halifax Children's Hospital. Ruth graduated in the fall of 1948 and received a special diploma for general proficiency. It was the second highest award given at the graduation ceremony.[11]

Racial discrimination in the Canadian nursing profession extended beyond the refusal to admit Black women to nursing schools. Once Black women were finally allowed to train and practice nursing in Canada in 1948, they were subjected to various forms of ridicule and discrimination. In 1964, a fictional article appeared in *Chatelaine* entitled the "The Glass Wall," in which the author, Sheila Mackay Russell, described the emotional tension and apprehension among hospital personnel following the hiring of a Black nurse.[12] In this fictional account, Lydia Sanford, a Black nurse, is described as friendly and having the highest qualifications; yet, after being hired, she is avoided and treated as though she was "invisible" by other hospital staff. The students at the hospital "made jokes that portrayed Blacks as barbaric, even as they admitted that Sanford was the best instructor they ever had."[13] Virginia Travis, one of Canada's first generation of Black nurses, describes a similar incident that happened while she was in nursing school. She found herself in a situation in which she was being unfairly criticized by her nursing supervisor, and when she asked for an explanation, her supervisor told her "quit acting like a monkey."[14]

The incidents described here illustrate the on-going struggle among Black nurses in Canada to overcome racial stereotypes and discrimination. In her study of Black nurses in Canada, Karen Flynn notes: "Nursing leaders in North America and Britain lobbied tirelessly to establish nursing as a White, middle-class, female occupation associated with respectability and gentility."[15] Canada's culture of racism was so pervasive in the nursing profession that it was not an uncommon practice for nursing students to perform as blackened faced actors in nursing school minstrel shows. Flynn describes a minstrel show that was depicted in the Atkinson School of Nursing yearbook for 1967. This demeaning and racist form of entertainment was performed "despite the visible presence of Black nurses on staff."[16]

Pearleen's fight to end racial discrimination together with her other community and church-related activities were part of her deep religious faith and her commitment to her husband's ministry and to the extended community of Black Baptists in Nova Scotia. Her faith was a source of strength that guided and inspired her social activism; it also opened an intellectual pursuit of interest for her in the researching and writing of church history. Pearleen wrote several important histories, including *A Brief History of the Colored Baptists of Nova Scotia 1782–1953*, which was written in commemoration of the centennial anniversary of the African United Baptist Association of Nova Scotia (AUBANS), and *Song of the Spirit* (1994), a history of the Beechville United Baptist Church. These histories build on the earlier work of Peter E. McKerrow, who published *A Brief History of the Coloured Baptists of Nova Scotia* in 1895.[17]

Pearleen begins her first narrative history with the arrival of Black Loyalists to Nova Scotia following the American Revolutionary War and continues it through the founding of the African Baptist Association of Nova Scotia (ABANS) under the leadership of Richard Preston in 1853 to the centennial year of 1953. She presents a vivid and intensely moving account of the struggles, hardships and triumphs of the Black Baptists who remained in Atlantic Canada following the exodus to Sierra Leone of the first Baptist leader David George together with many of his followers and other Black Loyalists in 1792.

Pearleen's church history is part of an epic but little known narrative that traces the emergence of Black spiritual identity among a handful of devout ex-slaves, under simple and trying circumstances, to the establishment and development of Black Baptist congregations throughout Nova Scotia, Prince Edward Island and parts of New Brunswick. It is a story that reiterates the theme and words of McKerrow, of religion born in "the forests behind stone walls, in the cane breaks, in the cotton fields, and in the swamps."[18] Historian James Walker notes that early Black Baptist preachers like David George, John Burton and Richard Preston built a Black church that "came to be a strong positive force in the development of Black community life."[19] Their success rested on the ability to inspire a personal relationship and experience with God. Walker states that it was not important if some of the early preachers were uneducated or even illiterate because "the Holy Spirit was believed to speak directly to the heart of the preacher," and through them, it was communicated to the congregation. "Untrained in formal theology, lacking perhaps a firm grasp of the bible's contents, the Black Christians were satisfied that theirs was a sanctified religion and even a superior one to that taught in white churches. This sense of confidence, this conviction that they were fulfilling God's intention, formed the cement of the Black communities' social structure."[20]

The history of the Black Baptists is similar to other New World religious ventures such as that of the Puritans who sought to build a city of Zion amidst the "howling wilderness" of New England. Pearleen's account of this journey into the "wooded wilderness" is a celebration, in her words, of "the Divine intervention of God in the deliverance of a remnant of Afro-American slaves to the cold and rocky shores of Nova Scotia."[21] These former slaves and their descendants survived the enduring hardships of climate, poverty and racial oppression, and to quote the words of a sacred AUBANS hymn, they have "come a mighty long way" in becoming, as they are today, an equal and essential part of Atlantic Canada's racially and culturally diverse society. Recent scholarship has reinforced the main elements of this narrative of church history, and it documents the vital role the Black Baptists had in creating a lasting sense of community and regional identity among Blacks.[22]

The following interview is a portion of a much longer interview with Pearleen that was conducted by Catherine Arseneau over several hours in 1991. This portion focuses mainly on Pearleen's campaign to allow Black girls to pursue a career in the nursing profession, which, until 1948, barred Black girls from training and practicing in Canada. She recalls the incident of a light-skinned Black girl from Guysborough who applied to the nursing program in the early 1940s. Italics have been added to provide background information and to improve the readability of the transcription from the oral interview.

Pearleen: *The girl from Guysborough matriculated from High School* and passed to go into nursing. If you were white and had grade 11, you could train. She was going to the V.G. [Victoria General Hospital] in Halifax *and when she arrived she was required to complete a registration form that asked for her racial identity.* She put "coloured" on it because her mother had coloured blood in her ... and when they saw that in the office ... they said you made a mistake. She said, "No, I'm coloured." *The Hospital staff member replied:* "Oh well then, we can't take you here. You cannot train."

[The girl had come to Halifax expecting to be admitted to the nursing program at the Victoria General Hospital, and when she was refused, she discovered she didn't have enough money for a return ticket home. She was then directed to seek help at the Cornwallis Baptist Church where Pearleen's husband Reverend William Oliver was the minister. Pearleen comforted the girl and later arranged for her to return to her home in Guysborough. After she returned home, her mother sent her to Boston where she could train.

Shortly after this incident in the early 1940s, Pearleen was asked to speak at a meeting of the Colored Citizens Improvement League at the Garrish Street Hall in Halifax.]

I was angry. Angry about *what happened to the girl*, angry about what was happening overseas, angry that my brothers were going *overseas*. My husband by that time was in uniform.

He became a chaplain to the coloured *people* coming in the port *of Halifax*. I said, "Here we are doing our best and we are buying *war* bonds *and* doing everything we could *in support of the war effort*" and then I said "but here's this little girl from Guysborough, she couldn't even train to ... be a nurse."

[Pearleen also raised the issues of racial discrimination in the schools. Her oldest son was 5 years old and he was now in school. One of the books he had to read was Little Black Sambo.]

When I saw the book with little black Sambo with his purple pants ... I said to my son, "You're not going to read this." So, when it came his time to read a line *from the book in class, he explained that* my mother said I am not to read *from this book*. And he didn't read it. *Later the school called about this incident and asked why I had interfered with the teaching of the class.* I said, "I'm not going to send my child to school to be reading about this little Black boy running around a tree with a tiger ... with purple pants and a pink umbrella." I said, "That is degrading!"[23]

In raising these issues in public, I thought I was really in it *and* I'm going to disgrace my husband. But then, in those days you couldn't get into any hotel. You couldn't eat in any restaurant. You could go to a fish chip joint and take things out, but not sit in any *restaurant. At this time,* an American Black doctor and his wife ... had motored down *from New York* to see ... this part of the world. They were elegant, well dressed and had a lovely car. *When they arrived at Cornwallis Street Church they said* they came down here and "We went to a hotel but the hotel told us we weren't allowed *to stay* here. We couldn't get into any hotel." And they said the best they could do was to send us up to the coloured minister. And these people were people of money. And I was embarrassed that they had come to my humble parsonage. But they were so sweet, and I was just myself, so I said, "That's true ... there's no hotel where you can stay and don't go into the restaurants, they won't feed you." And he said, "Well then we only want to stay here tonight. Is there some place where we could stay for the night?" *I was able to find them accommodation in the home of a West Indian woman.* I told them all they had to do was drive up this way, they were from New York, so *they were not familiar with* the little streets of Halifax ... and they found the house and the women was out looking for them and she put them up for the night.... But before they left, they shook hands with me *and* I said, "Don't worry about it, this is a fine women. She's got a nice house and she'll keep you for the night." I then said, "You might as well get out as fast as you can *and* get back to the States because you're not going to get a hotel anywhere here."

And so he went to shake hands with me, and I felt him putting something in my hand … and I didn't look but thought maybe it is a two-dollar bill. *When they left, I discovered* it was a fifty-dollar bill. I guess he felt sorry for us that we had to live under this oppression.

Catherine Arseneau: Where were you allowed to live then?

Pearleen: A certain part of Creighton Street and … Maynard Street and down by my Church on Cornwallis Street … that's all.

[*Returning to a discussion of her campaign to raise public awareness about racial discrimination*] I got this call from the businessman. They had their meetings during their lunch hour and he wanted to know if I would come to this hotel…. I didn't … know that I was breaking … down *the colour line.* It wasn't until years later, and I said, "My God, I was breaking it down and didn't even know it." He wanted to know if I would come to this hotel, the Lord Nelson Hotel, and speak to their dinner meeting … and just tell them about *the racial* conditions…. So I said yes.

[*Pearleen arrived at the hotel with her speech and was greeted at the entrance of the hotel and escorted into the lobby where no Black person was allowed*] Here I am *in* the dining hall *with* the beautiful tables *where* I had never been before. And I'm at the head table…. So I told them … what conditions were like when I grew up and what conditions are like today. And if we are fighting for democracy *overseas,* we'd better do something right here. They liked *my speech* … so I got invited again. *The next time,* I told them about the nurses.

[*After Pearleen first spoke in public about the nurses, she received a letter from Ruth Bailey in Toronto, which she said began:*] "Dear Mrs. Oliver, in our Toronto Newspapers we were reading about you talking about no hospital in Nova Scotia will train a Black girl…. But I want you to know," she said, "that I was born in Toronto and I've tried … every hospital from Vancouver down, and when I told them that I was coloured, they wouldn't accept me." So, she said, "Instead of … saying no hospital in Nova Scotia will train Black girls, you'd better say no hospital in Canada." I said that's a bigger gun for me and I needed all the ammunition I could get. So I was asked to go to another dinner. I went into every hotel. Went in the main door, was led in … and taken to the table where I wouldn't be allowed to sit ordinarily and served a beautiful dinner, and I got up and told them how bad things were for my people, and I was not nervous because I was telling the same story over and over. When Ruth [Bailey] said Canada, then I not only hit Nova Scotia, I hit Canada, and I said what's Canada doing sending troops overseas to fight the Nazis with their racism while we are doing the same thing. That's when it started, about 1941.

So, when I hear the kids today talking about racism … I just think, they don't even know. They weren't born, and … they don't even know what it was like. They can go into any hotel they want to go into, eat in any restaurant, live on any street they want to live. We couldn't do that, so we had a real battle to fight.

Catherine Arseneau: Was racial discrimination worse in Halifax than where you grew up in New Glasgow?

Pearline: Well, you just knew your place. In the towns it was terrible. You just lived in a certain ghetto … and that's where you lived. You were restrained. It takes leadership.

And … strong leadership, like Dr. Martin Luther King Jr., that's what it takes. Thank God we didn't … get shot here. But Dr. Oliver and myself just said, "Well that's what we are here for. We're born for this. It doesn't matter." Some people might say: "Look you're going too far. Don't say this, don't do that, you're making it harder for us…. Don't use the word 'Black' and all that." And we just looked at them and said, "We've got to." We had people turn against us. *Some of* our own people *were* turning against us. They didn't understand. They weren't awakened. But they know now. Young people today don't know what we had to go through.

[Pearleen's discussion returns to the subject of the nurses.] I was always hitting the nursing *issue* because that young girl that came to my house that day looking so white and yet because she put down 'coloured' they wouldn't take her *into the nursing program.* The patients wouldn't even have known she was coloured. I thought this is a terrible sin…. So, that's why I got in it.

[After Pearleen received a letter from Ruth Bailey, she stepped up her campaign on behalf of Black nursing school applicants and put pressure on board members of the Halifax Children's Hospital. Early in 1946, she received a phone call from a board member.] The phone rang and I took it, and it was the chairperson of the board of the Children's Hospital and he said, "Well, you've been doing a lot and you've been showing what conditions are like, and I brought it up to the board and they asked me to phone you and ask you to send us two of those girls to the Children's Hospital. You pick them." It happened that at that time, I only had two girls, Ruth Bailey from Toronto and Gwyneth Barton from Halifax, because the rest had gone to Boston. "You send us two with this stipulation: that the Children's Hospital will train them but we cannot give them … the guarantee that they can affiliate with the Victoria General, the Grace Maternity … or the Nova Scotia Hospital *in Dartmouth." [The Chairperson of the board indicated to Pearleen that once the two nursing students graduated]* "We will add our voice to yours … in the hope they … will get into these other hospitals."

[Pearleen immediately contacted Ruth Bailey and Gwyneth Barton informing them they had been accepted into the nursing program at the Halifax Children's Hospital.

When Ruth arrived in Halifax later in 1946, she stayed at the Oliver residence and later at a Church Deacon's home until she was able to move into residence at the Children's Hospital. Ruth and Gwyneth, were the first two Black nursing graduates to train and practice nursing in Canada.]

NOTES

1. For biographical information on Pearleen Oliver, see Colin A. Thomson, *Born with a Call: A Biography of Dr. William Pearly Oliver, C.M.* (Dartmouth, NS: Black Cultural Centre, 1986); Constance Backhouse, *Colour-Coded: A Legal History of Racism in Canada, 1900–1950* (Toronto: University of Toronto Press, 1999); George Elliott Clarke, ed., *Fire on the Water*, Vol. 1 (Lawrencetown Beach, NS: Pottersfield Press, 1991); Agness Calliste, "Women of 'Exceptional Merit': Immigration of Caribbean Nurses to Canada," *Canadian Journal of Women and the Law* 6 (1993), p. 85, 92; Barbara Hull, "How Pearleen Fought Discrimination," *Bedford-Sackville News* (12 November, 1975); Colin A. McCubbin, "The Women of Halifax," *Chatelaine*, June 1954, p. 16. Additional information regarding Pearleen Oliver was provided to the author by Pearleen's son Les Oliver in an oral interview conducted in Wolfville, NS on July, 16, 2014.

2. Pearleen played an active role in the public defence of Viola Desmond and in the fight to end racial segregation at the Roseland Theatre. See "Ban All Jim Crow Rules Is Comment on N.S. Charge," *Toronto Daily Star* (30 November, 1946) p. 3. She appears together with Viola Desmond in a photo with the caption "Fight Nova Scotia 'Jim Crow' Restrictions" in *Globe and Mail* (3 December, 1946).

3. This is according to Pearleen's own account as recorded in an interview conducted by Catherine Arseneau in 1991 (Beaton Institute Archives). A segment of the interview is included in this documentary chapter.

4. Karen Flynn, "Beyond the Glass Wall: Black Canadian Nurses, 1940–1970," *Nursing History Review* 17 (2009), p. 147; for information regarding Ruth Bailey and Gwyneth Barton's graduation, see "Given High Award to Negro Nurse," *Globe and Mail* (6 October, 1948).

5. Katherine McPherson, *Bedside Matters: The Transformation of Canadian Nursing, 1900–1990* (Toronto: University of Toronto Press, 1996); Karen Flynn, "Beyond the Glass Wall: Black Canadian Nurses, 1940–1970," 2009; Karen Flynn, *Moving Beyond Borders: A History of Black Canadian and Caribbean Women in the Diaspora* (University of Toronto Press, 2011)

6. Katherine McPherson, *Bedside Matters*, 1996, p. 211ff. The YMCA of Canada conducted a national survey in 1947 that documented the racially restrictive admission policy in nursing schools across Canada. For a summary of the YMCA survey, see "Negro Girls as Nurses Are Found 'Unwelcome' YMCA Survey Reveals" *Globe and Mail* (26 September, 1947).

7. This account is described in a letter written by the girl's father, Arthur C. Moore, to Mr. G. Roberts, president of the Toronto Coloured Liberal Association. See Karen Flynn, "Beyond the Glass Wall: Black Canadian Nurses, 1940—1970," pp. 131–32.

8. Julian Rezetnick, "Negro Reports Hospitals Refused His 2 Daughters," *Toronto Star* (18 October, 1947) p. 5.

9. Julian Rezetnick, "Negro Reports Hospitals Refused His 2 Daughters," 1947.

10. Julian Rezetnick, "Negro Reports Hospitals Refused His 2 Daughters," 1947.

11. "Give High Award to Negro Nurse," *Globe and Mail* (6 October, 1948).

12. Sheila Mackay Russell, "'The Glass Wall': A New Chapter in the Human Drama in a Hospital," *Chatelaine* (October 1964) cited in Karen Flynn, "Beyond the Glass Wall: Black Canadian Nurses, 1940–1970," 2009, pp. 133–34.

13. Cited in Karen Flynn, "Beyond the Glass Wall: Black Canadian Nurses, 1940–1970," 2009, p. 134.

14. See Virginia Travis' comments following The Promised Land Project Roundtable (below).

15. Karen Flynn, *Moving Beyond Borders,* 2009, p. 135.

16. Karen Flynn, *Moving Beyond Borders,* 2009, p. 137.

17. Peter E. McKerrow, *McKerrow: A Brief History of the Coloured Baptists of Nova Scotia, 1783–1895,* Frank Stanley Boyd, Jr. ed. (Halifax: Afro-Nova Scotian Enterprises, 1976); Pearleen Oliver, *A Brief History of the Coloured Baptists of Nova Scotia 1782–1953* (Halifax: African United Baptist Association of Nova Scotia, 1953); Pearleen Oliver, *Song of the Spirit: 150th Anniversary, Beechville United Baptist Church* (Hantsport, NS: Lancelot Press, 1994). For a historiographical discussion of Pearleen Oliver's work in relation to African-Canadian Church history, see George Elliott Clarke, "Introducing a Distinct Genre of African-Canadian Literature: The Church Narrative," in George Elliott Clarke, *Directions Home: Approaches to African-Canadian Literature* (Toronto: University of Toronto Press, 2012), pp. 46–57.

18. Peter McKerrow, *McKerrow: A Brief History of the Coloured Baptists of Nova Scotia, 1783–1895,* 1976, p. 11.

19. James W. St. G. Walker, *The Black Identity in Nova Scotia: Community and Institutions in Historical Perspective* (Dartmouth, NS: Black Cultural Centre for Nova Scotia, 1985), p. 10.

20. James W. St. G. Walker, *The Black Identity in Nova Scotia,* 1985, pp. 10–11.

21. Pearleen Oliver, *Song of the Spirit,* 1994, p. 7.

22. See Harvey Amani Whitfield, *Blacks on the Border: The Black Refugees in British North America 1815–1860* (Burlington: University of Vermont Press, 2006); George Elliott Clarke, *Directions Home: Approaches to African-Canadian Literature* (Toronto: University of Toronto Press, 2012).

23. *Little Black Sambo* was published in 1898 by British author Helen Bannerman. The story was originally set in India, but it was quickly adapted to the American context. It was published in the United States in 1899 and immediately became a popular children's book. The many American editions of the book frequently contained racially offensive illustrations that perpetuated Black racial stereotypes. Pearleen Oliver's comments before the Colored Citizens Improvement League resulted in the passage of a resolution asking the Nova Scotia Department of Education to remove the book from Nova Scotia schools. Following up on this resolution, the League's president, B.A. Husbands, wrote Premier A.S. MacMillan in 1944. A decade later, Black activist Daniel Braithwaite and his supporters led a similar campaign to remove the book from Toronto schools and

public libraries. In 1956, *Little Black Sambo* was officially removed from all Toronto public schools. See Sylvia Hamilton, "Stories from 'The Little Black School House'" in *Cultivating Canada: Reconciliation through the Lens of Cultural Diversity*, ed. Ashok Mathur, Jonathan Dewar and Mike Degne (Ottawa: Aboriginal Healing Foundation, 2011), n. 15, p. 110; Daniel Braithwaite, *The Banning of the Book 'Little Black Sambo' from Toronto Public Schools 1956* (Toronto: Overnight Typing and Copy Co., 1978).

Epilogue

The Black quest for the Promised Land, like other racial narratives in Canadian history, is still a journey in progress. Viola Desmond's free pardon in 2010 was a significant action in righting a longstanding wrong and in raising public awareness about the practice of racial segregation that existed in Canada for most of the twentieth century. In a matter of a few short years, Viola Desmond has moved from historical obscurity to an inspiration for all Canadians as well as a symbol of her generation's fight to end racial segregation and discrimination in Canada. In 2012, following the historic action of the Nova Scotia Government, Canada Post issued a commemorative stamp in Viola's honor. In 2014, the Museum of Human Rights in Winnipeg was officially opened to the public, and among the museum's exhibits is a permanent display commemorating the Viola Desmond incident as a uniquely Canadian story of courage. More recently, the Nova Scotia Government has created Heritage Day, a new provincial holiday in February, to honor persons of historical significance, and it designated February 16, 2015, as the first Heritage Day in honor of Viola Desmond. Also in 2015, the Historic Sites and Monuments Board of Canada accepted the nomination of Viola Desmond as a person of National historic significance.

Viola Desmond's Canada has documented the parallels between the narratives of race in the United States and Canada. Given these similarities in history, especially in relation to the practice of Jim Crow–style segregation and the struggle for racial equality in both countries, it is perhaps fitting for us to designate a figure like Viola Desmond as Canada's Rosa Parks. Interestingly, because Viola's singular act of courage at the Roseland Theatre occurred nine years before Rosa Park's similar act aboard a bus in Montgomery, Alabama, the historical timeline would suggest that Rosa Parks is America's Viola Desmond. Both these courageous Black women were catalysts in the larger collective struggle for civil rights and social justice. Following her arrest and release from jail, Viola took comfort and council from her family and members of the Cornwallis Street Black Baptist Church, particularly Pearleen Oliver and her husband the Reverend William Oliver. The NSAACP and the Black community also rallied in support of Viola, and although she lost the appeal of her case and the incident quietly receded out of public consciousness, the struggle for racial equality continued in Nova Scotia and elsewhere in Canada.

By the early 1950s, as we have seen, the winds of change were clearly in the air in both Canada and the United states. In 1954, the year of the watershed *Brown* decision that ruled for the end of racial segregation in schools in the United States, the Frost Government in Ontario strengthened earlier provincial civil rights legislation by enacting the *Fair Accommodation Practices Act*. In 1959, in response to the efforts of Rev. William Oliver and the NSAACP, together with the active support of Premier Robert Stanfield, the Nova Scotia legislature passed the *Fair Accommodation Act*, which prohibited discrimination in all public spaces on grounds of race, religion and nationality. By the early 1960s, the majority of the provinces enacted human rights legislation, and by the end of the decade, most overt forms of racial segregation had ended in all parts of Canada.

These historical developments, together with the recent public awareness regarding the Viola Desmond incident, have helped to ensure the history of the struggle for human rights in Canada will remain in the public consciousness as an important aspect of our national history. Race relations in Canada have undeniably improved over the years, but racial prejudice remains a deeply ingrained aspect of our culture. Combatting prejudice and eventually overcoming the legacy of racial discrimination in Canada will require continuing the efforts to raise awareness through education and engaging in an open and honest dialogue about race and the history of race relations in Canada.

Appendix

The Promised Land Project
Symposium Roundtable Discussion

The following discussion was part of the Fourth Promised Land Project Symposium that was held at the Black Cultural Centre in Dartmouth, Nova Scotia, May 6–8, 2011. The discussion focused on early recollections of racial discrimination among three Roundtable participants: Wanda Robson, author and the youngest sister of Viola Desmond; Sylvia Hamilton, African Canadian film maker and professor of journalism at Kings College in Halifax, and Marie Carter, community historian in the town of Dresden, Ontario. The discussion begins with introductory comments by the author who severed as the roundtable moderator.

Graham Reynolds: I want to begin our roundtable discussion by making a few observations that are relevant to several of the themes that have dominated many of the papers presented at this conference as well as the discussions that have followed. The first thing that strikes me is the fact that many Canadians are simply unaware of the history of race relations in Canada and that racial segregation existed in our country for most of the twentieth century. Viola Desmond's protest against the practice of racial segregation at the Roseland Theatre in New Glasgow, Nova Scotia, occurred in 1946, which was nine years before Rosa Parks refused to give up her seat aboard a racially segregated bus in Montgomery, Alabama. At the time, the Viola Desmond's incident received local and even national news coverage, but it was quickly forgotten, and the issue of racial segregation receded from our memories and out of public consciousness for more than half a century. It wasn't until 2010 that Viola Desmond finally received the recognition and justice she deserved, when she was granted, posthumously, a free pardon by the Nova Scotia legislature.

Another observation I would like to make that is relevant to the presentations and discussions at this conference is that I see many similarities between the narratives of race in Canada and the United States. Although we usually associate racism against Blacks with the United Sates, we are beginning to understand that a similar pattern of racism existed in Canada. It is still very much a part of the Canadian experience, and I think there is some urgency for us to begin a much-needed public dialogue about racism in our society today. I think there is no better place to begin this dialogue than in our schools. I also believe that the narrative of race is an integral part of Canadian history, and it needs to be taught to all students of Canadian history and not just to those specializing in African-Canadian studies.

I would like the members of the roundtable to begin by relating their earliest memories and personal experiences of racism.

Wanda Robson: My thoughts are with growing up in the '30s. I was born in 1926 in the west end of Halifax. There were no other Blacks there, and we lived in this neighbourhood until I was about 7 or 8, when we moved to Gottingen Street in the north end of Halifax. I noticed the difference right away between my old school and new school because there were no Black children in the west end school. I entered grade 3 at Alexander Elementary School in Halifax when I was 8, and instantly I knew that the teacher did not like Black students. When I walked into the classroom all the Black students were seated at the back of the room. They were not separated by ability or performance; they were just Black, and that's where this teacher believed they should be. The teacher said to me, "Take your things and go down there," so I went to the back of the room. But this teacher had a system of seating students according to how well you performed on her monthly test. Wherever you came, if you came first or second, you were put in the first or second seat of the first row. Well, I being the youngest of a very large family, I learned a great deal from my older siblings, and I seemed to know a lot for my age. I came first in our class, and she begrudgingly said to me, "Well you have to go to the first row in the first seat." So I left the so-called black leper colony and sat with the white students. That's a nasty word, but I think she felt that we lepers, and she didn't want anything to do with us. And some of those children wanted to learn. So I was sitting in the first row in the first seat, and one day I was doing what I am doing now, speaking. I turned around and said something to somebody behind me so the teacher said: "Were you speaking, Wanda Davis?" I said, "Well, yes." And she said: "OK get your things up and go back of the room again." So this carried on for quite a while. Back and forth back and forth; I tried to be good. And then came parent's day, when your parents would come to the school, and I was in the back row where all the Black students were. My mother knew I was in trouble because I was acting nervous. I knew that it would come out that when she came in the class she would see me there in the back and she knew the system about the first row and the first seat. So the night before, my mom said: "Is there something wrong?" I said, "Yes." I started crying and I told her that I was in the back of the class.

She said: "Did you speak?" I said: "Well, yes." She said: "Alright. Go to bed."

The next day when I walked into the classroom the teacher said: "You take your things and go in the first row in the first seat." Then when my mother came with Viola, who came when she could to check on the younger children, I was where I should have been. This teacher was just horrible to me, and I was always trying to figure out why. One day during an exercise in our class, I raised my hand and said: " I know, teacher." She said: "Well now, we have a genius in our midst, I guess. What do we do with people who are geniuses? Well, you pack up your things and you go to the next grade." So she took me to grade 4, and she said to the grade 4 teacher: "This is Wanda Davis and she is a genius, she thinks she knows more than I do so I think you can take her in the next grade." Luckily, the next grade teacher was very understanding. She saw me as a student, and she didn't care about colour. I came into her classroom and she kept giving me my grade 3 homework. Then toward grading day, the teacher, Ms. Reid, came and took me back to the third grade.

That was a big thing to inflict on a small child who wanted to learn, who was studying, only because of the colour of her skin. I'm 84, and I still remember her face today. These kinds of incidents stay with you the rest of your life. I once asked a little girl, when I told her the story about my sister Viola: "What do you think about that?" She said: "It's not fair." That's a small way of talking about racism, not being fair. Racism is certainly not fair; it's ugly, it's demeaning, and it is very hurtful. And that is what I learned in grade 3 when I was 8 years old in Halifax.

Sylvia Hamilton: Thank you and good afternoon everyone. It is a pleasure to be here. In relation to what Wanda was just saying, I remember growing up in Beechville, Nova Scotia. We went to a segregated school from grade primary to grade 3 and my "knock in the head" and the "knock in the head" to all the kids in our community came at grade 4 when we had to leave the segregated school in Beechville to go to Lakeside, which was the neighbouring white village. On our first day in grade 4, we were told to sit on one side of the classroom so the white children were on one side and we were on the other.

I'm very interested in legacies and how we understand the past. The past plays an important role in our contemporary mind, as you can see from these two brief stories, and no matter how long ago those stories took place, they left an imprint on us; it has left an imprint on me.

The other knock in the head, as I recall, came when I hit grade 9. When I went to Halifax West; it was quite exciting because no one else had gone into high school. The first day in grade 9, the teacher gave me a form, and this is one of those things that is burned into my memory, and she said: "Take this home and have your mother sign it, and if you can get through high school maybe you can get a little job for yourself." Now I don't know what the teacher's intentions were. I don't deal in intentions. I can only deal with the impact of that particular action on the part of that teacher.... Anyone who knows my late mother Marie knows that I didn't sign that form and it went into the trash. But the impact of that teacher's behaviour could have been devastating, and it was devastating for other students. So the question of the past and the way that past still plays a role in our lives has been a motivating factor in much of the work that I do. My work has been about uncovering and visualizing that past so that we can see it and create spaces for dialogue. I was often asked in the early stages of this research, especially by people of European descent, "Why are you people always digging up that past, like why can't you just let things be?" And my question and response would always be: "Well whose past is important? Why can't I dig up my past because you're digging up your past?" A lot of the past has been on display, but it's whose past has been on display and whose past has been privileged. I think about the kind of work that I do as a way of engaging in conversation and having people look at that past and think about it.

In one of my documentary films, *The Little Black School House,* I wanted to look at the role that segregation in education played in Black communities in Nova Scotia and in Ontario. I selected those two provinces because they were the two provinces that codified segregation in education in legislation. It wasn't simply happenstance; it wasn't simply geography; it was actually a concerted legal effort to segregate children on the basis of race.

Shooting the film here in Nova Scotia and in Ontario was a very emotional journey because I learned through that process about the struggle of Black teachers and the enormous role they played in those small Black schools that were without ample resources. They often had no heat and no running water, but at the core of those classrooms were people who looked like me and took my interests at heart. Uncovering many of the stories in the film was an emotional journey, but it was also provided room for people to speak to their own experiences, to do what I call "being witnesses within their own lives." And I began thinking about the buildings and other structures as being sites of memory. There is a French historian who has developed this concept that he has called "sites of memory." It can be a place, it can be a person, it can be an event, and so these old school buildings, a few of them in Nova Scotia that were still in existence, but also the physical geography and the location of those places have embedded memories; they have stories that are really important for us to think about. And at the same time as those embedded memories, in those buildings, in those sites, and in indeed the witnesses the people, there was also the question of the oral tradition. I was able to look at the archival record, and I saw petition upon petition from the early 1800s of Black people petitioning for education and ... for schools. And so those petitions supported the oral stories. Now there are many questions about audience and who looks at the kind of work that I do and the experiences of African Canadians. So often in question and answer periods, I get a lot of questions about why are you doing this. And one of the things I throw back at audiences, and especially audiences of people of European background, is for them to begin thinking about their ancestors who were responsible for the legislation and the kinds of segregation that existed so they might begin to ... interrogate the mindset of the people who did that. So people of African descent can do the work that we are doing, but there is an equal amount of work that can be done by European historians and people of other racial backgrounds in relation to those attitudes. It is that legacy that I don't think has been examined enough, and this is where I think the dialogue should continue to go.

Marie Carter: I just wanted to start by saying I feel a certain amount of humility being up here. My mom and dad are from Holland, and I am a first generation Canadian. We came into the community of Dresden, Ontario, in late 1949 in the midst of a civil rights struggle, so I have this odd sort of relationship to community. It is my community, but it's not my community. I'm Canadian, but I'm not Canadian. I have my own struggle with identity issues and cultural issues in terms of who I am. I think I needed to say that and also to tell you some more background about myself before I get into one particular story that I like to tell to high school students and to college students when I go to speak to them. Because it is primarily white audiences I speak to, I try and get them to objectively break open the whole issue around racism. I like to explore where is their attitude toward racism at their age and where is anyone's in terms of their attitude towards it. Just to share my own journey in terms of struggling with that and wrestling with who am I in all this? What is my role in all this? Other than that, I am fascinated by history and especially community history. I think everybody's history is a part of community history, and that has always been my approach.

I grew up in a rural area in what was formally the Dawn Settlement area. I think a lot of you have probably heard of Dawn from Revered Josiah Henson of the Uncle Tom story who was the inspiration for Harriet Beecher Stowe's character. I grew up literally right next door to Uncle Tom's cabin as a child. The neighbourhood I grew up in was very much a mixed neighbourhood. There were many people who were like my parents who were new immigrants. There were a few established Irish/Scottish type of settlers around, but there were a lot of African Canadians in our neighbourhood who I went to school with in our one-room schoolhouse. My experience of that was radically different from what I am hearing. There was a comment made in a *Maclean's* article [written by Sidney Katz in 1949 to expose the racism that existed in the town of Dresden] that the principal of the Dresden school at that point said that because we live and we are educated together we tend not to see people in terms of colour now. I would say that growing up that was my experience; it was never pointed out to me that you should feel differently about anyone. My dad's favourite saying was "You always judge people by the way that they treat you and how they relate to you." So that is the kind of upbringing that I had.

I should also say that within the rural community in that area there was a farmer-to-farmer network, and everyone helped one another. I know that the folks from Dresden might know the names of two Black residents, Mr. Bill Thompson and Mr. McCokel. Bill came to barrel the hay and Mr. McCorkel came to harvest our grain, and my mother would set out the table with the best silverware when they came because we were so happy that someone would come and help us with the harvest. Marie McCorkel use to drop in and keep my mother company. We European women weren't allowed to drive; that was our place; it was very old fashioned. Marie had a car and would come and visit mom and that was her lifeline back when we were children. Marie would take us to swimming lessons, and she would take us places where we would never have the opportunity to go if not for our Black neighbours. Anyhow, that's my background.

[Marie recounts that when she was a young girl in the 1970s, her parents told her about the practice of racial segregation that had existed in Dresden, a decade earlier. The same restaurant where she enjoyed eating ice cream with her friends had excluded Blacks.]

I had grown up in the town, and I knew nothing of this legacy; no one had ever said a word to me. So it tells you something of the extent of historical amnesia that an entire town that you know going around and being in that community, that growing up there, I had never of heard this…. I think that for me it was really a life changing moment when my parents said: "You know, this is what went on." … And … suddenly I said, "Oh my God, in all these years I never thought that this kind of thing happened here." I always thought it was Canada the good and that we were somehow morally superior to the U.S., and I had looked across the border and thought, oh yeah, there could never be a race riot here. Well guess what? We had race riots in the 1860s … just up the road from Dresden…. I would say it all happened here exactly the same way as it did across the border. It's very sobering. Talk about having your world being turned upside down. But I think when I tell this story and I tell the kids I don't tell them what date it is when I tell them the story. I just tell them the story about the National Unity Association. I tell them about Percy Carter and Hugh Burnett from the National Unity Association and how they challenged the practice of segregation in Ontario, starting with the town of Dresden.

At the time, Uncle Tom's cabin had just been recently purchased by a white man. It was actually one of the family homes of the Henson family that he wanted to turn into a national historic site and he was actively lobbying to get that done. I think people really seized on this and understood the symbolic value of this. And certainly when it was picked up in the press in 1949 in Maclean's magazine, the headline read "Jim Crow lives here in Dresden at the home of Uncle Tom." And you can understand the optics of that and how it set out to capture national attention. And it was the thing that really helped to capitalize on the status of Dresden being a terminus for the Underground Railroad and a wonderful place where freedom was supposed to be. The irony of this really gave it currency in the press. You need laws and you need outside attention to move that forward. You can't do it solely from within the community, as Hugh Burnett and Percy Carter tried.

They actually had a series of meetings with people in the town and they hoped to get public support to change things. After all, this was 1949, and we just fought a war in which we had all kinds of Black heroes in uniform going over to fight. And yet you go into a restaurant where men from work crews who were captured German soldiers could sit down and have a coffee, but not this war hero who had come home and couldn't have a coffee. This is not right. This is a reasonable argument, and you would think people would accept it. But the situation didn't change until the Jewish labour organization and newly formed civil rights groups began applying pressure. It left a painful legacy for a lot of people and some, like Mr. Carter and Mr. Burnett, left town. One of the local papers that sided with the National Unity Association ... closed because they lost their income base. So, fighting for freedom is not without its costs.... This was very painful for people in a town where you meet the same people and you go to the same grocery store and to the same church. In this situation, people just want to remain silent and not say anything. But issues like this need to be talked about, and we need to teach our children to be honest about what our histories are so that we can prevent it from happening again. It never completely goes away, and the minute we feel that we have some kind of moral superiority over someone else and point a finger and say it was their fault, we have lost sight of the truth. We are all part of the problem and we shouldn't lose sight of this.

Thank you.

Graham Reynolds: Thank you very much for your comments, Wanda, Sylvia and Marie. I think all of us have some experiences or if not an experience perhaps a question. I would like to try and facilitate some direction between the audience and our roundtable and get some feedback from all of you. I would like to begin by asking Virginia Travis for her comments. Virginia is a retired nurse and she was one of the first generation of Black nurses in Canada. She also grew up in Dresden during the 1930s and 40s.

Virginia Travis: Thank you panel. I can identify with each your experiences, and I believe I need to respond to the chair of this panel in terms of my experiences as a child and then as part of the nursing profession. As a child, I was raised in a home that I felt very trusted in, and I felt loved, and I felt that as a family of six children, I had a network of family with grandparents, aunts, uncles and cousins. Living in Dresden, as you know, age related experiences do matter. As a young child, it seems to me that I had wonderful life. I never really dwell on the racism, but I noticed it with playing with other children. There were certain children in my neighbourhood that were not allowed to play with me and the children who did play with me were also labelled for playing with me. When I was in school, the "N" word was used. And so on the playground and in school there certainly was a separation, and you identified with your cousins because they knew you and you felt that supportive feeling when you were in their company. Whenever possible, my parents made sure that we were all at the dinner table together until my other brothers started going out to work. In public school, during the Second World War, I was three years behind my brother Jarvis who was in grade 8. One day Jarvis had come home crying, which was embarrassing for a young man, and I asked openly at the dinner table, "What was wrong? Why was Jarvis crying?" My mom said: "Just let this be." I wasn't told until a couple days later but my father took my brother aside to find out why he was crying. On the way home from school the next day my father was dressed in his suit and hat, and it was not his time to leave work, it was early. So I said: "Dad where are you headed?" He said: "I am going to the school." And I said: "Well, I will come back with you." I lived at least a mile and a half from the schoolyard. He said, "No, you go straight home. I will see you at home." So the short and long of it is that we had Red Cross days every Friday in public school, and my brother was asked by the students who were responsible for the program to read a poem that had the "N" word in it. My brother was strapped for refusing to read that poem in front of the class. My brother gave the poem to my father and he took it to the school the day I met him and addressed the issue with the principal.

One thing I remember about being in school is that I was never asked to read. I noticed that as a 6-year-old, and I had the audacity to ask the teacher if I could read out of the reader, but she didn't let me do that that particular day. I think it was because her father and my father worked at the same factory and they both walked to work that made me think that this could be a possibility that I would eventually be asked to read....

During my high school years, I thought I could sing, and the the musicians selected for the play, *Pirates of Penzance*, tested us all, but we were not invited to participate in that play. Our parents organized a separate support group for our entertainment for the weekends.

We generally attended church, and I think that's where I drew the strongest support growing up. In high school, I said to my father: "Dad, I really want to be a nurse.... Do you think we can afford that? Because I have to pay to be a nurse. I have to have the right uniforms, pay for my shoes, buy a watch." And he said:

"Virginia you can do anything you want to do because if you put your mind to it you can do it." So I became a domestic in high school and earned enough money to get to the nursing program and buy books and my uniform.

In the nursing program, the first six months you are called a "probie." During the first three months, we were interviewed by the director of nursing to decide whether we would remain as a nurse probie or not. So, I had my interview, and I had been left on a surgical unit for most of that first three-month period. After about eight weeks, I was not moved, but other students were moved, and I asked the head nurse of that unit if I would be able to have a different patient; would I be able to do something different than what I was always assigned to do in one unit? So I had my evaluation, and I don't recall any discussion about discipline or criticism, but when I got to the interview with the director of nursing she said: "Just what do you think you are going to achieve if you do not accept criticism?" And I said, "I beg your pardon." And she said: "It's right here. You do not accept criticism." And I said: "I'm sorry I have not heard that before." So she said: "I will show it to you it's right here." And this evaluation system meant that you signed your name to it and that continues today. So the director of the school of nursing said "You will receive your cap, but for now on quit acting like a monkey." I went home and told my parents, and I said: "I'm not sure if I'm going to be staying." They said: "Yes you will. What's wrong?" So the incident triggered to me that there was going to be a difference.

The last experience I will describe for you happened after I had become head nurse. I had become proficient in operating room nursing and I was asked to teach operating room nursing after I graduated. I was then asked to become the head nurse and after that I was asked to become the nursing supervisor of the department. And at the time there was an incident in Chatham in which a teacher applied for job and she was not hired because she was Black. This story had become public information after the teacher took the school to court. When it became public in the paper the chief of surgery came to me and said: "Virginia, you have not had any problems because of the colour of your skin have you?" And I said: "Dr. Keeley it's something I choose not to talk about." There were six Black nurses in that school of nursing before me. My colleague who was called the "big sister" said to me the first month I was in the nursing program, "Virginia, from my experience," this is very difficult to say, "if you have a patient like I have who says to you when they wake up in recovery: 'Oh my God, they've given me darkie blood,' you have to be prepared for that, and it's my responsibility to teach you that so that you are prepared for whatever comes down the line." So I became prepared, but when I became a supervisor I really wasn't prepared for a professional person to go behind the scenes and ask me to be relieved of my job and use colour as an issue....

The last incident I will relate to you involves a patient who I knew in a progressive care unit who called me in one day when I was doing a quality-monitoring program.... And the patient said: "Virginia, come here." He happened to be the brother of a local minister. He said: "I just want you to know that the nurses were talking at the desk last night, and I overheard them, and they said: 'What are those people, those Black nurses doing? You would think that here trying to take over this hospital.'" And I said: "That's not what we're going to do, we are trying to do our very best and demonstrate that there is caring quality and quality assurance in this hospital."

The highlight of my experience was that I was elected to the College of Nurses of Ontario as a board member, and I decided that I would do my very best to make sure that equality, discipline and obligation to the professional standards of care would be practiced. And that was my opportunity then to become a teacher of nursing. I taught nursing at community college, and I taught nursing ethics and professional development....

Graham Reynolds: I would like to ask members of the audience if they have any questions for Virginia or our panel members.

Speaker 1: I don't have a question but I certainly have a comment. These are first-person accounts, and I would recommend that we make some effort to get these testimonies in print. I'm sure were hearing these kinds of testimonies at other Promise Land conferences, and they are contextual; they are the evidence of the past, and I don't think we should miss an opportunity to have these stories told and be made available for future generations.

Speaker 2: The lady that just spoke.

Graham Reynolds: Virginia.

Speaker 2: Yes. I knew her as a child, and I just wanted people to know that her experiences were never transferred to me. I was raised in Chatham, Ontario, and in fact her and my mother were quite good friends. So I was just sitting here thinking this sweet woman who went through all these things when she was at our Sunday school and at our church, we as children didn't know that. So Virginia I just wanted to thank you. I'm 62 now but I can't give Virginia's age. She would of known me when I was just a child, and I'm thinking she is 67 or maybe 68, but I don't want to date her. I just want to openly thank her for being so good to me and my peers who went to that same church in Chatham, Ontario. And when I think about this whole idea about the legacy of excellence and the legacy of competence and all those nice little things that we talk about all the time, I would say that it is easy to see from my experience why I became a school teacher was because of people like her. And thank you.

Speaker 3: I think that it is really interesting to listen to your story Virginia. I'm a nurse as well. But it's really interesting that after this length of time that the pain is still there. It was quite obvious how you felt that pain. It is important for us to acknowledge that this event has had a lasting legacy within the individual because in essence … it wounds the spirit and the soul, and that lasts a lifetime. But what I need to say is how important it was for us to be able to provide hope for people … So somewhere along the line we have to acknowledge the importance that spirituality plays within us and allows us be able to continue the journey in spite of traumatic events. It is about rising to the occasion, and at the same time, even though we may have a wounded spirit and a wounded soul, at the end of the day, we prevail. I just wanted to share that.

References

Amnons, Elizabeth. 2007. *Harriet Beecher Stowe's Uncle Tom's Cabin: A Casebook.* New York: Oxford University Press.

Archer, William. 1970 [1910]. *Through Afro-America: English Reading of the Race Problem.* New York: Negro Universities Press.

Arnesen, Eric. 2001. *Brotherhoods of Color: Black Railroad Workers and the Struggle for Equality.* Cambridge: Harvard University Press.

Ayes, Edward L. 1992. *The Promise of the New South: Life After Reconstruction.* New York: Oxford University Press.

Backhouse, Constance. 1999. *Colour-Coded: A Legal History of Racism in Canada, 1900–1950.* Toronto: University of Toronto Press.

____. 1998. "'I Was Unable to Identify with Topsy,' Carrie M. Best's Struggle Against Racial Segregation in Nova Scotia, 1942." *Atlantis* 22, 2 (Spring/Summer).

____. 1994. "Racial Segregation in Canadian Legal History: Viola Desmond's Challenge, Nova Scotia, 1946." *Dalhousie Law Review* 17.

Baron, W.R. 1992. "Historical Climate Records from the North Eastern United States, 1640–1900." In R.S. Bradley and P.D. Jones (eds.), *Climate Since A.D. 1500.* New York: Rutledge.

Bartley, Alan. 1995. "A Public Nuisance: The Ku Klux Klan in Ontario 1923–27." *Journal of Canadian Studies* 30, 3.

Bates, Beth Thompkins. 2001. *Pullman Porters and the Rise of Protest Politics.* Chapel Hill: University of North Carolina Press.

Baumann, Shyon, and Loretta Ho. 2014. "Cultural Schemes for Racial Identity in Canadian Television Advertising." *Canadian Review of Sociology/Revue canadienne de sociologie* 51, 2 (May).

Beaton, Elizabeth. 1995. "An African-American Community in Cape Breton, 1901–1904." *Acadiensis* xx, 1 (Spring).

Berton, Pierre. 2001. *The Last Spike: The Great Railway, 1881–1885.* Toronto: Anchor.

____. 2001. *The National Dream: The Great Railways, 1971–1885.* Toronto: Anchor.

Best, Carrie M. 1977. *The Lonesome Road: The Autobiography of Carrie M. Best.* New Glasgow, NS: Clarion Publishing Company.

Bogle, Donald. 1994. *Toms, Coons, Mulattoes, Mammies, and Bucks: An Interpretive History of Blacks in American Films,* 3rd edition. New York: Continuum Publishing.

Bordewich, Fercus M. 2005. *Bound for Canaan: The Epic Story of the Underground Railroad, America's First Civil Rights Movement.* New York: Harper Collins.

Braithwaite, Daniel. 1978. *The Banning of the Book 'Little Black Sambo' from Toronto Public Schools.* Toronto: Over Night Typing and Company.

Bridgen, Loren. 2012. "A Membership for Manhood: Masculine Cultures in Nineteenth Century African-Canadian Organizations." Paper presented to *Claiming the Promise: A Retrospective on African Canadian History and Invitation to New Research,* 5th Promised

Land Project Symposium. Chatham, Ontario, June 14–16.

Bristor, Juila M., Renee Gravois Lee and Michelle R. Hunt. 1995. "Race and Ideology: African-American Images in Television Advertising." *Journal of Public Policy & Marketing* 14, 1 (Spring).

Bristow, Peggy. 1994. *We're Rooted Here and They Can't Pull Us Up: Essays in African Canadian Women's History.* Toronto: University of Toronto Press.

Cahill, Barry. 1995. "Habeus Corpus and Slavery in Nova Scotia: *R v. Hecht Ex Parte Rachel, 1798.*" *Unviversity of New Brunswick Law Journal* 44.

Calliste, Agnes. 1993. "'Women of Exceptional Merit': Immigration of Caribbean Nurses to Canada." *Canadian Journal of Women and the Law* 6.

Canada's Digital Collections. "Black Loyalists." <blackloyalist.com/Canadiandigitalcollection/index.htm>

Canadian Human Rights Commission. "Human Rights in Canada: A Historical Perspective." <Chrc-ccdp.ca>

Canadian Negro. 1956. "Churches Rapped!!! Grizzle and More Speak Out of Against Minstrel Shows." *Canadian Negro* 4, 1 (March).

Canadian Press. 2013. "Employees at Leon's Furniture Outlet Fired for Lynching Black Statue." *National Post,* September 5.

Carson, Jenny. 2002. "Riding the Rails: Black Railroad Workers in Canada and the United States." *Labour/Le Travail* 50 (Fall).

Carter, Marie. 2012. "Re-visioning the Dawn Settlement: Part III: A Black Utopia or Early Multicultural Experiment?" Paper presented to *Claiming the Promise: A Retrospective on African Canadian History and Invitation to New Research.* Chatham, ON, June 16.

Clairmont, Donald H., and Dennis William Magill. 1999. *Africville: The Life and Death of a Canadian Black Community,* 3rd edition. Toronto: Canadian Scholars Press.

Clarke, George Elliott. 2012. "Introducing a Distinct Genre of African-Canadian Literature: The Church Narrative." In George Elliott Clarke (ed.), *Directions Home: Approaches to African Canadian Literature.* Toronto: University of Toronto Press.

____. 2011. "'Indigenous Blacks': An Irreconcilable Identity?" In Ashol Mathur, Jonathan Dewar and Mike De Gagne (eds.), *Cultivating Canada: Reconciliation Through the Lens of Cultural Diversity.* Ottawa: Aboriginal Healing Foundation.

____. 1991. *Fire on the Water,* Vol. 1. Lawrencetown Beach, NS: Pottersfield Press.

Colley, Sherri Borden. 2010. "Unintentional Activist; By All Accounts, Viola Desmond Was Ahead of Her Time, Making Inroads as a Woman and as a Black. A Sister Remembers Canada's Rosa Parks." *Chronicle Herald,* March 6.

____. 2010. "Desmond Should Be Pardoned; Case Helped Eliminate Segregation in Province, Says Retired Judge." *Chronicle Herald,* March 6.

Cooper, Afua. 2006. *The Hanging of Angelique: The Untold Story of Canadian Slavery and the Burning of Old Montreal.* Toronto: Harper Perennial.

Cooper, John. 2007. *Season of Rage: Hugh Burnett and the Struggle for Civil Rights.* Toronto: Tundra Books.

Crawford, Killian. 2008. *Go Do Some Great Thing: The Black Pioneers of British Columbia,* expanded edition. Vancouver: Commodore Books.

Darwin, John. 2009. *The Empire Project: The Rise and Fall of the British World-System 1830–1970.* New York: Cambridge University Press.

De B'beri, Boulou Ebanda, Nina Reid-Maroney, and Handel Kashope Wright. 2014. *The Promised Land: History and Historiography of the Black Experience in Chatham-Kent's Settlements and Beyond.* Toronto: University of Toronto Press.

Dixon, Thomas Jr. 1905. *The Clansman: A Historical Romance of the Ku Klux Klan.* New York: Grosset & Dunlap.

Donovan, Ken. 2013. "Female Slaves as Sexual Victims in Cape Breton, 1713–1810." Paper presented to the Old Sydney Society, February 28.

____. 2010. *Marie Marguerite Rose and Slavery in Louisbourg, 1713–1768.* Parks Canada, Fortress of Louisbourg, unpublished manuscript.

____. 2004. "Slaves in Ile Royale, 1713–1758." *French Colonial History* 5.

____. 1995. "Slaves and Their Owners in Ile Royale, 1713–1760." *Acadiensis* 25, 1.

Douglas, Orville Lloyd. 2013. "Why I Hate Being a Black Man." *The Guardian,* November 9. <theguardian.com/commentisfree/2013/nov/09/i-hate-being-a-black-man>

Dowden, Cara, and Shannon Brennan. n.d. "Police-Reported Hate Crime in Canada, 2010." Statistics Canada. <statcan.gc.ca/pub/85-001-x/2012001/article/11635-eng.htm#5>

Doyle, Bertram. 1937. *The Etiquette of Race Relations in the South: A Study in Social Control.* Chicago: University of Chicago Press.

Du Bois, W.E.B. 1970. *The Soul of Black Folk.* New York: Washington Square Press.

Ebert, Roger. "Great Movie: 'The Birth of a Nation.'" Retrieved from <rogeredbert.com/reviews/great-movie-the-birth-of-a-nation-1915>.

Elkins, Stanley M. 1976. *Slavery: A Problem in American Institutional Life,* 3rd edition. Chicago: University of Chicago Press.

Eltis, David, and David Richardson (eds.). 2008. *Extending the Frontiers: Essays on the New Transatlantic Slave Trade Database.* New Haven: Yale University Press.

Ely, Melvin Patrick. 1991. *The Adventures of Amos 'n' Andy: A Social History of an American Phenomenon.* New York: Free Press.

Equiano, Olaudah. 2004. *The Interesting Narrative of the Life of Olaudah Equiano: Or, Gustavus Vassa, The African (1789).* New York: Random House.

Evans, Doris, and Gertrude Tynes. 1995. *Telling the Truth. Reflections: Segregated Schools in Nova Scotia.* Hantsport, NS: Lancelot Press.

Fanon, Frantz. 2008. *Black Skin, White Masks,* revised edition. New York: Grove Press.

Fingard, Judith. 1992. "Race and Respectability in Victorian Halifax." *Journal of Imperial and Commonwealth History* 20.

Flynn, Karen. 2011. *Moving Beyond Borders: A History of Black Canadian and Caribbean Women in the Diaspora.* Toronto: University of Toronto Press.

____. 2009. "Beyond the Glass Wall: Black Canadian Nurses, 1940–1970." *Nursing History Review* 17.

Frost, Karolyn Smardz. 2007. *I've Got a Home in Glory Land: A Lost Tale of the Underground Railroad.* New York: Farrar, Strauss and Giroux.

Globe and Mail. 2013. "'I Didn't Sign Up for This': Nova Scotia Liberal Breaks Down Discussing 'Black Pete' Photo. December 2.

Globe and Mail. 1948. "Given High Award to Negro Nurses." October 6.

Globe and Mail. 1947. "Negro Girls as Nurses Are Found 'Unwelcome' YMCA Survey Reveals." September 26.

Globe and Mail. 1946. "Fight Nova Scotia 'Jim Crow' Restrictions." December 3.

Greer, Allan. 1997. *The People of New France*. Toronto: University of Toronto Press.

Grekel, Jana. 2009. "The Right of Consent? Eugenics in Alberta, 1928–1972." In Janet Miron (ed.), *A History of Human Rights In Canada*. Toronto: Canadian Scholar's Press.

Grizzle, Stanley G. 1998. *My Name's Not George: The Story of the Brotherhood of Sleeping Car Porters in Canada*. Toronto: Umbrella Press.

Halifax Gazette. 1752. "African Nova Scotians." May 17. <gov.ns.ca/nsarm/vitual/africans/archives.asp?ID=4>

Hamilton, Sylvia. 2007. *The Little Black Schoolhouse*. Halifax, NS: Maroon Films.

Harding, Kimberly L. 1998. "St. Philip's African Orthodox Church: A Case Study of a Unique Religious Institution." Unpublished masters of arts thesis in Sociology, Acadia University, Wolfville, NS.

Henson, Josiah. 1876. *"Uncle Tom's Story of His Life:" An Autobiography of the Rev. Josiah Henson*. London: Christian Age Office.

Henson, Tom M. 1977. "Ku Klux Klan in Western Canada." *Alberta History* 25, 4.

Hill, Lawrence. 2007. *The Book of Negroes*. Toronto: Harper Collins.

Hochschild, Adam. 2006. *Bury the Chains: Prophets and Rebels in the Fight to Free an Empire's Slaves*. New York: Houghton Mifflin.

Hull, Barbara. 1975. "How Pearleen Fought Discrimination." *Bedford-Sackville News*, November 12.

Innis, Harold Adams. 1954. *The Code Fisheries: The History of an International Economy*. Toronto: University of Toronto Press.

Jefferson, Thomas. 2002. *Notes on the State of Virginia and Related Documents*. Edited with an introduction by David Wallstreiker. New York: Bedford/St. Martins Press.

Jenkins, William. 2007. "Views from 'the Hub of the Empire': Loyal Orange Lodges in Twentieth-Century Toronto." In David A. Wilson (ed.), *The Orange Order in Canada*. Toronto: Four Courts Press.

Jobb, Dean. 2009. "Ticket to Freedom." *The Beaver, Canada's History Magazine* April–May.

Johnston, A.J.B. 2011. "Matheiu Da Costa and Early Canada: Possibilities and Probabilities, Canada." Retrieved from <pc.gc.ca/ihn-hhs.ns/portroyaledu.edu1/edu1f.aspx>.

Jonah, Anne Marie Lane. 2010. "Unequal Transitions: Two Metis Women in Eighteenth-Century Ile Royale." *French Colonial History* 11.

Jonah, Anne Marie Lane, and Elizabeth Tait. 2007. "Filles D'Acadie, Femmes De Louisbourg: Acadian Women and French Colonial Society in Eighteenth-Century Louisbourg." *French Colonial History* 8.

Katz, Sidney. 1949. "Jim Crow Lives in Dresden." *MacLean's* November 1.

Kelly, Ninette, and Michael Trebilock. 2010. *The Making of the Mosaic: A History of Canadian Immigration*, 2nd edition. Toronto: University of Toronto Press.

King, Boston. 1796. "Memoirs of Boston King." Black Loyalists. Canada's Digital Collections. <blackloyalist.com/cdc/documents/diaries/king-memoirs.htm>

Lamberston, Ross. 2001. "'The Dresden Story': Racism, Human Rights, and the Jewish Labour Committee." *Labour/Le Travail* 47 (Spring).

Larson, Kate Clifford. 2004. *Bound for the Promised Land: Harriet Tubman, Portrait of an American Hero*. New York: Random House.

Lemons, J. Stanley. 1977. "Black Stereotypes as Reflected in Popular Culture, 1880–1920." *American Quarterly* 29, 1 (Spring).

Lhamon, W.T. Jr. 2000. *Raising Cain: Blackface Performance from Jim Crow to Hip Hop.* Cambridge: Harvard University Press.

Litwack, Leon F. 1998. *Trouble in Mind: Black Southerners in the Age of Jim Crow.* New York: Alfred A. Knopf.

MacKey, Frank. 2006. *Done with Slavery: The Black Fact in Montreal 1760–1840.* Montreal and Kingston: McGill-Queen's University Press.

Madeleine, Dobie. 2010. *Trading Places: Colonization and Slavery in Eighteenth Century French Culture.* Ithica: Cornell University Press.

Marano, Carla. 2010. "'Rising Strongly and Rapidly': The Universal Negro Improvement Association in Canada, 1919–1940." *The Canadian Historical Review* 91, 2 (June).

Marquis, Greg. 2014. "A War Within a War: Canadian Reactions to D.W. Griffith's Birth of a Nation." *Histoire Sociale/Social History* XLVII, 94 (June).

Marston, Benjamin. 1784. "Diary." August 26 and September 14. Black Loyalists. Canada's Digital Collections. <blackloyalist.com/cdc/documents/diaries/marston_journal.htm>

Mathieu, Sarah-Jane. 2010. *North of the Color Line: Migration and Black Resistance in British North America, 1870–1955.* Chapel Hill: The University of North Carolina Press.

McCubbin, Colin A. 1954. "The Women of Halifax." *Chatelaine* June.

McKerrow, Peter E. 1976. *McKerrow: A Brief History of the Coloured Baptists of Nova Scotia, 1783–1895.* Frank Stanley Boyd Jr. (ed.). Halifax: Afro-Nova Scotian Enterprises.

McLaren, Angus. 1990. *Our Own Master Race: Eugenics in Canada, 1885–1945.* Toronto: McClelland & Stewart Inc.

McPherson, Katherine. 1996. *Bedside Matters: The Transformation of Canadian Nursing, 1900–1990.* Toronto: University of Toronto Press.

Mensah, Joseph. 2010. *Black Canadians: History, Experience, Social Conditions,* 2nd edition. Black Point, NS: Fernwood Publishing.

Moogk, Peter N. 2000. *The Making of French Canada: A Cultural History.* East Lansing: Michigan State University Press.

Moore, Oliver. 2010. "Burning Cross Ignited Racial Tension in Nova Scotia." *Globe and Mail,* February 24.

Nelson, Jennifer J. 2008. *Razing Africville: A Geography of Racism.* Toronto: University of Toronto Press.

Nerbas, Don. 2013. *Dominion of Capital: The Politics of Big Business and the Crisis of the Canadian Bourgeoisie 1914–1947.* Toronto: University of Toronto Press.

Nova Scotia News. 2010. "The Late Viola Desmond Granted Apology, Free Pardon." April 15. <novascotia.ca/news/smr/2010-04-14-pardon.asp>

Oliver, Pearleen. 1994. *Song of the Spirit: 150th Anniversary, Beechville United Baptist Church.* Hansport, NS: Lancelot Press.

____. 1953. *A Brief History of the Coloured Baptists of Nova Scotia 1782–1953.* Halifax, NS: African United Baptist Association of Nova Scotia.

Pachai, B. 1993. *Peoples of the Maritimes: Blacks.* Tentallon, NS: Four East Publications.

Palmer, Howard. 1994. "Reluctant Hosts: Anglo-Canadian Views of Multiculturalism in the Twentieth Century." In R. Douglas Francis and Donald B. Smith (eds.), *Readings in Canadian History: Post Confederation.* Toronto: Harcourt Brace & Co.

Patten, Lesley Ann. 1999. *Loyalties.* Toronto: National Film Board of Canada.

Philpot, Thomas Lee. 1991. *The Slum and the Ghetto: Immigrants, Blacks, and Reformers in Chicago, 1880–1930*, 2nd edition. New York: Wadsworth Publishing Company.

Pitsula, James. 2013. *Keeping Canada British: The Ku Klux Klan in 1920s Saskatchewan.* Vancouver: University of British Columbia Press.

Promised Land Project. <huronuc.on.ca/research/promised_landproject/>

Reid, Jennifer. 1999. "A Toolshed from Gate #4: The Dominion Iron and Steel Company and the Formation of an African American Church." In Bruce L. Guenther (ed.), *Historical Papers 1999: Canadian Society of Church History.* Langley BC: Canadian Society of Church History.

Reid-Maroney, Nina. 2013. *The Reverend Janice Johnson and African Canadian History, 1868–1967.* Rochester: University of Rochester Press.

Reitz, Jeffrey G., and Raymond Breton. 1998. "Prejudice and Discrimination in Canada and the United States: A Comparision." In Vic Satzewich (ed.), *Racism and Social Inequality in Canada.* Toronto: Thompson Educational.

Reynolds, Graham, and Richard MacKinnon. 2000. *The Peopling of Atlantic Canada* [CD ROM]. Sydney, NS: Folkus Atlantic.

Rezetnick, Julian. 1947. "Negro Reports Hospitals Refused His 2 Daughters." *Toronto Star,* October 18.

Robson, Wanda. 2010. *Sister to Courage: Stories from the World of Viola Desmond, Canada's Rosa Parks.* Wreck Cove, NS: Breton Books.

Schama, Simon. 2006. *Rough Crossing: Britain, the Slaves and the American Revolution.* New York: Harper Collins.

Scott, William D. 1914. "Immigration and Population." In Adam Shortt and Arthur G. Doughty (eds.), *Canada and Its Provinces: A History of the Canadian People and Their Institutions by One Hundred Associates,* Vol. II. Toronto: Glasgow, Brook & Co.

Shadd, Adrienne. 2010. *The Journey from Tollgate to Parkway: African Canadians in Hamilton.* Toronto: Dundurn.

Stokes, Melvyn. 2007. *D.W. Griffith's 'The Birth of a Nation': A History of the Most Controversial Motion Pictures of All Time.* New York: Oxford University Press.

Sydney Record. 1918. September 3.

Thomas, Owen. 1996. "Cultural Tourism, Commemorative Plaques, and African-Canadian Historiography: Challenging Historical Marginality." *Social History/Histoire Sociale* 29.

Thomson, Colin A. 1986. *Born with a Call: A Biography of Dr. William Pearly Oliver, C.M.* Dartmouth, NS: Black Cultural Centre.

Thordarson, Thorvaldur, and Stephen Self. 2003. "Atmospheric and Environmental Effects of the 1783–1784 Laki Eruption: A Review and Reassessment." *Journal of Geophysical Research* 108 (D1).

Toronto Daily Star. 1946. "Ban All Jim Crow Rules Is Comment on N.S. Charge." November 30.

Toronto Daily Star. 1915. "Coloured People Protest." September 17.

Toronto World. 1915. "The Birth of a Nation." December 18.

Toronto World. 1915. "Birth of a Nation Beyond Promises." September 21.

"Torture and the Truth: Angelique and the Burning of Montreal." Great Unsolved Mysteries in Canadian History. <canadianmysteryseries.ca.>

Trans-Atlantic Slave Trade Database Project. <slavevoyages.org>

Trudel, Marcel. 1960. *L'Esclavage Au Canada Francais: Histoire et Conditions de L'Esclavage.* Quebec: Les Presses Universitaires Laval.

Truth and Reconciliation Commission of Canada. <trc.ca/website.trcinstitution/index. php?=3>

Turner, Patricia A. 1994. *Ceramic Uncles & Celluloid Mammies: Black Image and Their influence on Culture.* New York: Anchor Books.

Tuttle, William M. Jr. 1996. *Race Riot: Chicago in the Red Summer of 1919.* Chicago: University of Illinois Press.

United Federation of Workers. 2013. "By the Numbers: Facts about Racial Discrimination in Canada." March 17. <Ufcw.ca/index-php?option=com_content&viewart icle&id=3324Aby-the-numbers-facts-about-racial-discrimination-in-can>

Wade, Wynn Craig. 1998. *The Fiery Cross: The Ku Klux Klan in America.* London: Simon and Schuster.

Walker, James W. St. G. 1999. "African Canadians." In Paul Robert Magocsi (ed.), *Encyclopedia of Canadian Peoples.* Toronto: University of Toronto Press.

____. 1997. *Races, Rights and the Law in the Supreme Court of Canada.* Toronto: The Osgood Society for Canadian Legal History and Wilfred Laurier Press.

____. 1993. *The Black Loyalists: The Search for a Promised Land in Nova Scotia and Sierra Leone.* Toronto: University of Toronto Press.

____. 1985. *The Black Identity in Nova Scotia: Community and Institutions in Historical Perspective.* Dartmouth, NS: Black Cultural Centre for Nova Scotia.

____. 1984. *The West Indians in Canada.* Ottawa: Canadian Historical Society.

____. 1976. "The Establishment of a Free Black Community in Nova Scotia, 1783–1840." In Martin L. Kilson and Robert I. Rotberg (eds.), *The African Diaspora: Interpretive Essays.* Cambridge: Harvard University Press.

Ward, Samuel Ringgold. 1852. "Canadian Negro Hate." *Voice of the Fugitive* October 21. <ink.ourontario.ca/brouse/vf/reel1/00118>

Weeks, Joan. 2007. *One God, One Aim, One Destiny: African Nova Scotians in Cape Breton.* Sydney, NS: Centre for Cape Breton Studies.

White, Deborah Gray. 1999. *Ar'n't I a Women? Female Slaves in the Plantation South.* New York: Norton.

Whitefield, Harvey Amani. 2012. "The Struggle Over Slavery in the Maritime Colonies." *Acadiensis* 41 (Summer/Autumn).

____. 2008. "Reviewing Blackness in Atlantic Canada and the African Atlantic Diaspora." *Acadiensis* 37 (Summer/Autumn).

____. 2006. *Black on the Border: The Black Refugees in British North America.* Burlington Vermont: University of Vermont Press.

Whitehead, Ruth Holmes. 2013. *Black Loyalists: Southern Settlers of Nova Scotia's First Free Black Communities.* Halifax: Nimbus Publishing.

Wilkerson, Isabel. 2010. *The Warmth of Other Suns: The Epic Story of America's Great Migration.* New York: Random House.

Williams, Dorothy. 1997. *The Road to Nowhere: A History of Blacks in Montreal.* Montreal: Vehicule Press.

Wilson, David A. 2007. "Introduction: 'Who Are These People?'" In David Wilson (ed.), *The Orange Order in Canada.* Toronto: Four Courts Press.

Winks, Robin. 1997. *The Blacks in Canada: A History*, 2nd edition. Montreal: McGill-Queen's Press.

Woodsworth, James S. 1909. *Strangers Within Our Gates or Coming Canadians*. Toronto: Stephenson.

Archival

African Nova Scotians Collection, Beaton Institute, Cape Breton University.

Immigration Branch Records, Government of Canada, Beaton Institute, MB66-MG16, Reel No. 6 (RG 76, Volume 566, File 810666, pt. 1).

Pearleen Oliver interviewed by Catherine Arseneau, 8 November 1992. Beaton Institute.

Memorandum Brief presented to the Prime Minister and Minister of Citizenship and Immigration by the Negro Citizenship Association, April 27, 1954. City of Toronto Archives, Fonds 431, file 1.

Wanda Robson, personal communication to the author.

The National Archives of the United Kingdom (TNA) Public Record Office (PRO) High Court of the Admiralty (HCA) 30/264/ Letter 32, Pierre Lapouble to Madame Labatiste Laurens, negresse.

William D. Scott to F.C. Knight, 25 April 1916. Archives Canada, RG. 79, Vol. 566, File:81066, pt. 2. Beaton Institute

Scott to F.C. Knight; see also (below) Scott's letters of 17 November 1914 and 16 September 1915. Archives Canada, RC. Vol. 566 File: 81066, pt. 2. Beaton Institute

J.B. Williams to William D. Scott, "Report of the Landing of Negroes at Nova Scotia Ports," 29 June 1909. Archives Canada RG. 76, Vol. 566, File: 81066, pt. 1. Beaton Institute.

William D. Scott to L.M. Fortier, 10 August 1916. Archives Canada, RG. 76, Vol. 566, File: 81066, pt. 2. Beaton Institute.

Marcus Garvey, Speech at Melnick Hall, Sydney Nova Scotia, *The Black Man: A Monthly Magazine of Negro Thoughts and Opinions*, Vol. 3, n.10 (July 1938). Beaton Institute.

"Administrative History/Biographical Sketch: Ku Klux Klan of Kanada fonds." Provincial Archives of New Brunswick, MC 2604. Description retrieved from <archivescanada.ca/English/search/item Display.asp?>.

Index

A Brief History of the Colored Baptists of Nova Scotia 1782-1953,167
abolition (see also anti-slavery sentiments, *Anti-Slavery Act of 1793*, Somerset case, John Graves Simcoe, John Robinson), 22-26, 30
African Baptist Association of Nova Scotia (ABANS), 167
African Diaspora, 5-6, 11n21, 14
African Methodist Episcopal Church, 52, 155
African Orthodox Church (AOC), 142
African United Baptist Association (AUBANS), 142-143
Africville, 31, 50, 42-43
   city of Halifax apology, 4
   early history, 42
   expropriation and destruction 4, 43
Alexander, Philip, 5
Alexandra Elementary School, 71-72
Ambersburg, Ontario, 25
Amos 'N' Andy, 160
Angelique (Marie-Joseph-Angelique), 89-92, 90-91
   comparison to Marie Marguerite Rose, 91
   trial, torture and execution, 90-91
Anti-Slavery Act of 1793, 2n3, 25
anti-slavery sentiments, 24-25
Apex College of Beauty Culture and Hair Dressing, 76
Arnold, William, 42
Arseneau, Catherine, 168ff
Association of Canadian Clubs, 148
Atkinson School of Nursing, 167

Backhouse, Constance, 3, 10n12
Bailey, Doris, 165-166
Bailey, Joe, 165-166

Bailey, Ruth, 165-166, 171-172
Barton, Gwyneth, 165,171,172
Beechville United Baptist Church, 163, 167
Belleville General Hospital, 166
Bennett, R.B., 153
Best, Carrie, M. 53, 59, 61, 78, 80
Bibb, Henry, 30, 40
Bigot, François, 15
Birchtown, 19-23
"Birchtowners", 19
Birth of a Nation (see also D.W. Griffith, racial stereotypes, Ku Klux Klan), 47,154-158
   first Hollywood "Blockbuster" movie, 155
   in Canada, 157
   protests among the Black community, 154-155
   racism and sympathetic portrayal of the Old South, 155-157
   reception and popularity in the U.S., 157
Black battalion (Halifax), 23
Black Belt, 52-63
Black Code (see *Code Noir*)
Black Cross Nurses (see also Universal Negro Improvement Society), 142
Black fraternal organizations (see fraternal associations)
Black immigration, 8, 39-40, 45, 48, 49, 114 (see also West Indian immigration)
Black Loyalists, 2-4, 6, 17-22
Black settlers to Alberta (see also Henry Sneed), 45
Black (Victoria) Pioneer Rifle Corps, 39
Blackburn, Thornton, 31, 40
Blacks in Canada: A History, 2, 114

Blacks on the Border: the Black Refugees in British North America 1815-1860, 2
Blanchette, Arthur R., 58
Blowers, Sampson, 23
Borden, Robert, 48, 51
British-American Manuel Training Institute, 30
British and North American Settlement Company, 54-55
British Banner, 31
Brown v Board of Education (1954), 56, 176
Brown, William, 42
Bureau of Social Research, 147, 148
Burnett, Hugh (see also National Unity Association), 1, 58
Burning of Old Montreal, 90
Burton, John, 167
Buxton, Ontario, 31, 50

Canadian Brotherhood of Railway Employees and Other Transportation Workers (CBRE), 50-51
Canadian History Magazine (formerly *The Beaver*), 82
Canadian League for the Advancement of Colored People (CLACP), 134, 143
Canadian Pacific Railway, 44, 48
Cape Breton Post, 81
Cape Breton University, 7, 82, 83
Caplan, Ron, 84-85
Carter, Bill, 56
Carter, Marie, 54-55, 181-183
Charter of Rights and Freedoms, 57, 160
Chatelaine, 166
Chatham, Ontario, 30, 41
Chronicle Herald, 83
Civil Rights Act of 1964, 56
civil rights legislation (see also individual civil rights acts), 56-57, 179
Clarke, George Elliott, 39, 40
Clarkson, John, 21
Clarkson, Thomas, 21
Code Noir, 88-89
Coffin, Levi, 26, 30

Cokeville, 52
Cokovia School, 52
Colaiacova, Tony, 82-83, n585
Colley, Sheri Borden, 83
Colored Political and Protection Association, 134
Colored Protection Association, 134
Colored Regiment, 41
Colour-Coded: A Legal History of Racism in Canada, 3
Common School Act of 1850, 50
Conveyance and Law of Property Act, 57
Cooly, Chloe, 24
Cooper, Afua, 2, 90
Co-operative Commonwealth Federation (CCF), 147
Cornwallis Street Baptist Church, 54, 70, 163, 179
cotton gin (see also Eli Whitney), 25
Couagne, Therese de, 89-90

Da Costa, Mathieu, 64n15
Daily Record, 52
Davis, James Albert, 69-70
Dawn of Tomorrow, 134
Dawn Settlement, 30, 49-50
Department of Immigration (see also Frank Oliver, William D. Scott), 50
Desmond School of Beauty Culture (see also Viola Desmond), 61, 76-77, 79
Desmond, Viola, 1, 7, 60-63, 77-81, 175-176
  career as a teacher, 75
  comparison to Rosa Parks, 175
  Desmond School of Beauty Culture, 61, 76-77
  early life, 75
  Free Pardon, 1, 83
  inspired by Madam C.J. Walker, 75-76
  Roseland Theatre incident, 1, 61, 77-81
  Viola's arrest and appeal 1, 78-81, 175-176
  visit to her sister Wanda's school, 72

Dexter, Darrell, 83
Diallo, Aminata (Laurence Hill's fictional character), 3, 6
Dixon, Thomas, Jr., 47, 65n47, 146
Dominion Iron and Steel Company (DISCO), 49, 51-52
approval to employ West Indian workers, 120
employment of African American workers, 49, 51
William D. Scott's letter approving the landing of West Indian workers, 132
Donovan, Kenneth, 15, 16, 17, 94
Douglas, Frederick, 28
Douglas, Orville Lloyd, 85n1
Douglas, Sir James, 39
Douglas, Tommy, 57
Dresden, Ontario, 1, 30, 31, 54-56, 57
Du Bois, W.E.B., 35, 36, 134

Edmonton Board of Trade, 46
Emancipation Proclamation, 35
Equal Pay Act, 57
Equiano, Olaudah, 6
eugenics movement, 147-148

Fair Accommodations Act, 57, 62, 160, 176
Fair Accommodations Practices Act, 57, 59, 176
Fair Employment Practices Act, 57, 62
Female Employees Fair Remuneration Act, 59
Female Employment Practices Act, 59, 59
Field Beauty Culture School, 76
Fingard, Judith, 41, 42
first battalion of Halifax, 23
First Nations, 4, 39, 55
Fisher, E.D., 45-46
Flynn, Karen, 166-167
Fortress of Louisbourg (see Louisbourg)
Foster, W.E., 152
Francheville, François Poulin de, 89
Francis, Mayann, 85
fraternal associations, 41-42, 143

Free Pardon (see also Viola Desmond), 1, 7, 62-63, 83, 84
Frost Government of Ontario, 59
Frost, Karolyn Smartz, 27
Fugitive Offenders Act, 25, 28
Fugitive Slave Act (1793), 25, 28
Fugitive Slave Law (1850), 29

Galton, Francis, 147
Garvey, Marcus, 134-135, 141-142
speech at Menelik Hall, 136-140
George, David, 19, 21, 167
Grand Trunk Railway, 44
Great Migration, 49, 120
Griffith, D.W. (see also Birth of a Nation), 47, 154-157
Grizzle, Stanley, 58, 158-159

Hackley, Rev. W., 155
Halifax, 4, 21-22, 170-171
Africville Apology, 4
Black population in the Victorian era, 41-43
departure of Black Loyalists, 21-22
pattern of racial segregation, 4, 43, 54, 170-171
Halifax Children's Hospital, 166, 171
Halifax Gazette, 17
Hamilton Spectator, 158
Hamilton, Sylvia, 179-181
Hammonds Plains, Nova Scotia, 42
Harewood, Adrien, 82
Harker, John, 83
Harlem Renaissance, 120
Harris, Walter, 144
Henson, Josiah, 18, 26-27, 28, 31, 54
Hill, Lawrence, 3-4, 6
Hochschild, Adam, 24
Homestead policy, 45
Horne, William Van, 48
Human Rights Act, 57

Île Royale (see also Louisbourg), 6, 15-17, 88ff

Immigration Acts
  1906, 48
  1911, 48
  1923, 67-68n97
  1962, 144
immigration policy and Blacks, 48-49
Imperial Order of the Daughters of
  Empire (IODE), 46
industrialization and the rise of Jim Crow
  in Canada, 43-46
integration (see Petition to Halifax school
  authorities [1883] and *Brown v Board
  of Education*)
Inter Colonial Railway, 50

Jean-Francois, 16
Jefferson, Thomas, 18
Jenkins, Gwen, 77
Jewish Labor Committee, 58
Jim Crow (see also racial segregation,
  Plassy v Ferguson), 36-39, 36, 49-56
  in Canada, 36, 49-56
  in Southern United States, 36-39
  origin of term, 35
"Jim Crow Lives in Dresden", 55-56
Johnson, Gwendolyn Irene, 69-70
Johnson, Henry Hatcher, 70

Kaplansky, Kalmen, 58-59
Katz, Sidney, 55-56
Kay's Café and Grill, 55, 57, 58-59
King, Boston, 19, 20-21
King, Mackenzie, 146
King, Martin Luther Jr., 1, 7
Ku Klux Klan (see also racial stereotypes),
  46-47, 149-154
  and *Birth of a Nation*, 149, 154
  in New Brunswick, 150-154
  in Ontario, 149
  in western Canada, 149-150, 151
  revival of the Klan in the United
  States, 35, 46-47
  the KKK and cross burning, 65n47

Laki eruption in Iceland and the winters
  of 1783 and 1784, 20, 33n21
Lane-Jonah, Anne Marie, 112n24, n26
Lapouble, Pierre, 94-95
  letter to Marie Marguerite Rose, 94-
  95, 110, 112n24
Laurent, Jean Baptiste, 16, 92, 112n26
Laurier, Wilfred (see also Homestead
  Policy), 45-46, 50
  order-in-council to prohibit Black
  immigration, 50
Lincoln, Abraham, 35
Little Black Sambo, 73
  campaign to remove from schools
  and public libraries, 173-174n23
Litwack, Leon, 37, 38
Lochhead, W.L., 147
Long, Walter, 156
Loppinot, Jean Chrysostome, 16, 91, 92,
  95
Lord, J.S., 153
Louisbourg (see also Île Royale), 6, 15-17
Loyalists (see Black Loyalists)

MacDonald, Clyde, 83
MacGregor, Rev. James, 23
MacKay, Peter, 85
MacLean, Anne, 82
Maclean's, 55-56
MacMillan, Barrie, 82, 85
Mansfield, Lord Chief Justice, 24
Maritime Religious Education Council,
  164
Marley, Bob, 142
Maroons, 22, 31
Marrant, John, 19
Marston, Benjamin, 19-20
Mason, Norman, 159-160
Masonic lodges (see fraternal associa-
  tions)
Mathieu, Sarah-Jane, 2
Mauger, Joshua, 17
McGuire, George Alexander, 142
McKay, Morley, 55, 58-59
McKerrow, Peter E, 167.

Means, John H., 49
Minstrel Shows (see also racial stereo-
   types), 35,47, 158-160, 167
Moore, Donald Wilfred, 58, 67-68n97
Morton, H.H., 152-154
Mosher Aaron, 50-51
movie houses 158-160
Murray, Stuart, 83
Museum of Human Rights, 83, 175

National Association for the
   Advancement of Colored People
   (NAACP), 80, 134
National Unity Association, 1, 58-59
Native Sons of Canada, 148
Negro Citizen Association, 67-68n97
"Negro Problem" and Canada's racially
   restrictive immigration policy, 46-49,
   115ff
New Glasgow, Nova Scotia (see also
   Roseland Theatre), 78, 82, 83, 85
"New Negro" movement, 120
No2 Construction Battalion, 51
North of the Color Line: Migration and
   Black Resistance in Canada, 1870-
   1955, 2
Nova Scotia Association for the
   Advancement of Colored People
   (NSAACP), 59, 61, 80, 163-164, 175
Nova Scotia Education Acts of 1836 and
   1865, 50
Nova Scotia government's apology and
   Free Pardon (see Free Pardon)
Nova Scotia Museum Black Heritage
   Resource Data-Base, 6, 10n16
Nova Scotia Training School for Girls,
   164
nursing profession and racial discrimina-
   tion, 164-166

Oddfellows (see fraternal associations)
Oliver, Frank, 46,48, 50
Oliver, Pearleen Oliver, 8, 54, 59, 60, 61,
   168-174, 176
   campaign to remove Little Black

Sambo from schools, 73, 173-174n23
   fight to allow the training and
   practice of Black nurses in Canada,
   164-165, 168-172
   history of Black Baptists of Nova
   Scotia, 167-
   support of Viola Desmond, 164, 176,
   168
Oliver, Rev. William Pearly, 54, 61, 80,
   163, 164, 176
Orange Order, 148-149
Order of Sleeping Car Porters, 51

Pak, Laurie, 85
pardon (see Free Pardon)
Parks, Rosa, 1, 175
Patrollers, 28
petition to Halifax school authorities
   (1883), 42, 50
Pitsula, James, 150
Plassy, Homer, 38
Plassy v Ferguson, 38
Point Douglas, 52
Preston, Nova Scotia, 21, 42
Preston, Richard, 167
Promised Land defined, 2, 9n3
Promised Land Project, 10,n14
Pullman, George 48
Pullman sleeping car porters, 48-49

Racial Discrimination Act, 56, 59
racial segregation (see also Jim Crow,
   Roseland Theatre, Africville,
   Cokeville, Dresden, Halifax), 2, 8, 49,
   170-171
   railroads, 44-45
   voluntary segregation, 36, 49-50
racial stereotypes (see also Jim Crow, Ku
   Klux Klan), 8, 18, 46, 48, 155-158,
   160, 179 Birth of a Nation, 155-
   158,162n29
   "Black Pete", 63n2
   in media and advertising, 160,162n37
   "Sambo", 18, 46,48, 65n44

Tom and Topsy in *Uncle Tom's Cabin*, 179, 162n29
"racial uplift", 134
racial violence, 5, 19-20, 53, 142, 153-154
  Chicago (Red Summer), 20, 53
  east St. Louis , 20
  Glace Bay, Nova Scotia, 53
  Pictou, Nova Scotia, 53
  recent incidents in Nova Scotia, 10n19
  Shelburne, Nova Scotia, 19-20
Rebellions of 1837–1838, 40-41
Reconstruction Era, 36
"Redemption Song" (see also Bob Marley), 142
revival of Black culture in Montreal, 120, 177ff
Revolutionary War, 40-41
Reynolds, Graham, 81-82, 176-177,183, 186
Rice, Thomas D., 35
Robertson, Carmelita Carvey, 6-7
Robinson, John A., 58
Robinson, John Beverly, 27
Robson, Wanda, 5, 7-8, 69-85, 178-179
  family background, 69-70
  first experiences of racial prejudice, 71-75
  personal journey of self-discovery, 81-85
  recollections of her sister Viola and her arrest, 75-81
Rose, Marie Marguerite, 6, 8, 15-17, 88, 91
  African identity, 16-17, 95-96
  comparison to Angelique, 91
  inventory of material possessions, 16, 92-94, 97-109
  life as a slave and free woman, 16-17, 91-92
  success as a businesswoman, 16-17, 93-97, 112n24
Roseland Theatre (see also Viola Desmond, racial segregation), 59, 61, 155, 159-160

as a venue for *Birth of a Nation*,155
during the silent movie era, 159-160
minstrel shows, 159-160
the Viola Desmond incident, 61-63
Roseway Harbour, 19-29
Royal Alexandra Theatre, 155
  ad for the premier of *Birth of a Nation*, 156
Russell, Sheila Mackay, 166

School Act of 1865, 42
school segregation, 42, 50
Scott, William D., 8, 48, 117ff, 146, 147
  correspondence, 121-132
Seaview African United Baptist Church (see also Africville), 43
segregation (see racial segregation, Jim Crow)
Shelburne, Nova Scotia, 19-20
siege of Louisbourg, 16
Sierra Leone, 4, 21, 31, 46
Simcoe, John Graves, 24-25
Sister to Courage: Stories from the World of Viola Desmond, Canada's Rosa Parks, 84
slavery (see also Transatlantic Slave Trade, *Code Noir*), 5-6, 11, 14-26
  and sexual exploitation, 18
  and the Loyalist migration, 17-22
  decline of slavery, 23-26
  sale and purchase of slaves, 17-18
  under British rule, 17-26
  under French rule, 14-17
Smith, Susan Irene, 69-70
Sneed, Henry (see also Black settlers to Alberta), 45
Somerset Case, 24, 25
Somerset, James, 24
Song of the Spirit, 167
Souls of Black Folk, 35
St. Antoine, 52
St. Philip's Church (see African Orthodox Church)
Stanfield, Robert, 176
Stowe, Harriet Beecher (see also *Uncle*

Tom's Cabin), 18-19, 54
Strange, Thomas Andrew, 23
Strangers Within our Gates or Coming
    Canadians, 147

The Black Loyalists: The Search for the
    Promised Land in Nova Scotia and
    Sierra Leon, 2
The Black Man, 135-140
The Book of Negroes, 3-4
The Clansman, 47, 65n47, 149
The Clarion, 59, 60, 62, 80
The Hanging of Angelique: The Untold Story
    of Canadian Slavery and the Burning of
    Old Montreal, 2
The Liberator, 47
The Negro Citizen, 59
The Times of African Nova Scotians, 82
The Toronto Star, 165-166
Thibault, Claude, 91
Thornton, Henry, 40
Toronto General Hospital, 165
Toronto Mail and Empire, 46
Transatlantic Slave Trade, 6, 11n21, 14-15
Travis, Virginia, 5, 166, 183-186
Trinity Anglican Church, 70, 74
Trudel, Marcel, 89
Tubman, Harriet, 28-29, 30

Uncle Tom's Cabin (see Harriet Beecher
    Stowe), 18-19, 54
    adapted for stage, 159-160
Underground Railroad (see also Josiah
    Henson, Levi Coffin, Harriet
    Tubman), 3, 8, 26-31
    origin, 26
    organization, 28
Universal Negro Improvement
    Association (UNIA), 134-143
    UNIA marching band (1921), 143
Upper Hammonds Plains, 75

Vancouver Island, 39
Veniot, Peter, 152-153
Victoria, British Columbia, 39
Voice of the Fugitive, 30

Waddell, Dr. Alfred E. (see also Viola
    Desmond's arrest), 79-80
Walker, James W. St. G., 2, 22, 135

Walker, Madam C. J. (see also Viola
    Desmond), 75-76
War of 1812, 23, 31, 39, 42
Washington, Brooker, T, 134
West Indian immigration, 8, 49, 115ff
White, Portia, 77
Whitehead, Ruth Holmes, 10n16, 11n23
Whitfield, Harvey Amani, 2, 18
Whitney, Eli, and the cotton gin, 25
Whitney Pier, Nova Scotia, 52, 142
Wilberforce, William, 24
Wilkinson, Moses, 21
Williams, J. B., 116
    report to William B. Scott, 117-119
Winks, Robin, 2, 114
Woodsworth, J.S., 147-148